'You wo   ours
security   be
there are bureaucrats trying to stop you.'

The words of Glyn Michaels, a friend, a colleague,
David's mentor, my boss and one of the most capable
MI5 officers we ever came across, July 1997

'How can ministers assert that the services operate
within the law, if they simply ignore evidence that
they do not?'

David Shayler, on many occasions

'[The law/UN diplomacy] offers the best foundation
for resolving prolonged conflicts – in the Middle East,
in Iraq, and around the world. Those who seek to
bestow legitimacy must themselves embody it, and
those who invoke international law must themselves
submit to it.'

UN Secretary General Kofi Annan, address to the UN,
21 September 2004

'We know that dictators are quick to choose aggression,
while free nations strive to resolve differences in peace.
We know that oppressive governments support terror,
while free governments fight the terrorists in their
midst.'

US President George Bush, address to the UN, 21
September 2004

SPIES, LIES AND WHISTLEBLOWERS

MI5, MI6 and The Shayler Affair

Annie Machon

The Book Guild Ltd
Sussex, England

First published in Great Britain in 2005 by
The Book Guild Ltd
25 High Street
Lewes, East Sussex
BN7 2LU

Typesetting in Times by
Keyboard Services, Luton, Bedfordshire

Printed in Great Britain by
CPI Bath

A catalogue record for this book is available from the
British Library

ISBN 1 85776 952 X

I dedicate this book to
Herbie Machon (1919–2004),
a man who fought for this country,
and to
Amy Shayler
May her world be safe

Contents

Acknowledgements

It is difficult to know where to begin. I owe a debt of gratitude to so many people who have helped me survive the tumultuous seven years since we went on the record.

First of all, the Shayler and Machon families. Without their practical and emotional help, I doubt we would have survived. Phil and Nick have both been on the receiving end of the authorities' bully-boy tactics, but they have given us rock-solid help and support; Michèle, Ron, Anne, and Jem, who between them have helped me move home when Dave was 'unavailable', not once but twice; Becky, for allowing us to live in hers; and Rich and Juliet, for moral support. I must not forget Etienne for his help in Paris. Thanks also to Jeremy and Annu for their support, letting me stay at their house, for Jeremy's work as The Webmaster, and for the cats.

I must also thank our lawyers, particularly John Wadham and Gareth Peirce and the barristers in England, and Anne-Sophie Levy and Willy Bourdon in France. They all worked above and beyond the call of duty.

Many journalists deserve honourable mention for their dedication to the pursuit of the truth: Mark Hollingsworth, who has been a rock over the last seven years; Martin Bright and James Steen, who have both felt the full force of the law because of David's case; Richard Norton-Taylor; Mark Urban; Francis Wheen; Nick Cohen; Nick Davies; Mark Lloyd; Mark Thomas; Ben Ando; Paul Brennan; Yosri Fouda; Christophe

Deloire; Mark Skipworth, Chris Anderson and Michael Smith. My thanks also go to those in the National Union of Journalists who have supported us, particularly Barry White, Tim Gopsill, Jeremy Dear and Tim Lezard.

Finally, I should like to thank The Book Guild. Without the vision and courage of Carol Biss and her team, the facts in this book would have remained shrouded behind a veil of secrecy, spin and lies. We all owe a great debt to Tom Paine.

Other friends and supporters would prefer not to be named in this book. You know who you are – thank you.

Introduction

Q: Which organisation out of MI6, Gaddafi's External Security Organisation and Saddam's Mukharabat (secret police) has the most recent record of sponsoring international terrorism?

A: MI6, when it funded the plot to assassinate Colonel Gaddafi in 1995/96.

Q: Which organisation out of the Provisional IRA, the Loyalist paramilitaries and Army intelligence targeted civilians for murder, and tortured and executed effective IRA informants?

A: The Loyalist paramilitaries and Army intelligence, and their agent Stakeknife.

Q: Which state funds the security forces of a certain Middle Eastern country, which has the worst record for the terrorist murder of innocent civilians?

A: The USA. It gives Israel $3 billion annual military aid, which allows it to carry out its 'pinpoint prevention' policy and which has led to the deaths of innocent Palestinian civilians.

The answers to the above questions may seem shocking but they are absolutely true. And they are not isolated examples. The US/UK intelligence establishment is responsible for creating

1

more threats to world security than it prevents. The reason Saddam could invade Kuwait in 1991 was precisely because he had been funded by the UK and the US in the Iran–Iraq war. The reason that Al Qaeda is such an effective terrorist grouping is because the CIA and MI6 funded and trained the Mujahadeen in the Soviet–Afghan War. Veterans of that are now using that knowledge to cause murder and mayhem across the world.

As a result of the intelligence-led UK/US invasion of Iraq, we only have to watch the nightly news footage detailing endless murders and kidnappings in Iraq – largely carried out by Al Qaeda affiliates – to see the dangers of upsetting the equilibrium of a region. Saddam Hussein was a dictator but, having been in power for 40 years, he did provide a certain amount of stability to the region, in the same way that Libyan leader, Colonel Gaddafi, continues to provide stability to North Africa. It is also true that by the standards of the region, they could in some ways be considered liberals, as they provided education and health care programmes to their people, unlike western allied states such as Saudi Arabia.

Although Tony Blair has claimed that Libya renounced its support for terrorism and its weapons of mass destruction (WMD) programmes because of the invasion of Iraq, the reality is rather different. Gaddafi had been trying to come back into the diplomatic fold since the mid-1990s, when I worked in MI5's G Branch, the section responsible for investigating international terrorism. It proved to be rather easy for Gaddafi to give up his WMD programmes, as, like Saddam Hussein, he did not actually have any weapons, or indeed programmes, to give up.[1]

It is no good Blair claiming that other Western intelligence agencies shared the same assessment of Iraq. The truth is they did not. The US relied heavily on British intelligence and

---

[1] Although the Butler inquiry praised MI6's 'success' in countering the Libyan WMD threat, the UN International Atomic Energy Authority, which sees all the intelligence, did not share the British assessment that Gaddafi's programmes existed.

analysis to justify the war in Iraq, and Bush's motives were different. He unashamedly called for 'regime change', while Blair insisted the war was necessary because of Saddam's supposed WMD. The French and Germans opposed the war, partly because their assessed intelligence did not justify it.

Although Iraq and Libya have both in the past posed threats to the lives and security of the British people, the contrast between the two could now hardly be starker. As a result of the invasion of Iraq in 2003, hundreds of US and UK servicemen, and tens of thousands of civilians, have been murdered and maimed, and many more live in fear of their lives. The ensuing chaos has created the ideal breeding ground for Al Qaeda in Iraq. At the same time, the illegal invasion has radicalised otherwise moderate Arabs, fuelling a conflict that will last for at least a generation. Even though Iraq has a new government, insurgent activity is on the increase, and its future hangs in the balance. The only guarantee that the country will not ultimately fall into the hands of Al Qaeda, in the same way that Vietnam fell into the hands of the Viet Cong, is the US has a need for its oil.

The occupation could, though, ultimately cost the USA trillions, while stretching its forces to breaking point as it tries to cope with the world-wide threat from Al Qaeda.

Violence always begets more violence. The UK-aided US bombing of Tripoli in 1986 prompted the murder of 270 people, most of them British and American, when Libya took its revenge by bombing Flight PA103 over Lockerbie. Contrast that with Libya now. Diplomacy has given us an ally with which we can trade and conduct cordial diplomatic relations. More crucially, Colonel Gaddafi is an ally in the war against Al Qaeda. In five years' time Libya will almost certainly be a more stable and liberal country than Iraq.

Anyone with knowledge of counter-terrorism work knew the risks of invading Iraq. The Joint Intelligence Committee (JIC) even warned Blair that it could lead to an increase in terrorist activity. David and I have been active in the Stop the War Coalition for precisely these reasons.

The role of the spies

To counter the increasing terrorism threat, the UK has three primary intelligence agencies:

- The Security Service (MI5) is the domestic agency responsible for identifying, investigating and assessing threats to our national security. For the bulk of its ninety-five-year history it primarily investigated espionage and political subversion. For the last fifteen years it has moved into what were traditional areas of police work – terrorism, organised crime and proliferation of WMD.
- The Secret Intelligence Service (SIS or MI6) is responsible for gathering intelligence abroad on terrorist, political, economic, and organised crime targets.
- The Government Communications Headquarters (GCHQ) is responsible for intercepting communications. It shares its product (intelligence) with its American sister organisation, the National Security Agency (NSA).

In addition to these, there is a plethora of smaller intelligence outfits in the UK. Each police force has its own Special Branch (SB). The Northern Ireland Police Service (formerly the RUC) gathers intelligence. The armed forces have a Military Intelligence wing, and HM Customs and Excise (HMCE) has its own Investigations Department. All these competing organisations, working to their own agendas, leads to duplication of work and obfuscation.

Since the early 1990s, the domestic security service, MI5, and the overseas intelligence agency, MI6, have put an enormous PR effort into trying to convince the public that they have changed since the excesses of the 1950s to the 1980s. They would now have us believe that they are efficient and professional organisations which work calmly *within the law* to protect us from the horrors of terrorism.

The idea that our intelligence services should work within

the law, that they should be accountable to our elected government, is not based on naïve idealism. Nor does it spring from any 'hand-wringing liberalism', as certain sections of our esteemed national press may claim. We live in a western democracy, not a totalitarian regime such as the former Soviet Union, where the KGB had unlimited powers. Checks and balances must exist to ensure that, on the one hand, the intelligence community can work effectively to protect us from today's threats, but on the other, that it does not needlessly infringe our liberties. A whole raft of legislation has been passed by Parliament in an attempt to get this balance right. As I shall demonstrate in this book, I do not think we are there yet.

In comparison with other western democracies, our intelligence services work behind an unprecedented veil of secrecy. There may have been an argument for this in the days of cold war espionage and mole hunts within the services. However, MI5 and MI6 are now primarily involved in work traditionally carried out by police. Why should intelligence officers be any less accountable than police Special Branch officers who do the same work?

When faced with the threat of modern terrorism, nobody would argue against the need for our intelligence services to carry out covert operations, such as bugging telephone lines and property, or secretly searching someone's home when there is a good intelligence case to do so. However, for such operations to be legal, intelligence officers have since 1985 been required to gain the permission of government ministers before going ahead with such intrusive investigations. Additionally, under the 1994 Intelligence Services Act, MI6 has an immunity from prosecution in this country for any illegal acts it carries out abroad, provided it has gained the prior permission of the Foreign Secretary. These laws at least give us a notional democratic oversight, and a degree of protection from violations of our rights.

However, David's and my experiences working at the heart of the intelligence community have shown us that MI5 and MI6 have repeatedly broken these laws.

MI5 when I joined

When I was being recruited in 1990 as part of a new generation of officers, I was told repeatedly that MI5 must work within the law. I was also assured that it only had a lingering interest in 'reds under the bed', and instead its work was increasingly focused on terrorism. My time there proved this claim was, at best, misleading, while also giving me access to files on some of MI5's less savoury activities in the past.

However, I was troubled most by an organisation which would not learn from its mistakes, which lied to government, seemed resistant to change, did not care about getting the best from its staff, and never considered ways of making better use of its resources in its fight to protect us. If MI5 had been a private company, the brighter members of staff would have left to set up their own outfit and blown the old organisation out of the water in any head-on competition.

Add to all this an institutional arrogance, which ignored absolutely any media, Parliamentary or internal criticism, and there is the worst kind of small-minded bureaucracy.

MI5 was founded in 1909 to counter the threat from German spies in the run-up to the First World War. For the next eighty years it worked to its own agenda in the shadows. Its primary function was as a counter-espionage agency. Following the damage caused by the Cambridge spy ring, MI5 further broadened its investigations into extreme left-wing political parties in an attempt to ensure any future Philby, Burgess and Maclean types could not slip through the net. Despite comprehensive coverage of these groups, they were not altogether successful. George Blake operated as a soviet agent for a number of years before his arrest and conviction in the 1960s. A number of other traitors evaded their clutches, and to this day have not been prosecuted.

The 1989 Security Service Act merely enshrined its highly secretive practices. The act did not make any attempt to reform the service, nor did it allow anyone else to assess threats, review MI5's methods and performance, or judge its effectiveness. In

6

fact, MI5 is the envy of other Whitehall departments. It decides which 'threats' it should investigate, secretly carries out these investigations, and then reports to its political masters on how well it is doing. Politicians may delude themselves that they hold our intelligence services to account, but they are only told what the services think they should know. Within this book are examples of MI5 and MI6 lying to government.

The majority of those promoted rise not on the strength of their performance but on the length of time served and their capacity not to rock the boat. *Open Secret*, former MI5 chief Dame Stella Rimington's breathy, jolly-hockey-sticks account of her years in the service confirms this. She tells us that in her day recruits were chosen because they were reliable – read pliant – rather than for their enquiring intellect or for standing up for what is right:

> 'I soon realised that people regarded you with suspicion if you asked too many questions so I learnt to keep quiet,' she observes, without ever analysing the drawbacks and pitfalls of such a decision. 'I knew that open protest was not likely to be successful. If one got a reputation as a revolutionary, one would be regarded as suspect and written off.'[2]

Is that not the very definition of the kind of 'Stalinism' that David referred to when he went on the record in *The Mail on Sunday* (*MoS*)? To see just how true that is, look at the appointment of John Scarlett as head of MI6.

Open Secret reveals little of the abuses of power which David and I saw during our time in MI5 – the very years when Dame Stella was in charge. That is why my private sub-title for this book is *What Dame Stella didn't tell you*. In fact Rimington is disingenuous when she describes her visit to the post-Soviet Russian intelligence services:

---

[2] *Open Secret*, pp. 98, 121.

'We had come prepared with scripts about the need for laws and oversight in democracies... We in this country had quite recent experience of setting up systems which were working well. We had up-to-date advice to offer.'

Very commendable, you might think. But this was 1991, when the head of the SVR, MI5's equivalent in Russia, could be named in the British press but the Director General of MI5 could not. So much for openness. (Stella became the first head of MI5 to be named publicly, but only later that year.)

The visit took place when MI5 had spent a single year as a legally constituted organisation after spending 80 years breaking the law ('bugging and burgling its way around London' as Peter Wright so succinctly put it in his book *Spycatcher*). In the process MI5 had violated minimum democratic rights standards, now recognised by the Human Rights Act. Dame Stella's visit came less than two years after the passing of the 1989 Official Secrets Act, which makes it an offence, for example, for an MI5 officer to blow the whistle on MI6's funding of Al Qaeda to assassinate a foreign head of state. It was three years before there was any democratic scrutiny of the services at all in the UK, when the Intelligence and Security Committee (ISC) was set up in Parliament under the 1994 Intelligence Services Act.

That committee is sometimes referred to as a 'Parliamentary' committee but is appointed by and reports only to the Prime Minister (PM), who can vet its findings. In this book, I quite properly refer to it as the PM's ISC. The committee cannot properly carry out its oversight function because it has no powers to compel intelligence officers to answer questions or hand over documents. Unlike just about every other Western democracy, the intelligence services – not our elected representatives – appear to have the upper hand. Otherwise why have our MPs not passed laws making the agencies properly accountable to them?

8

Blair and his legal responsibilities

When David went on the record in August 1997, he hoped that Prime Minister Tony Blair, a man newly elected on a platform of human rights, freedom of information and an ethical foreign policy, would take possession of his evidence. (If ignoring the MI6-funded assassination of a foreign head of state and illegally invading a sovereign country is his idea of an ethical foreign policy, I wonder how Blair would have behaved if he was following an unethical one?)

The PM – who in opposition had voted against the removal of a public interest defence in the 1989 Official Secrets Act – has repeatedly refused to take any notice of David's evidence, even though he has a *duty*, not a choice, to ensure that the intelligence services work within the law of the land under the:

- Common law.
- Human Rights Act.
- 1989 Security Service Act.
- 1985 Interception of Communications Act (now superseded by the 2000 Regulation of Investigatory Powers Act).
- 1994 Intelligence Services Act.

There can be no doubt he has failed to discharge his legal duty. If a Health and Safety manager ignored his legal responsibilities, he would quickly find himself in trouble, if not in court. Why not the PM? If Blair is allowed to get away with this, we might as well forget democratic accountability. It is worth pointing out that in recent years, Blair, bolstered by the whip system in parliament, has passed the 2000 Terrorism Act, the 2000 Regulation of Investigatory Powers Act and the 2001 Anti-Terrorism Act. All these Acts increased the powers of the intelligence services – in some cases to invade privacy without a warrant. Would MPs have passed them if they had known that MI5 and MI6 regularly abused their powers?

In fact, we have obtained further proof of the authorities' inability to understand their responsibilities to the rule of law when David applied for information from the Home Office under the Data Protection Act:

'Shayler and the ISC

[Name Withheld]'s intention is that the [committee's] taking evidence will ease other political pressures for an enquiry – a victory [Name Withheld] did not want to give Shayler in any case.'[3]

This appears to demonstrate that officials were more interested in covering up for the intelligence services than holding an enquiry to establish the truth. Instead of taking David's evidence when it was offered, the government took out a wide-ranging, interim injunction,[4] preventing the media from reporting any information David had learnt in MI5, even where this concerned murder, illegal investigations and the failure to prevent IRA and Middle Eastern terrorist attacks.

While David was gagged, the spin-doctors went to work on the media, briefing against him, with untruths and misrepresentations. For the record, I know David was *not* too junior to know the information he disclosed; he *did* have regular and formal access to MI6 and its work; it was *not* bar-room gossip; he was *not* overlooked for promotion; he was *not* sacked; and he certainly is *not* a 'Walter Mitty' character – all claims made about him by the government in an attempt to discredit him.

These off-the-record criticisms of David now have an eerie familiarity. Ministers used the same techniques to undermine Dr David Kelly, calling him 'middle ranking', 'disgruntled' and

---

[3] As you can see with the [Name Withheld]s, the restrictive nature of the Data Protection Act, which we used to access this document, is rather hazy about those involved in this meeting. We of course will seek full disclosure of this document when the Freedom of Information Act comes into force. The date of the document was also removed.

[4] Order of Mr Justice Hooper, 5 September 1997.

'a Walter Mitty'. Recent history has already shown us that Kelly's allegations were correct.

The Blair government has also taken *The Guardian* and *The Observer* to court because they sought to expose the crimes of the intelligence services. The latter was also threatened with an Official Secrets Act (OSA) prosecution. At the same time, James Steen, the former editor of *Punch* magazine, now has a criminal conviction for revealing how the agencies failed to prevent the IRA's 1993 Bishopsgate attack, which caused one death, cost the country £350 million, and drove John Major's government to the negotiating table with the IRA.

At the time of writing, the Blair government is again threatening to use the OSA to silence its critics on the *Sunday Times*, particularly its managing editor, Mark Skipworth. Blair's use of the OSA has had a chilling effect on free speech, particularly with regard to the crimes of the intelligence services. Editors now self-censor rather than risk legal action and prosecution. The consequences of this were seen when the government first published the September dossier on Iraq's WMD. No newspaper was able to expose the truth about the document's lies and shortcomings. When a whistleblower did belatedly appear in the form of Dr Kelly, various sources reported how Blair's government used the OSA to either drive him to his death or create the circumstances for the intelligence services to murder him.[5]

Blair, free speech and collusion

In July 1998, David used a legal route to report the MI6/Al Qaeda conspiracy to try to assassinate Colonel Gaddafi in Libya. Blair did not take his evidence. He did not call in the police

---

[5] As the Hutton 'washes whiter than white' enquiry was used to prevent a proper inquest into Dr Kelly's apparent suicide, we are no wiser about the real circumstances leading to his death.

to investigate conspiracy to murder. Instead, he had David thrown in prison in France, with a view to extradition. Also without taking the evidence, Foreign Secretary Robin Cook immediately claimed it was 'pure fantasy'.

Over a year later, when a MI6 document largely confirming the conspiracy was leaked and appeared on the Internet, the Foreign and Commonwealth Office (FCO) pretended it had not happened. Cook continued to tell journalists that the plot was 'pure fantasy'. However, he did tell journalists off the record that MI6 had given him a 'bum briefing'. Nevertheless, he still did not call in the police.

By failing to hold an enquiry into the Gaddafi plot, the government has literally allowed MI6 to get away with murder. Our intelligence services have wide-ranging powers to do their job effectively. However, they are required to operate within the laws of the land, and to gain the permission of ministers if they want to perpetrate an act which would otherwise be illegal. By failing to gain this permission, they commit a crime. In the case of the Gaddafi plot, this involves terrorism and murder.

The government has spent the last seven years using threats, legal action, arrests and imprisonment to prevent the public and Parliament from hearing the evidence of intelligence service crimes. They have, I believe, perverted the course of justice.

As Parliament has no authority to order the intelligence agencies to give evidence or hand over documents, the only individuals who could order an enquiry into the MI6 funding of Al Qaeda were the Prime Minister and the Foreign Secretary. They have failed to do so.

Tony Blair has sent a clear message to the services: they do not have to obey the rule of law or respect democratic rights, as the government will simply refuse to hear evidence against them. At the same time, their critics will be prosecuted.

This has not just happened in David's case. Former Lt-Colonel Nigel Wylde, decorated for his bravery in bomb disposal, was arrested in 1999 and charged under the OSA by the Ministry of Defence (MoD) police, although his case was dropped shortly before trial. The journalist he was alleged to have worked with, Tony Geraghty, was also arrested and had his computer seized by police.

The same happened to *Sunday Times* journalist Liam Clarke, who had written extensively about collusion between the security forces and Loyalist terrorists in Northern Ireland, breaking former Force Research Unit whistleblower Martin Ingram's story. In 2003, Clarke was arrested and had his computer seized for revealing that the security services had bugged a conversation between Mo Mowlam, when she was Northern Ireland minister, and Martin McGuinness, the Education Secretary of the new Northern Ireland Cabinet. There cannot be any damage to national security in that disclosure. In fact, we have to ask why the security services were bugging a conversation between two politicians in the first place, as this cannot be 'necessary in a democracy'.[6]

At one point, *The Sunday People* newspaper had to produce a blank page because Blair's government had injuncted the paper not just to prevent it from exposing collusion between the security services and the Loyalist paramilitaries, but also to ban any mention of the injunction.

As well as intimidating journalists who tried to expose the truth about MI6's funding of Al Qaeda, Blair's actions have stopped the press from getting at the truth about Army intelligence's collusion with terrorists to murder agents and civilians.

The PM's ISC is no better. Tom King, then chair of the committee, refused to hear David's evidence when offered it repeatedly from August 1997 onwards. That did not stop members of the ISC from blackening David's character. One member, Michael Mates MP, erroneously stated on television that David was motivated by spite, as he had been sacked from MI5. Another alluded to his supposed venality in a House of Commons debate without ever bothering to check his information with

---

[6] The test of whether a telephone tap is lawful under the Human Rights Act (HRA), and the European Convention of Human Rights (ECHR), Article 8(2).

David first. Not one MP has asked a question about MI6's funding of Al Qaeda or even about the 'enquiries' Cook made which led to his wholly false claim that the plot was 'pure fantasy'. Tom King has since received a peerage.

The situation is, of course, very different in the US. In May 2002, Coleen Rowley, an FBI officer in Minnesota, blew the whistle on the FBI's failure to tackle Zacarias Moussaoui (the alleged '20th hijacker' and the sole person charged in the 11 September attacks), even though French intelligence had reported that Moussaoui was a suspected terrorist. She also accused FBI directors of making 'misleading' statements on how the agency handled the Moussaoui case, before and after 11 September, in an effort to cover up FBI mistakes.

In the case of her whistleblowing, she was allowed to give her evidence to a congressional hearing. The US has re-organised its agencies to ensure that in future intelligence is properly shared and exploited.

Why we need whistleblowers

There will be those who continue to condemn whistleblowers. I wonder though if these individuals would condemn whistle-blowers if their children had been murdered in a terrorist attack funded by MI6. In fact, without whistleblowers, we would know nothing of Israel's illegal development of nuclear weapons; we would not know that the 45-minute claim in Britain's notorious September dossier referred to battlefield munitions not long-range WMDs; and we would continue to be in ignorance of how the Blair government was secretly massaging immigration figures.

In 1998, the Public Interest Disclosure Act became law. For the first time in Britain, the law gave statutory protection to employees who blow the whistle, as long as the information is disclosed reasonably and responsibly and is in the public interest. If their employers then victimise them, shooting the messenger as so often happens, whistleblowers can sue for damages.

14

Unfortunately, the Act does not apply to the intelligence services. If the services murdered Tony Blair, any MI5 whistleblower who reported this to the media would leave himself open to charges under section one of the 1989 OSA. Before David went through the courts, it was a crime for an MI5 officer to go to the police or ministers with a similar claim.

So for now, the excessive secrecy in Britain continues to create the need for principled whistleblowers. We hoped that our whistleblowing could make some small contribution to opening up a debate in Britain and making it more democratic. Blair clearly hoped that the appalling way David has been treated would deter other whistleblowers. Instead, our actions have created the climate for others, such as Katherine Gun (formerly of GCHQ) and Clare Short, to blow the whistle about illegal activities within the intelligence community.

The misinformed and the ignorant continue to say that David is a traitor. But by covering up the crimes of the intelligence services, Tony Blair is the person who has really betrayed our democracy.

Some hope

In July 2003, MP Andrew Mackinlay told the House of Commons that the latest ISC report was 'dotty and barmy' because of the large number of redactions, including:

> '*** continues to deliver considerable value to GCHQ...
> As a consequence, GCHQ expects to extend the expected life of *** and make corresponding accounting changes.
> *** will start later this year.'

I doubt any of those deletions are actually necessary to protect national security. However, there is some hope. The same report admits:

15

'The Committee has not yet taken formal evidence on the Official Secrets Acts and their usefulness. However, we believe that the legislation could benefit from a review, *as it does not seem to produce a balanced regime*. We will return to this subject in due course.'

I hope that, if and when this review takes place, David and I will be able to contribute to it.

Just the girlfriend

When David went on the record in 1997, the government portrayed him as a lone voice criticising MI5. I was dismissed as 'just the girlfriend' who supported him out of love. I'm sorry, but you do not give up your whole way of life – jobs, home, friends and family – go on the run from the intelligence services, and face an uncertain future, risking imprisonment or worse, merely because you count the world well lost for love. I worked in MI5 for almost six years. I saw the same abuses as David, and I left in disgust, as did so many of our peer group. Even if David and I had separated under the pressure of the last seven years, I would still have written this book. The whole appalling story needs to be told.

The government has throughout this case pursued a policy of shooting the messenger rather than addressing the very serious issues he has raised. As well as attacking his character, the government spin machine has claimed he did it for the money. This is a lie. *The Mail on Sunday* did indeed offer him some money to survive on (half the amount claimed by the spin doctors), but only *after* he had agreed to go on the record. We both gave up our well-paid jobs in London and faced an uncertain and dangerous future. The money allowed us to survive until we could give our evidence of the most serious crimes to the government. During our first year in France, David and his

16

lawyer, John Wadham, negotiated for David's return to the UK without immediate imprisonment and prosecution, so that he could present this evidence. As a condition of his return, he offered to give back the money he had taken as expenses, including any he had already spent. The government has consistently refused, and to this day David has still not given his evidence.[7]

In spite of the personal attacks on us, our period of exile and David's two spells of imprisonment, we still believe we made the right decision. Whichever way you cut it, our disclosures have highlighted to the British public the failings of our intelligence services, not only through abuses of democratic rights but also through an institutional inability to protect the lives of the innocent. I hope that the vast majority of the British people want to know the truth, so they can insist negligent ministers in future make informed decisions about the way we are protected from terrorism and whether our country goes to war. That is the purpose of this book.

Annie Machon
Osea Island
October 2004

Note: all names of intelligence officers have been changed, unless they are already in the public domain. I have also followed MI5's practice of writing operational names in capital letters.

We are also indebted to Swallow Tail, a former officer who was so shocked at David's treatment that he came forward to

---

[7] If David had legally been allowed to take his information to an independent body to investigate he would have followed that route. In the absence of such a body, he was forced to go to the media. If David had been in it for the money, he could have sold his information to the IRA and the Libyans for millions. When the Libyans approached him after he came out of prison, they offered him millions to betray his country. David of course turned them down and reported the matter to the UK authorities.

provide information for this book. I have been deliberately scant about his position as I do not want another Dr Kelly scenario.

Chapter 1

Recruitment and Indoctrination

My first steps

Growing up on the somnolent Channel Island of Guernsey, I had no real awareness or conception of the spying game. I occasionally watched a new James Bond film, and I do remember sitting up with my father watching John Le Carré's spy drama, *Tinker, Tailor, Soldier, Spy*, on television in the early 1980s. Dad was riveted; my impression was of a dark, menacing world peopled by paranoid misfits. Not exactly a dream job.

After graduation from Cambridge in 1989, I moved to London and took up a job in a small publishing house. However, with a degree in Classics and some knowledge of French, German and Russian, I had always been interested in working for the FCO.

After sitting the Foreign Office exams, I received a letter on MoD-headed notepaper which said 'there may be other jobs you would find more interesting'. Although the letter didn't mention the actual job, it did give a MoD-switchboard number. I still do not know why, but my instinctive, startled reaction was 'Oh Christ, it's MI5!' Then I told myself not to be absurd. I had a friend who worked for the MoD. I thought he was probably winding me up. But I *was* intrigued and curiosity got the better of me. I rang the number and soon found myself sitting in an anonymous building in Tottenham Court Road being grilled about my life from the age of twelve.

Daphne Green, my interviewer,[8] was not at all what I had expected: a tall, slim, 30-something woman with hair down to her hips, and a layered hippy skirt. I found that reassuring. (It was only after I had joined MI5 that I found that she was not at all representative of MI5 officers and that all those recruited by her in fact were viewed as 'mavericks'.) She told me that the service was looking for a new breed of officers with a more rounded view of the world and some work experience outside the service, rather than wet-behind-the-ears graduates straight out of college.

Throughout the recruitment process, she was at great pains to emphasise the changing nature of MI5's work. She pointed out in broad terms that the service had virtually ceased to investigate 'subversion' – Communists, Trotskyists, anarchists and right-wing extremists or 'the enemy within' – as Mrs Thatcher had dubbed them during the miners' strike. MI5 was no longer obsessed with 'reds under the bed'. MI5 was bidding to take over areas of work previously handled by the police, such as the Provisional IRA. Most of the work of MI5 in the 1990s – I was assured – would be in counter-terrorism. More importantly, the service had finally been put on a legal basis a year or so earlier in the 1989 Security Service Act. This meant that for the first time MI5 was formally accountable.

David and I agree that we would not have joined a service which investigated individuals simply for holding political opinions that the government thought 'subversive'. We could see that MI5's work against terrorism was legitimate, as it set out to protect democracy from those who use violence rather than argument to make their point.

Although the pay was not brilliant, this was important work in defence of democratic values and human life. Call me old-fashioned, but I was attracted to serving my country.

---

[8] The fictitious name I first used was vetoed by MI5. This is another fictitious name.

David's first steps

His background and recruitment were very different from mine. At college, he had been editor of his student newspaper and passed stories to the national press. Shortly before graduating in July 1989, he had won a student journalism award. Three months later he joined *The Sunday Times* on its graduate training scheme. In April 1990, along with another trainee, he was sacked. With a friend, he then raised the capital to start a small business publishing a free-sheet to 25,000 students across Scotland. Although he had some success to start with, the business went down in the recession.

Then, on 12 May 1991, an advertisement in the media section of *The Independent* newspaper caught his eye. Entitled 'Godot isn't coming' it asked if he was interested in current affairs, had common sense and an ability to write. Although the ad seemed tailor-made for his skills, it did not feature a company name. David assumed it was telesales and didn't bother to send an application. His mother later persuaded him that there would be 'no harm' in exploring further as in many ways the position seemed ideally suited to him.

First interview

Still unaware of the 'company' which had placed the advert, David went to T G Scott recruitment in Soho Square, London. After passing a couple of intelligence tests, he was briefly interviewed. When asked what he had done to 'change the world', he replied that he had published extracts of Peter Wright's book *Spycatcher* when it was under injunction in 1988. Still believing the job involved journalism or media, David told the interviewer that the security services had no reason to destabilise democratic government. David says:

'This question came up at every stage of the recruitment

21

process. Each time I gave the same answer. They would then go on to ask what about national security and I would tell them that the information would have been gleaned by Britain's enemies, long before I published the information.'

It was at my first interview in July 1990 that I was asked to sign the OSA. I was told that they wouldn't go any further unless I did. Being intrigued, I signed it. I expected my interviewer to lead me through my first steps into the charmed circle. But the only specific information they allowed me to know – until the day I joined MI5 – was the grade I'd been recruited at. The OSA document I signed has no validity under criminal or contract law. It is a piece of theatre designed to demonstrate to the wide-eyed recruit that he or she will be entering the secret world.

At this stage of the process, David and I also learnt that we would have to give up any employment rights, including the right to belong to a trade union or staff federation, on joining. If you were, for instance, in dispute with management, there would be a far greater sensitivity on the part of management. I can specifically recall from my own interview that the phrase 'you will be looked after' was used to justify any qualms potential officers had about their employment rights being undermined. However, the experience of the next six years was a direct contradiction of all this. Because employees had no employment rights, they could be treated arbitrarily and in effect persecuted for pointing out what was wrong with the organisation. They could be compelled to follow orders even where they knew that this might be unlawful.

Any request to honour what had been promised in interview, – for example, a sensitive response to complaints about difficult ethical situations and work-related problems – was ignored. There is absolutely no reason why members of MI5, like GCHQ staff, should not in this day and age be allowed to join a union or federation to represent their interests at work.

Second interview

David had similar experiences when he attended his second interview in Tottenham Court Road in June 1991. He takes up the story:

> 'The interview took place at an unmarked empty building. I was greeted by the epitome of the patrician intelligence officer: tall, thin, swept-back silver hair and chalk pinstripe suit.'

Some commentators have expressed astonishment that David was surprised at MI5's legal shortcomings, yet during our separate recruitment processes, the service went to great pains to point out that it observed the rule of law. At his second interview, David was asked about Kevin Barry O'Donnell, a young IRA suspect who had been shot dead with others in Dungannon, County Tyrone, by the SAS. As all the suspected IRA men had been killed outright, it had led to speculation that the SAS had shot to kill, rather than in self-defence. David gave the interviewer his analysis:

> 'If terrorists engage SAS operatives, the soldiers are of course entitled to defend themselves. But we are not at war with the IRA under the terms of the Geneva Convention, so the SAS are not allowed to assassinate suspects. In a democracy, terrorist suspects must be arrested and brought to trial under the criminal law. It is only in totalitarian states that law enforcement agencies summarily execute suspects without trial.'[9]

In my case, I was asked about the ethics and legality of internment and replied similarly. In each case the interviewer confirmed that it was MI5's policy to work within the rule of law in the ways we had discussed.

---

[9] The service can't say that it didn't know what it was getting in David.

CSSB

In September 1990, I attended the Civil Service Selection Board (CSSB). Although MI5 is not part of the mainstream Civil Service and the job requires very different skills, the intelligence services still use CSSB to select candidates. In fact, the two days of tests were gruelling – far harder than the actual desk work of an MI5 officer. They involved:

- verbal, numerical and spatial tests;
- a written exercise, in which candidates have to summarise a dossier of information and make recommendations to ministers. There is only enough time within the two hours to skim read the dossier before writing the summary and recommendation in one draft;
- management exercises based on the dossier in chairing and contributing to meetings;
- interviews with a member of the service, a member of the civil service, and a psychologist.

A month later, I attended the Final Selection Board. The same day, they phoned to offer me a job as a GI5 – a fast track entrant as an officer at grade 5^{10} – pending security clearance. This was the only concrete information I had been given about the service at this stage. However, by now I had successfully completed such an intensive recruitment process over a period of eight months that I felt the job had to be right for me. I was also by now thoroughly intrigued.

Security vetting

Both David and I had to undergo security vetting to what was

---

[10] A member of the General Intelligence Duties group, grade 5, shortened to GI5. GI6 was the lowest and GI1 the highest. Senior management started at grade SM4. The DG was SM1.

24

RECRUITMENT AND INDOCTRINATION

then called Enhanced Positive Vetting (EPV) level, the highest level of security clearance. This included sending a Special Branch officer to David's neighbours' homes to ask them about his family's behaviour and character. The service also interviews four nominated friends from different phases of your life, and then interviews other friends whom they nominate, until a full picture of your character has been drawn up. I was also interviewed, and had the embarrassment of being asked all about my sex life by a sweet little old lady who, despite looking just like my grandmother, had the gently probing technique of Miss Marple.[11]

In preparation for David's security interview, he bought a *Daily Mail*, which he left on the table where the interview was to take place, and served coffee in old Royal Wedding mugs belonging to his mother. In addition to being quizzed about his private life, he was asked the inevitable: 'Have you or any members of your family been members of the Communist Party?' David admitted to being a former member of CND and the Anti-Apartheid movement.

About a month later, David was called into the unmarked building on Tottenham Court Road for a second security interview. The interviewer began by asking about one of his referees, a close friend from school days, Matthew Guarente, and his political affiliations.

David: He's a member of the Labour party but that can't be of any importance, can it?
Interviewer: He may have had more extreme views than that.
David: He once went to a few meetings of the Socialist Workers' Party, but surely that can't bother you.
Interviewer: The SWP is an extremist organisation. Your referee has a file with the service. Did you ever join him at the meetings?

---

[11] There used to be Positive and Normal – not Negative – Vetting, until Normal Vetting was declared unlawful as it took place without the consent or knowledge of the applicant.

David: No, because he became involved at college when
we briefly drifted apart.
Interviewer: You must never tell him this.

David passed his final board in summer 1991.

Induction and indoctrination

On 29 January 1991 I walked into MI5's training office in
Grosvenor Street, Mayfair. Beyond my grade of GI5 I knew
nothing of what my job would entail. However, I felt confident
that I was right for the job, as the recruitment process had been
in-depth and long drawn out. The first two weeks were taken
up with Training Course (TC) 101, MI5's induction course. As
a foretaste of the desk work, the bulk of the course was taken
up with paper-handling skills; how to write a loose minute or
a note for file, and how to accurately identify the subject of a
Personal File (PF) – ie a target of MI5. This may sound basic,
but the trainers highlighted how easy it was to make simple
mistakes and wrongly target innocent people. To drive home
this point we had to examine real files where mix-ups had
occurred. Our trainers told us this happened with surprising
frequency. As light relief from all this desk work, we were also
taken to meet specialist sections of the office, such as A4
(mobile surveillance), A2 (telephone tap transcribers) and A1
(gadgets).
   My TC101 group was a strange mix of people. It was the
first intake to include the new grade of GI6, the bottom grade
for MI5 officers. The distinction between graduates being
recruited at GI5 or GI6 appeared to be based on which university
had been attended. Those who had studied at Oxbridge and
redbrick universities entered MI5 at a higher level than those
who had attended the newer establishments, regardless of age
and experience. Sir Humphrey would have approved. My TC101
was a disparate group, which never built up the usual *esprit*

de corps. However, I was pleased to see that Rob Webb,[12] whom I had met on both CSSB and the Final Selection Board, had made it into the office as a GI5. He had also been recruited by Daphne.

David joined MI5 eight months later. After delays in travelling back after a break in Scotland, he arrived home in the early hours of 11 November 1991 to find a letter from the Director of Establishments, confirming he had a post at GI4, a higher grade than expected of a 25-year-old. Later that day – some seven months after David first saw the 'Godot isn't coming' advert – he walked into MI5's old training building in Grosvenor Street, SW1, carrying his birth certificate as the requested means of identification. David met five other trainees:

Jestyn Thirkell-White, 23, Philosophy, Cambridge, GI5
Linda,[13] 31, English, Reading University, GI4
Penny, 24, Oxford (Poly), GI6 (daughter of former senior
    MI5 official)
Caroline, 29, Marketing, Birmingham, GI4
Damien, 27, History, Cambridge, GI4

In late November 1991, David took up his first post in the service in C3, the vetting section, which assessed the notional security threat from any government job applicant. He says of this period:

'My first STAR designation (job title assigned by the office administration system, STAR) was C3P/3. Unfortunately, although there was a C3P/1 and a C3/0, there was no C3P/0. But there was an R2, if not an R2D/2. Glyn Michaels, a colleague, used to joke: 'For all the sense you get out of R2, they might as well speak the same language as the robot.'

'I was delighted to be taken out for a "beer and a

---

[12] Not his real name.
[13] Real first names changed on orders of MI5.

27

sandwich" during my first lunch break. As the lunch hour finished though, there was no sign of the fabled sandwich. Rather than returning to the office, the group – which included senior managers – ordered another beer. And another, bringing the lunchtime total to 5 pints each. C3/0, the section head, then retreated to his office where he fell asleep for the afternoon.[14]

'In a scene out of a *Dilbert* cartoon, Jeremy, my line manager and "mentor" who was a youngish looking 48-year-old, told me I should get out while the going was still good, while still young. At the time I laughed, thinking he was just an old cynic. Now I wish I had heeded his advice. Ironically, he also gave me a copy of a book which, he said, contained everything I needed to know about vetting. It was called *Blacklist* by Mark Hollingsworth and Richard Norton-Taylor, two journalists who were later involved in my story.'

David's job in C3 was largely paper pushing. However, he soon came across his first experience of MI5's strange attitude to individual liberties. Under MI5 and government policy, an individual cannot be refused Positive Vetting clearance – to see material classified SECRET or below – if his membership of a subversive group had lapsed for more than five years. One such former member of Militant Tendency (MT) had applied for clearance. Although he had been recorded as a 'member: Trotskyist organisation' many years before, in the previous five years he had only come to attention once, and then only to make a brief, social telephone call to MT HQ. MI5's counter-subversion department, F2, did not normally consider a one-off phone call to MT HQ to be evidence of membership of the organisation. However, at one point during the conversation, the file holder had referred to his contact at MT as 'comrade',

---

[14] The abuse of alcohol continued to be a problem for the services, leading to headlines about the loss of security laptops and briefcases by drunken MI5 and MI6 officers in 2000.

a term used by many on the Left, including the Labour party and the trade union movement. On the basis of this fraternal use of the word 'comrade' C3, the vetting section, ignored service policy and recommended to his employers that he be refused security clearance and therefore be barred from the job for which he had applied.

Although this is a minor example, it still forms an infringement of an individual's right to pursue a private and professional life within a democracy. It is also clear evidence that MI5 makes intelligence assessments on the flimsiest of information

A brush with DG Stella and 'Dir T' Lander

A month after joining, David had his first encounter with the then Director General (DG)-designate, Stella Rimington, at the outgoing DG's sherry party. David describes the moment:

> 'Sir Patrick Walker [the former DG] was talking to a group of us, me and my fellow recruits, when suddenly I heard this booming yet shrill voice. Ann Widdecombe's bossy sister emerged in front of us and virtually shouted, "My name is Stella Rimington. I'm about to become DG." She then shook us all firmly by the hand, barely having time to catch our names, before turning to Penny, one of the new recruits. As Stella knew her father, a former Deputy DG, she spent her time chatting to her.'

A month later David had his first encounter with another officer destined to become DG. In January 1992, David was told he would be posted to T branch to work against the Provisional IRA (PIRA), if the Home Secretary gave MI5 primacy – or lead responsibility – for PIRA investigations on the British mainland. While waiting for official confirmation that MI5 would be taking on this work, David was 'parked' in the counter-subversion section, F2.

29

At the Irish Background briefing course, David found himself sitting next to a curious figure with untucked shirt and messy hair, who proceeded to fiddle with his shoelaces during the final lecture. The mysterious figure then got up to address the course. It was David's first encounter with Stephen Lander, then Director T, head of the domestic counter-terrorism department, known in the service as 'Dir T', pronounced 'dirt'.[15]

During a question and answer section, David asked Lander about Operation Flavius, which had led to the deaths of three Irish citizens in Gibraltar in 1988. While they were members of PIRA, at the time of the shooting they were unarmed. As a student journalist, David had keenly followed the news coverage. He was particularly concerned that information that could only have come from security sources had come to be aired in the press so fully, especially as it turned out to be 'disinformation'. David explains:

'I asked if the service had played any part in these briefings or whether it had launched an enquiry to identify those responsible for the leaks of information. Lander was reluctant to comment, but I tried to push him. He denied that MI5 played any part in the misinformation so I asked him where he thought it had come from. He declined to reply more fully, other than expressing his belief that the service had done nothing wrong in Gibraltar. It was, he claimed, all the fault of the SAS because they took over responsibility for the operation as soon as executive action[16] was imminent.[17]

'I later discovered that he had in fact been the officer in charge of MI5's contribution to the Gibraltar operation.'

---

[15] His opposite number in G Branch, International Terrorism was known as 'Dir G', pronounced 'dirge'.

[16] The phrase used to describe arrests. As MI5 has no powers of arrest, it hands operations over to the police or the SAS to carry out this responsibility.

[17] In McCann v. UK (1995) 21 EHRR 97, the European Court of Human Rights (ECtHR) held that there had been a violation of ECHR, Article 2, the right to life. In other words, the British state was responsible for three unlawful killings.

David and I later learnt from Joe Hartley,[18] a colleague in MI5, that he had earned himself a 'black mark' regarding Gibraltar. He had resigned from the service because he did not want to work for an organisation involved in an ethically dubious operation. Having re-joined the service a year later, he found that Personnel Section had placed a note on his record of service, indicating that he had had moral qualms about the operation and that he therefore wasn't entirely to be trusted. As a result, he found that each new boss had pre-conceived ideas about him. His career was blighted in a number of ways. On his return to the service he received postings to deeply unpopular sections such as H4, financial administration.

Even during our first year in MI5, it was becoming obvious to David and me that MI5 was not like its portrayal in books or the media. Nor was it the scrupulously law-abiding service it told us it was. Instead of listening to concerns from officers about civil liberties, it punished those who ventured them. At the same time, drunken officers ruled a former activist out of a government job because he had called someone 'comrade' and a senior manager – later DG, Sir Stephen Lander – had refused to answer questions about MI5's role in an unlawful killing.

Given the hoo-hah created by the Gibraltar operation, it is a wonder that Lander was ever promoted again. But in 1996, Lander, then Director H, Administration, became DG after he and Eliza Manningham-Buller, then Director A, Operations, threatened to resign from MI5's six-person board of directors. Manningham-Buller supported Lander in this palace coup. In 2002 she succeeded Lander as head of MI5.

---

[18] Not his real name.

Chapter 2

The Enemy Within?

ORBAT[19]

F Branch	Counter-subversion section
Director F	
F2/0	Paul Slough. Assistant Director (AD) in charge of counter-subversion investigations and operations
F2/1	Steve Canute. AD's second-in-command
F2B/1	Hilda Trimble. Group Leader in charge of investigations into Trotskyist groups
F2B/4	Joe Hartley. In charge of investigations into Militant Tendency (MT). Succeeded in post by Sarah Knight
F2B/5	Alison Pomdeterre. In charge of investigations into the Socialist Workers' Party (SWP). I took over from her in February 1991
F2C/1	Glyn Michaels. In charge of investigations into extreme right-wing groups. He was promoted and became my group leader
F2C/7	David Shayler. In charge of investigations into Communist and anarchist groups
F4/0	Assistant Director in charge of the agent running section for F Branch, including my recruiter, Daphne Green, who was posted to F4 in 1991. The role merged with F2 as the branch was reduced in late 1991

---

[19] ORBAT stands for Order of Battle, a military term used by MI5 to describe the enemy's command structure. All names are fictitious.

Background to subversion

In 1991 MI5 was still using the same criteria for recording individual subversives and their sympathisers as was set out by Home Secretary David Maxwell-Fyfe in 1952. He called on the services to identify any individual engaged in undermining Parliamentary democracy, national security and/or the economic well-being of the UK by violent, industrial or political means. In fact, many would argue that groups who used only political means to get their point across were merely exercising their democratic rights. In fact, MI5 used photos of demonstrations, copies of election lists and even lists of subscribers to radical left-wing book clubs as indicators of subversive sympathy and membership. Of course, the world was a very different place when I joined the section, almost 40 years after Maxwell-Fyfe's declaration, not least because of the disintegration of the Soviet Union and its Eastern bloc allies.

From Maxwell-Fyfe's statement to Parliament, which was never made law, MI5 and subsequent governments used to argue that *all members* of certain parties – such as the Communist Party of Great Britain (CPGB) or later the bewildering array of Trotskyists, with names like the International Marxist Group (IMG), Workers' Revolutionary Party (WRP) Major and Minor, Revolutionary Communist Party (RCP) and Revolutionary Communist Group (RCG), anarchists and the extreme right – were threats to the security of the state or our democratic system. This in itself is a contentious proposition. None of these Trotskyist groups was cultivating Eastern bloc finance or building bombs in smoky back rooms, but were instead using legitimate democratic methods to make their case, such as standing in elections, organising demonstrations and 'educating' the workers. They certainly had no allegiance to a foreign power, the primary *raison d'être* for the investigation of subversion, because, unlike the Communist Party, they abhorred the Eastern bloc.

Since MI5 was effectively investigating individuals for holding opinions the government did not like – a very un-British position – it was always at pains to point out that it took its responsibilities with regard to human rights very seriously, although not seriously enough to ensure that these activities were regulated by a legal framework. All the service's phone taps prior to the passing of the Interception of Communications Act (IOCA) in 1985 were unlawful because there was no legislation governing the interception of communications.[20] In fact, the Home Office Warrants (HOWs) used to justify phone tapping and covert entry were so vague as to be meaningless. There was certainly not enough information for the minister signing a warrant to make an informed decision about letting the service break into an individual's home or bug their phone.

During publicity interviews for her book, *Open Secret*, the former head of MI5, Dame Stella Rimington, demonstrated that she at least was far from sensitive to the illegality of the activities of the service:

'I still thought the essence of the Cold War and spies and stuff was fun,' she said. 'You know, going around listening to people's telephones and opening their mail and stuff.'[21]

The HRA provides a number of reasons why a security service is allowed to invade the privacy of an individual. The standard is 'necessary in a democracy'. It does not include 'fun'. Dame Stella also admitted that files were opened on individuals who posed no threat to the state, undermining the authorities' previous assurances that files were only opened on members of subversive organisations or their sympathisers. This means that MI5 monitoring included legitimate political activists:

'You can say from the position of 2001 that *files were opened on people who were not actively threatening the*

---

[20] Under Article 8 of the European Convention of Human Rights (ECHR), incorporated into English law by the Human Rights Act (HRA), this is a violation of the right to privacy.
[21] *The Guardian*, weekend supplement, 8 September 2001.

state, but nevertheless, in the context of those days, I think the files that were opened fitted that definition of subversion. I think, in the past, some of *our predecessors may have been a bit over enthusiastic (in opening files),* but by the time I got there we were very focused on this definition and what we were doing.'[22] [My italics]

She tries to wriggle off the hook by referring to 'that definition of subversion' as if it somehow changed over the years. The truth is, it did not. In August 1997 David disclosed in *The Mail on Sunday* that files were opened on such individuals as Jack Straw and Peter Mandelson. Either they were innocent victims of MI5's over-zealous investigation of subversives, in which case they should demand an explanation from the service and should establish how many others were wrongfully investigated, or they really were a threat to our national security, in which case the British people have a right to know.

In fact, MI5 devoted such significant resources to subversive groups from the 1940s to 1993, when subversion was finally downgraded, that F2 claimed to know more about the finances of the CPGB than the Party did itself! In communism's heyday from the 1950s to the 1970s, around 60 desk officers – each with a number of support staff – spied on the CPGB alone, although F Branch had dwindled to around nine or ten desk officers and agent runners, plus around 20–30 support and secretarial staff by the time I arrived in 1991.

As public support for communism began to fade during the 1970s and 80s, F2 had become increasingly concerned with MT because of its entryist or 'False Flag' tactics, in which MT members who had infiltrated the Labour Party stood as candidates for Parliament and other bodies without declaring their association with Militant. However, by the early 1990s the Soviet bloc had collapsed; the ageing CPGB had become the Democratic Left, and MT was on the point of abandoning

[22] *The Guardian*, 11 September 2001.

entryism. As a result, everyone in F2 believed that there was no justification to continue the investigation of subversion – with the exception of Director F, the man in charge of the Branch. He seemed to have no idea that the work of MI5 should be in defence of democratic values. He was rather more concerned about his standing in the service pecking order alongside other MI5 directors. He saw any reduction in his branch's resources as an attack on his power base in MI5, so he fiercely resisted any attempts to transfer his staff to other branches.

In addition, MI5 management wanted to retain personnel so it would not need to take on extra staff, in the event of it winning the lead in the investigation of the PIRA[23] from the Metropolitan Police Special Branch (MPSB). That was where the SWP came in.

My role against the SWP

To my dismay, as I had always been completely apolitical, my first posting after the induction course was to F Branch, the counter-subversion section. During my recruitment, I had been told that MI5 no longer took much interest in subversion, instead focusing increasingly on such threats as terrorism. I had therefore hoped to go straight to a counter-terrorism branch or, failing that, to K Branch (counter-espionage) where I could use my Russian. It was some consolation to find out subsequently that MI5 had a policy of posting those deemed to be 'clear thinkers' to this section, because of the political sensitivity of its work. Perhaps we should infer that the counter-terrorism branches were staffed by muddled thinkers?

In February 1991 I joined F2. The section was tucked away in a little-known MI5 building in Bolton Street, Mayfair. The office was a classic, run-down civil service affair, with battered old wooden desks, lime green wall paint and threadbare carpets.

---

[23] This was finally announced to Parliament in May 1992.

37

The section when I joined had no computer system; all its records were on paper, a fact which surprised me, as easily accessible information is essential to an intelligence service. This also meant that all my work had to be written out in longhand and passed to my secretary for typing, before coming back to me for correction. Having worked in other offices with computers, I found this all painfully slow.

My 'job title' was F2B/5, and I was in charge of a small team investigating the SWP. David joined F Branch a year later as F2C/7, to study anarchists, communists and extreme right-wingers. David and I met in F2 but we didn't start going out with each other until spring 1993. Our eyes met across a crowded operations room, he always likes to joke.

All new MI5 officers are 'mentored' by a more experienced officer, usually of the same grade, over a period of six months. Some new recruits are lucky. David had Glyn Michaels,[24] my boss at the time, who took his mentoring duties very seriously. I was unlucky. I had Alison Pomdeterre, who appeared completely uninterested in the mentoring process. After only a month of mentoring, I took over the desk and the management of three clerical workers who did the painstaking work of formally identifying 'subversives'.

Like any other job, the MI5 desk officer has an IN tray and an OUT tray and processes information. (Officers always also made great use of the PENDING tray for anything that might look difficult.) The difference between MI5 and a normal job is that the information comes in the form of reports from agents in the field or GCHQ 'sigint'.[25]

As well as routinely processing vast quantities of Linen (product from telephone taps), Chalis[26] (letters), and source (agent) reports, in my first year in F2 I was tasked to research each area of the SWP's activities: finance, membership, student numbers, and industrial relations among others, in order to

---

[24] F2 officers' names are fictitious.
[25] Signals intelligence as opposed to 'humint', human intelligence.
[26] Codeword changed on orders of MI5, even though codewords are not security classified.

assess whether the party was a threat to national security. It was a moot point whether the SWP had ever posed a realistic threat to the state. But after I'd carried out months of painstaking research, I was in no doubt. Although individual members of the party were committed, the SWP was small, relatively poor, and their politics fell outside MI5's criteria for investigation – they neither had links to a foreign power, like the communists, nor did they practice entryism, like MT. Their policies advocated educating people so that they could take part in a *democratic* movement to replace the existing political system. This was hardly the stuff of revolutionary nightmare.

Despite my assessments, senior management in F2 ensured that the SWP assumed an increasingly prominent role in the work of the branch. MI5 management unremittingly applied pressure on me to beef up the case for the study of the SWP, particularly after its (legitimate) support for a number of industrial disputes in the early nineties, which of course posed no threat to national security or Parliamentary democracy. Despite the pressure, I still succeeded in terminating the last remaining telephone tap targeted against an individual subversive in the UK – Tony Cliff, the SWP's founder – and drastically reducing the number of agents who for decades had been run against the SWP at great cost to the taxpayer. However, senior managers still insisted that a telephone tap stay in place on the party's HQ.

Even then, F2 policy dictated that any individual who attended six or more meetings of the SWP was recordable as a 'member: Trotskyist organisation', even where the service knew that many individuals attended these meetings to protest against specific issues such as the NHS cuts or the poll tax, subjects of legitimate dissent.

Failure to transcribe telephone taps

When MI5 took over primacy for the IRA in October 1992, a number of telephone intercept transcribers were transferred to

39

the new T Branch section from F Branch work. English-speaking transcribers were at a premium in T Branch in the service's work against PIRA. As a result, F2 simply did not have the resources to transcribe the vast amount of intelligence gathered from the intercepts on the SWP and MT HQs. Therefore a backlog of untranscribed tapes built up over several months. Although F2 claimed in its HOW[27] applications that these intercepts were absolutely necessary to protect national security and other democratic rights, in 1993 Director F ordered that the untranscribed tapes be destroyed without ever being listened to, even though he had insisted on the phone lines being tapped.

If the SWP and MT really had been in the process of undermining the state, then MI5 would have lost vital intelligence and put the security of the state at risk. This was confirmation, if any were needed, that the intercepts on the SWP and MT were not 'necessary in a democracy' – they could only be destroyed precisely because they were *unnecessary* – and were therefore unlawful under the ECHR.

But the problem was compounded when MT abolished its policy of entryism in late 1992. Since MT's membership had dwindled to less than a thousand and entryism within the Labour movement was MI5's only legitimate reason for investigating MT, the desk officer, F2B/4, Sarah Knight, recommended that there was no longer a case to justify the telephone and letter intercept on the party's HQ. Her minute went through the management chain. In each case, the line manager agreed with her assessment until it reached Director F. He ordered the desk officer to go and 'make a case'. Under mild protest, she went off to seek out any nuggets of intelligence from the material that had been transcribed. She then squeezed a case for revalidation of the intercept warrant out of it, even where this meant exaggerating the importance of facts and taking them out of context or 'sexing up', as it is now known.

---

[27] Home Office Warrant, the name MI5 gives to its applications to the Home Secretary to tap telephones.

The Home Secretary approved the warrant in ignorance because he simply did not know of the desk officer's reservations or, I suspect, that months of untranscribed tapes had been destroyed.

The illegal and unjustified files

On our TC101 induction courses, David and I were told that MI5 has opened more than a million PFs. We were also exhaustively taken through case studies of incorrect identification. If MI5 were 99.9% accurate in its work that would still mean that there would be over a thousand files containing information that is factually incorrect. Of course, no organisation is 99.9% accurate and the inaccuracies would be spread across a much greater number of files. As we had seen on TC101, this was remarkably easy to do. This means that there must be thousands of files in the MI5 archives which contain inaccuracies about British citizens. Even where the information is accurate, its collection and retention is clearly unlawful under the HRA. After all, the difference between a democratic and non-democratic or totalitarian state is that legitimate political dissent and the privacy of those involved is protected in the former and not in the latter. Dame Stella Rimington has – we have already seen – admitted that she thought MI5 was 'over-enthusiastic' in its targeting of left-wing activists.[28] David and I can confirm that this is the case.

On one occasion, for example, a schoolboy had written to the Communist Party asking for information for a topic he was preparing at school. His letter was copied (all mail to the CPGB was copied by MI5) and used to create a PF, where he was identified before being recorded as a '?communist sympathiser'. On another occasion, a man divorcing his wife had written to MI5 claiming she was involved in communism.

---

[28] *The Guardian*, 8 September 2001.

For that, his wife got a PF again as a '?communist sympathiser'. In both cases, the suspect only came to the attention of the service on that one occasion. So why was this information still available to desk officers some twenty years after these individuals had first come to attention, in less than suspicious circumstances?

It is also of enormous concern in a democracy that MI5 continues to hold private information about our elected representatives which could be used to influence ministers and MPs in secret. In October 2002, *The Mail on Sunday* reported that Jack Straw had leaked information in connection with the Jeremy Thorpe/Norman Scott affair when he was PPS to Barbara Castle. As this information also features in his PF, we have to ask whether it was used to influence the then Home Secretary's policy towards hearing David's evidence, which he has declined to do, and seeing him prosecuted, which he has endorsed.

Even where MI5 was justified in holding files – as in the case of Vladimir Ilych Lenin (PF2) or Leon Trotsky (PF3), who actively worked to undermine this country – it cannot reasonably argue that it must still keep these files and their contents secret. However, the intelligence services are so resistant to scrutiny that these files remain in the registry of MI5's new HQ, Thames House, even though their subjects have been dead for years. MI5 has claimed that opening up these files will reveal sensitive operational techniques. The use of carrier pigeons perhaps?

In fact, the intelligence agencies are in the peculiar position of not just holding files on individuals who no longer pose a notional 'threat' but of holding files even though *the actual threat itself, such as state communism, no longer even exists.*

It cannot be therefore 'necessary in a democracy' for the services to continue to hold private information about individuals on outdated files which are still accessible to intelligence operatives. The gravity of this abuse of power is compounded by the fact that the material was unlawfully gathered in the first place.[29]

To comply with the conditions of the HRA, MI5 should notify every individual on whom a file was created before the passing of the 1989 Security Service Act that they have a right to remedy, and therefore compensation, for:

- MI5's initial unlawful invasion of their privacy.
- Any interference with their freedoms, such as being blacklisted because of alleged subversive sympathies. There are a number of BBC applicants who were affected by this.
- The service's continued invasion of their privacy by retaining personal information which could be used against them.

Files on public figures

In the course of my work in F2, I came across many files on media figures, celebrities and prominent politicians, particularly when we were asked to research candidates standing in the 1992 General Election. Our job was to summarise MI5's security history of an individual and assess the threat they might pose to national security. F2 management then passed the assessment and summary – but not the original material or file – to the Prime Minister and the leader of the opposition. They would use them when deciding on the suitability of a particular candidate for government or the shadow cabinet. Because the PM or the leader of the opposition did not see the raw intelligence or the detail of the security case against the individual concerned, they were in no real position to make an informed assessment of that individual. It was all too easy for the services to cherry pick intelligence or 'sex up' a case by omission, if they didn't

---

[29] See the case of Harman and Hewitt v. UK.

like a prospective minister or thought that his presence in government might mean that MI5 was more closely scrutinised or held to account.

F2, being tucked away in the little-known MI5 building on Bolton Street off Piccadilly, was a relaxed section, with quite an *esprit de corps*. Consequently, during our time there David and I either personally reviewed or were shown by our colleagues the following PFs. Few of those listed actually belong or belonged to subversive organisations. According to MI5, they have or had 'sympathies' with these or other groups and are therefore worthy of MI5 investigation:

John Lennon
Jack Straw MP
Ted Heath MP
Tam Dalyell MP
Gareth Peirce (solicitor)
Jeremy Corbyn MP
Mike Mansfield (barrister)
Geoffrey Robertson (barrister)
Patricia Hewitt MP
Harriet Harman MP
Garry Bushell (journalist)
Peter Mandelson (European commissioner)
Peter Hain MP
Clare Short MP
Mark Thomas (comedian)
Mo Mowlam (politician)
Arthur Scargill (NUM leader, who famously had his own recording category: unaffiliated subversive)
Neil Kinnock (politician)
Bruce Kent (peace campaigner)
Joan Ruddock MP
Owen Oyston (businessman)
Cherie Booth aka Blair
Tony Blair MP

David Steel (politician)
Teddy Taylor MP
Ronnie Scott (jazz musician)
Robin Cook MP
John Prescott MP
Mark Steele (comedian)
Jack Cunningham MP
Mohamed Al Fayed (businessman)
Mick McGahey (former union leader)
Ken Gill (former union leader)
Michael Foot (politician)
Jack Jones (former union leader)
Ray Buxton (former union leader)
Hugh Scanlon (former union leader)
Harold Wilson (politician)
James Callaghan (politician)
Richard Norton-Taylor (*Guardian* journalist)

David and I also came across a file called 'Subversion in contemporary music', which consisted of press clippings about Crass, then a well-known, self-styled 'anarchist' band; the Sex Pistols; and, rather surprisingly, UB40. You can almost imagine the *what's-the-country-coming-to?* Colonel Blimp type opening the file because the Sex Pistols performed shocking songs like 'Anarchy in the UK' – the lyrics of the song were on the file after being snipped from *Time Out* magazine – and (their version of) 'God Save the Queen'. But does any reasonable person believe that the Sex Pistols were actively trying to damage national security?

Unlawful investigation of non-subversives

The 'subversion' of cabinet ministers Harriet Harman and Patricia Hewitt was to have been leading members of the National Council for Civil Liberties (NCCL – now Liberty), the very

45

organisation designed to protect us from such unwarranted abuses of our liberties. At one point, David came across a series of minutes on a file dating from the early 1980s. They were written by Charles Elwell, a publicly named and notoriously paranoid former head of F2 who saw a red under every bed, and who had successfully argued that members of the executive of the NCCL were recordable as 'suspected sympathiser: communist', *simply for being members of the executive*. He based this assumption on the fact that, as one or two leading members of the NCCL had communist sympathies, the organisation was therefore by definition a communist front organisation.

This went beyond MI5's own rules. It justified its work against legitimate non-subversive organisations such as trade unions, CND, the NCCL and the Greenham Common women by saying that it was not investigating these organisations or their members *per se* but was investigating subversive penetration of these groups.

As a result, MI5 gathered ten thick volumes on both the Greenham women and CND. Inevitably, as a result of this, F2 gathered personal information on and details of legitimate political activists, which were passed to ministers in official Security Service reports – then known as Box 500 reports – under the guise of revealing subversive penetration of these organisations. The service also had a history of gathering information on trade union activity and industrial disputes on the same basis. However, it again went beyond a strict study of subversive activity, and passed information relating to legitimate industrial protest to ministers and the police.

The decision regarding the Executive of the NCCL meant that MI5 could investigate an individual – that means tap their phones, follow their movements, break into their houses, place a bug in their homes – simply for being a member of the Executive of the NCCL, without having to establish any other connections to communism. This was clearly a breach of democratic rights.

It cannot be 'necessary in a democracy'[30] to investigate the leading members of an organisation charged with upholding democratic rights, in the absence of other security information. Harriet Harman and Patricia Hewitt learnt of the infringement of their rights when former MI5 officer Cathy Massiter blew the whistle on the services in 1984. As a result, they took their case to the European Court of Human Rights (ECtHR) and won because MI5 was not a legally constituted and democratically accountable organisation, the minimum standard in a democracy. It was only as a result of this ruling that Parliament finally put MI5 on a legal footing for the first time and made it accountable to ministers in the 1989 Security Service Act.[31]

F2/URG

While in F2, I also came across files detailing the activities of the Universities Research Group. Although it referred to 'universities' it was only concerned with the activities of alleged communists at Cambridge and Oxford. As late as the mid-1980s, MI5 officers were still interviewing individuals who had been – or were alleged to have been – members of the Cambridge University Communist Party and the Cambridge University Socialist Party in the 1930s and 1940s, the time that Burgess, Philby, Maclean *et al.* were there.

If the individual could establish he had belonged to the Socialist Party, he was cleared of subversive suspicion. Those deemed to have been members of the Communist Party were interviewed and recorded as 'member: subversive; communist' and, if they were still working in public service or the BBC, had their vetting clearance secretly withdrawn. They were then moved to other positions, where they had little or no access to sensitive material.

---

[30] Article 8(2) ECHR.
[31] MI6 and GCHQ followed with the 1994 Intelligence Services Act. We have to wonder why it took five more years, as the same arguments apply to them as to MI5.

Considering the damage the Cambridge spy ring did to our national security, it is not surprising that MI5 had an interest in any possible 'fellow travellers'. However, you would have thought that, given the potential gravity of the situation, the service would have treated as a high priority the rapid identification of any further spies from that era. Instead, MI5 was still investigating potential suspects when they were at the end of their careers or already retired. If any had been spies, the damage would have already been done.

How MI5 vetoed Wilson's choice of a Cabinet minister

Another example of MI5's abuse of its powers is the case of Judith Hart, a minister in Harold Wilson's government in the 1970s. She was refused a particular ministerial post because MI5 alleged that she had connections with communists. Hart denied this and the case became a *cause célèbre* for the left. Many believed she had been mixed up with another Judith Hart who was a well-known member of the Communist Party. In fact, that is what many assert to the present day.

However, the truth is stranger still. Wilson, ever suspicious of MI5, asked for further details of the 'secret and reliable source' which had reported Hart's connections to communism. MI5 refused, so Wilson told them he was not prepared to infringe a minister's right to pursue her career in politics without further evidence. After a stand-off, the service reluctantly agreed to furnish Wilson with the raw intelligence in its original form. This was one of the first and only times that a prime minister had seen actual MI5 intelligence. (The little which ministers are usually allowed to see is always summarised, with sources disguised). The intelligence consisted of a couple of transcripts of telephone taps on the Communist Party HQ in King Street. It established that Hart had indeed been in contact with the CP but only to talk to a friend who worked there. As Wilson pointed out to MI5, this was hardly evidence of communist sympathy or connections. He nevertheless agreed to post Hart to a less sensitive area of government.

Creating bureaucracy: the traffic light system

As part of our work in F2, David and I had to review the 'traffic light' status of PFs. In the late 1980s, the service set up a system for its files, giving them a green, amber or red card, which dictated whether the service would carry out enquiries. It was largely a bureaucratic exercise which did nothing to protect civil liberties. In fact, it allowed the service to maintain all its files, rather than destroying them or opening them up to public scrutiny, after their targets had ceased to be of security interest. Red-carded files remained open for inspection by any officer requesting the file, even though red-carding was supposed to mean that the file was closed and the target had not come to attention for twenty or thirty years in some cases.

The retention of these files also slowed down counter-terrorist investigations because, if officers were trying to identify, say, Patrick Jones, registry would send them files concerning every Patrick Jones or P Jones the service had ever come across. The desk officer then had to look through these files to 'clear the trace' or confirm that the subject of the file was not identical with the suspect in the investigation. The last thing an officer facing tight investigative deadlines needed was to have to plough through files made in the 1940s on the off-chance that one of these communist targets was the same person as an IRA suspect, who had recently come to attention. Interestingly, Jan Taylor and Patrick Hayes, the two PIRA members convicted of the 1992 bombing of Harrods, were both well-known to MI5 for their membership of Red Action, a 'subversive' group which campaigned on Irish Republican issues. MI5 never considered them as suspects for the bombing. They were convicted on the basis of evidence gathered by the Metropolitan Police Anti-

Terrorist Squad. I am not criticising MI5 with the benefit of hindsight for failing to apprehend them. I am merely pointing out that a subversive record means nothing in the context of terrorism and is not therefore a reason for retaining files on individuals with 'subversive' records, as some officers in MI5 tried to argue.

As part of reviewing the traffic lighting of files, F2B officers saw some frighteningly anachronistic files. David came across a minute on the minute sheet which recommended that the target of the file be placed on a certain list because she had been promoted to district organiser of the CPGB. In the event of a state of emergency being declared, anyone holding the office of district organiser or above in the Communist Party was to be detained without trial. We also saw vetting files where individuals were denied promotion or dismissed because they were not 'the right sort', or because they had what MI5 called 'character defects'. As late as 1994, MI5 considered homosexuality, debt and promiscuity as evidence of a defective character.

Failure with IT

Despite the massive reduction in the perceived threat from subversion at this time, MI5 persisted in developing a new national database of 'subversives' in the UK. The computer system, Hawk, had been under development for a number of years by the time I joined F2. As with all MI5 systems, it was an in-house development designed at vast expense by technicians who could not find employment in the more lucrative commercial sector and overseen by an intelligence officer who resented being posted away from a more mainstream line of work. It was anachronistic before it even came online in 1992. However, F2 management still insisted that clerical workers spend valuable man-hours inputting irrelevant data to justify Hawk's development.

50

Of course, when the study of subversion was eventually shut down in 1996 it became apparent that the technology of Hawk was too out of date to be transferred to other sections in MI5. This was a pattern which could be seen in MI5's IT strategy across the service.

Class War and the Communist Party

David's main area of responsibility in F2 was for the anarchist group Class War and the rump of the Communist Party, which had decided to plug on with Marxism–Leninism, after the rest of the CPGB had renounced it and become the Democratic Left. He was surprised that MI5 still devoted such extensive resources to these groups. During recruitment, he had been told that MI5 was no longer looking in any great depth at subversives. MI5 lore had it that the study of Class War was beefed up in the wake of the Poll Tax riot in London in 1990, after the group's posters and banners were seen on the news coverage. However, according to Special Branch officers, the violence in Trafalgar Square had started when front-line anti-riot police had lost control and turned on the demonstrators.

By early 1992, Class War was a disorganised collection of around 200 anarchist individuals. As such, it posed no real threat to Parliamentary democracy or national security. F2 had no phone intercept on Class War because it did not have an HQ. However, the authorities did devote considerable resources to the group.

Some years before David had joined F2, a Metropolitan Police Special Duties Section (SDS) agent, codenamed M2589, had penetrated Class War. Unlike the vast majority of agents recruited by MI5, he was not a member of an organisation who had been 'turned' by the service. He was a full-time policeman from Special Branch under deep cover. For six days a week, he lived, ate and breathed the life of a class warrior before returning to his normal life with friends and family for a day. Whether Class

51

War merited this kind of resource intensive coverage is open to debate. I quote David:

'When I met M2589 in February 1992, at a safe house in London, it was quite obvious that this peculiar arrangement had affected the agent psychologically. After around four years of pretending to be an anarchist, he had clearly become one. To use the service jargon, he had gone native. He drank about six cans of Special Brew during the debrief, and regaled us with stories about beating up uniformed officers as part of his "cover". Partly as a result, he was "terminated" after the 1992 General Election. Without his organisational skills, Class War fell apart.'

Did the agent make Class War more effective while he was there? In other words, did the state actually provide resources which contributed to the spread of anarchism?

Another anarchist source was run by Daphne. It is doubtful whether any useful information ever came from him, as Daphne spent most of her time acting as his counsellor cum therapist, sorting out problems with his rent, his girlfriends and even having to get worm pills for his dog.

After the 1992 General Election, David carried out two research projects into Class War and the Communist Party which I read after he had left the section because I had taken over the study of the former group. David's research had clearly established that Class War was moribund and recommended that M2589 was not replaced. In practice, this meant that MI5 kept only a 'watching brief' over the group. David came to the same conclusions regarding the Communist Party. It had fewer than 1,000 members, half of whom were over 65. He recommended the termination of agent M148, who had been reporting on communists for thirty years. M148 had spent nearly his entire working life as an agent.

F2/0, Paul Slough praised David for this work after he left the section, accepting all his recommendations, although I later found that a colleague still in F2, Sarah Knight, had been tasked to copy out his assessments word for word. She explained that although David's work was a thorough, accurate and pertinent research project – and his recommendations had been accepted – it was felt that he was too new to the service to command the necessary authority in his assessments. His work was therefore copied, but presented as her work as she had been in the service longer.

David says:

> 'It was extremely frustrating not being credited for good work. The Class War research paper did though have a funny side. When I first read the typed draft of the paper I came across the line: "Class War sees the women's movement as clitist." Thinking I had take leave of my senses, I checked it against my handwritten version, which said: "Class War sees the women's movement as *élitist*." God knows what my secretary, an innocent 18-year-old from Essex, thought I was trying to say.'

Just before David left F2, he played an anarchist in a police agent running exercise. He was so convincing that a uniformed police officer outside Charing Cross station moved him on, making the exercise more of a challenge to the trainee. On his return to his Bolton Street office, one of the older officers remarked that he had 'now seen everything – a member of the officer class wearing an ear-ring' after catching sight of David's ear-ring which had been re-inserted purely for the role play.

Preparations for PIRA primacy

In 1991 and early 1992 expectations had been high within the service that it would be given the lead responsibility for the investigation of PIRA on the UK mainland. Traditionally the MPSB had the lead and MI5 merely acted in support. In order to ensure that enough officers would be available to form the new section, T2, when primacy was handed to MI5, other sections of MI5 had their staff quotas artificially inflated, particularly in the counter-espionage K branch and counter-subversion F branch.

However, directors' and assistant directors' prestige within the service depended on their staff numbers. So when the call came from the newly formed T2, some senior managers refused to allow their staff to be posted elsewhere. Even though T2 was desperately stretched, directors of other branches regularly turned down requests for help even in the form of temporary secondments.

In May 1992, Home Secretary Kenneth Clarke finally announced to Parliament that MI5 was taking over PIRA investigations in Britain, bringing to an end MPSB's 106-year lead responsibility for Irish Republican matters. MI5 officers were informed of the decision over the office tannoy, as part of an office[32] security announcement. Journalists looking for a quote, it told us, might doorstep us as we left the building because MI5 had been awarded primacy.

As PIRA was at this time regularly carrying out bombings and endangering the lives of British citizens, it was no longer a proportional – or, indeed, sane – response to continue to deploy vital resources like telephone tapping against Trotskyists rather than terrorists. The service conveniently decided that that subversion no longer posed the same serious threat as it had less than a year before – exactly what we desk officers had been arguing. In August 1992, just nine months after joining the service, David was posted to T2A.

Even though my two years as F2B/5 were up by February 1993,[33] and I had received a performance-related bonus and promotion, Director F turned down a request for my transfer from one of T2's senior managers because he had already seen

---

[32] Officers always call MI5 'the Office', a habit particularly useful in public places.
[33] Officers normally spend two years in a posting before moving on.

his empire shrink too much. I finally joined T5E, studying Irish terrorist logistics, in August 1993.

David's and my experiences in F2 had opened our eyes to state abuses of power, which most recruits in the 1990s just did not see. These ranged from the continuing and unlawful existence of files made before 1989, through the absurd files made on the basis of little security information, to the retention of deeply embarrassing personal material on influential figures. Both David and I hoped that this work now belonged to another era and that MI5 was finally ceasing such contentious operations. In the context of subversion, it all begged the question:

'In the 1980s, who really was the Enemy Within?'

Was it the miners struggling to protect their jobs and communities? Or political activists holding meetings, peace demonstrations and standing in elections? Or was it the state, with its undemocratic, unaccountable, law-breaking secret spies?

Chapter 3

MI5 Fails to get to Grips with the IRA

ORBAT[34]

Dir T	Director T, Head of T Branch. Responsible for investigating all Irish terrorism. At the time, Stephen Lander, the recent Director General
T2/0	Assistant Director – head of T2 (grade: SM4).[35] At the time, Eliza Manningham-Buller, the current Director General. Replaced by Nick Kent after she took over as Dir T
T2/1	Deputy Head of Section responsible for investigations and liaison. (GI1). At the time, Steve Canute
T2/2	Deputy Head of Section responsible for research and threat assessments (GI1)
T2A	Investigations into Irish Republican terrorism in the UK. Split into four subsections: **T2A/London Group**: investigations in London **T2A/Northern Group**: investigations in North of England and Scotland. Headed by T2A/2, Wendy Probit (GI2). David was T2A/11, grade GI4 **T2A/Southern Group**: investigations in South of England **T2A/Northern Ireland Group**

---

[34] Fictional names.

[35] SM stands for Senior Management, thus SM4 is a senior manager, grade 4. The Director General of MI5 is grade SM1. GI stands for General Intelligence (Duties). GI1 is General Intelligence Duties, grade 1, the highest before senior management. The GID group later became the General Duties (GD) group, and an officer's grade would be abbreviated as GD4, not GI4.

T2B	Liaison with local Special Branches and agent runners with responsibility for above
T2C	Assesses threat from Irish terrorist groups
T2D	Research into Irish terrorist groups
T2E	Liaison with MPSB (based at New Scotland Yard)
T5/0	Assistant Director of T5, Peter Clarke.
T5B	Investigations into arms trafficking
T5C	Counter-Irish terrorism in continental Europe (including the Irish Republic)
T5D	Counter-Irish terrorism in the rest of the world
T5E	Study of Irish terrorist logistics. I was T5E/2 (GI4)
T1/A	Investigation of Loyalist terrorism
T1/B	Police liaison
T8	Agent running for T branch, includes ███[36] based in Northern Ireland

Mistakes from the past, lessons for today

Given the current war against terrorism – in the form of Al Qaeda – it is worth looking at the mistakes that helped to create the environment in which PIRA could flourish. This led to thirty years of civil war in the UK, which we rather quaintly refer to as 'The Troubles'.

The army was after all sent to the province in 1971 to protect Catholics from attacks from Loyalist Protestants, which the RUC either turned a blind eye to, or actively joined in. The decision resembles that taken by the US Federal government in the 1950s when it sent troops to Alabama to protect the rights of African-Americans against the white majority. But there the resemblance ends. While the troops protected civil

---

[36] Removed on orders of MI5.

58

rights activists in the Deep South, allowing them to call on the Constitution's right to free speech and association to further their cause, the army in Northern Ireland lost the support of Catholics when its intelligence was used to imprison so-called PIRA suspects without trial. This flouted one of the fundamental rights of a democracy: no detention without fair trial.[37]

Up until that point, a clear majority of Catholics wanted to model themselves on the American civil rights movement, even adopting the anthem used by US activists: 'We Shall Overcome'. Once Catholics had been interned, they saw little point in trying to behave democratically towards a state which had infringed their basic rights by putting men in prison without trial. Ironically, the Bloody Sunday march in 1972, which saw 13 innocent and unarmed Catholics gunned down by the British Army in Derry, was in protest at arbitrary detention. Once the British had carried out what many in the international community called extra-judicial executions, some Catholics felt that they could only protect themselves by resorting to or supporting the armed struggle, while still trying to use the democratic process to raise awareness of their plight. This became known as the 'bullet and the ballot box' strategy.

By imprisoning so-called suspected PIRA members, the British government helped to light the blue touch paper to 30 years of conflict. It shaped the conditions for a civil war which has resulted in the deaths of around 3,000 individuals on both sides. 'The Troubles' have also cost the taxpayer insurance payouts of over £175 million in the Six Counties of Northern Ireland and around £400 million on the British mainland. Of course, those figures do not include the extra costs of policing terrorism, as well as lost tourist revenue and investment from those scared off by this instability.

In fact, it would be true to say that the British state had no strategy for bringing the terrorist conflict in Northern Ireland to

---

[37] Some have pointed out that the Republic of Ireland also interned PIRA suspects, but it did so on a far smaller scale and without prejudice: in Northern Ireland, Loyalist terrorists who indiscriminately murder Catholic civilians have never been interned.

an end, other than trying to bring convictions of individual terrorists and – later – trying to obtain prior intelligence about planned attacks (which as we shall see in this book was done in the most dilatory fashion possible). Certainly little was done to detect and cut off the flow of support to PIRA, which came principally from the US and Libya, until well into the 1980s. In fact, Libya's leader, Colonel Gaddafi had been moved to support the Irish Republican cause precisely because the UK authorities had taken the decision arbitrarily to imprison Catholics without trial. It was not until 1987 that a shipment of Libyan arms and explosives destined for PIRA in the Republic was intercepted off the coast of Brittany on board the MV *Eksund*, and then it was the French coastguards who acted, rather than the British police or customs.

If the British government had been serious about stopping the conflict, it would have set up a dedicated organisation to defeat PIRA. Instead, it failed to rationalise its response and continued to rely on a piecemeal group of organisations. These included, with shifting degrees of involvement and responsibility: the Army, the RUC (the Royal Ulster Constabulary, now renamed the Northern Ireland Police Service), MI5, MI6, the Metropolitan Police Special Branch (MPSB), SO13 (the Met's Anti-Terrorist Squad), the 40-odd Constabulary Special Branches (SBs), the Garda in the Irish Republic, and HMCE, all with their own chain of command, all duplicating each other's work and stepping on each other's toes, all with their own discrete archive of records.

Of course, none of these organisations trusted each other. They jealously guarded their sources. In fact, a great deal of the work in T2 involved acting as a conduit between the local SBs and the RUC, the Army and the Garda. I stress that this function was performed at the expense of actually investigating terrorists. It would have made far greater sense to have a single organisation with its own archive and single management chain, which could act effectively and efficiently against terrorist targets. I mention all this because there is an obvious lesson to be learnt for combating Al Qaeda.

The civil war in Northern Ireland was also a dirty war. Although the security services claimed that they worked within the rule of law, bringing suspects to trial and imprisoning them on conviction, in 2003 the Stephens Report refuted their claim. The investigation by Sir John Stephens has established that Army intelligence actively conspired with Loyalist terrorists to murder innocent Catholics, most notably the lawyer, Pat Finucane. That is exactly what happens in tin-pot dictatorships and other tyrannical regimes.

The building in Northern Ireland holding the evidence Stephens had gathered was burnt down. Martin Ingram, a former soldier and member of the organisation most heavily implicated in collusion, the Army Forces Research Unit (FRU), has disclosed that members of Army intelligence were responsible. At the same time, Sir John was also subjected to the same sort of smear campaign as David and other people who have dared to dissent over the security services. The Stephens Report has also established that MI5 obstructed the enquiry, when it withheld crucial reports concerning agents involved in the collusion. So much for its adherence to the rule of law, which MI5 insisted it observed when we were being recruited.

Rather conveniently for Army intelligence, Brian Nelson – the FRU agent most heavily implicated in collusion and whom Stephens wanted to interview – died just before the report came out. There has yet to be an enquiry into his death.

In 2003, it emerged that Stakeknife (aka[38] Steak Knife or Steaknife), an agent of the FRU, had been a leading member of PIRA's 'Nutting Squad'. As such, he had been responsible for the interrogation, torture and execution of a number of brave agents who reported back to the Army, RUC and MI5 on PIRA activities. The real damage to national security from his actions is incalculable.

PIRA, unlike the smaller Republican splinter groups, soon learnt to avoid deliberately targeting civilians and to give code-

---

[38] Also Known As, used by MI5 for targets with multiple names or identities.

worded warnings at least an hour before attacks, so that police could close the area. This was not so much out of respect for human life but rather a tactical decision designed to minimise opprobrium, not just in Britain, but also primarily in its financial support bases overseas. That is not just my view. It is MI5's official assessment of PIRA. Of course, these measures did not always work and innocent people were killed. And terrorism is still terrorism. David and I joined MI5 to help prevent such atrocities.

Stephens also concluded that the shoot-to-kill policy only served to prolong the conflict, a clear indication – along with the inefficient and ineffective duplication of responsibilities – that the British intelligence establishment never wanted an end to the civil war in Northern Ireland. It wanted jobs for the boys and of course the suspension of civil liberties and secrecy made possible by the conflict.

MI5 taking over from the Met

MI5's T5 section had traditionally had lead responsibility for the investigation of Irish Republican terrorism abroad, but had supported the MPSB in Britain and the RUC in Northern Ireland. Similarly, T1 had supported the RUC in investigating Loyalist terrorism in Northern Ireland, but had had the lead in the rest of the UK and abroad. In the two years before handover, MI5 had been working in support of MPSB, which was supposed to share all its intelligence with the service. In practice, MPSB shared rather less intelligence than it should with MI5.

That said, MPSB and T1 were so inept at recruiting agents – the best way to gain prior intelligence on attacks – that they had little intelligence about the mainland campaign. Where it was available, it had come from a 'walk-in' or volunteer rather than as a result of concerted targeting of PIRA members vulnerable to recruitment. Even then, the two services had lost control of the individual concerned.

In August 1992, David was posted to the new section, T2A, to investigate PIRA activity in the north-east of England. It was his first substantive posting in MI5. He was the least experienced officer in the section, having been in the service for fewer than nine months. I do not believe that personnel would have let him join such a high-profile section, if it had not had confidence in his abilities. On 1 October 1992, MI5 officially took over primacy. This meant that MI5's T2 section took over lead responsibility for all investigations into PIRA and other Irish Republican terrorism in Britain, but the RUC remained in charge in Northern Ireland.

T Branch's new responsibilities included:

- Coordinating mainland investigations, which included applying for telephone and letter intercept warrants and property warrants (T2A).
- Liaison with local SBs (T2B).
- Recruitment of new agents to obtain better intelligence (T1 and T8).
- Threat assessments (T2C).[39]
- Research and analysis (T2D).
- Liaison with MPSB (T2E).

Although MI5 had had nearly six months to get ready for the take over, it was woefully ill-prepared to begin investigating Irish suspects on 1 October 1992. I stress that these were not one-off mistakes borne of inexperience with a new target, but were the result of institutional failure. As a result, in the following six months, PIRA planted bombs in London at a greater rate than before or since, culminating in the Bishopsgate attack which cost the British state around £350 million.

---

[39] It is also worth pointing out that T2C holds files on each individual member of the Royal Family, including Princess Diana, for the purpose of assessing threats to their security. The files contain details of associates of the Royals and their movements.

MI5's failure to get to grips with PIRA

In her memoir, *Open Secret,* Stella Rimington tells us: 'A security service lives by its records.' Yet, as DG, she failed to put this truism into practice.

From the outset, T2 had its work cut out, not just as a result of MPSB's and MI5's failure to recruit human sources but because the service had failed to incorporate any of MPSB's records into its own. As a result, MI5 operations against PIRA targets were slowed down because T2 officers had to write to the Met to check for security traces against an individual. MPSB often gave brief and inadequate replies, which meant that the desk officer had to follow the matter up again. Sometimes, MPSB would reply to a request with a series of file references from its own archives. As these files were only available at New Scotland Yard, the MI5 officer would physically have either to go from Curzon Street House, where T2 was based, to New Scotland Yard or seek out T2E's help to obtain the correct traces, again slowing down the investigation of targets. This meant that even routine enquires could take weeks to be completed.

As MI5 only saw a précis of the original Met intelligence, there was a danger that a key corroborating fact could have been missed or the original intelligence misrepresented, leading to resources being allocated to the wrong targets. On one occasion, MPSB records indicated that a particular suspect had Irish Republican sympathies and was in possession of a gun. When David checked the intelligence, it turned out that the source had reported that a PIRA suspect had parked his red car outside a certain pub. Police National Computer checks on cars outside the pub had revealed a red car registered to the suspect, among others. There was no other information on him and no further enquiries had been made. The lead had not been properly followed up and resolved.

T2 management set a performance objective to incorporate MPSB and local SB records into the MI5 archives by the time of each T2 officer's annual assessment (to take place around summer 1993). David had seven force areas, more forces than many other T2A officers, and with more work because his area included large forces like Northumbria, West Yorkshire and South Yorkshire. Yet he managed to incorporate the records from five force areas. Other officers simply ignored the objective, perhaps only incorporating records from one or two forces.

The Records Review, as it was known in the service, was not completed until long after David left T2 in October 1994. For the first two years, hard-working, motivated T2 officers were effectively fighting PIRA with one hand tied behind their back.

'Palace Revolution' over out-of-date investigations

But by far the worst example of MI5's inability to get to grips with the very serious threat they were supposedly policing concerned the HOWs[40] MI5 inherited from MPSB for the handover of primacy in October 1992.

> 'They were out of date and inaccurate,' says David. 'In some cases, the intelligence on which the warrant was based was years out of date. At the same time, the intercept had produced very little – and in some cases, no – intelligence to support the original application to the Home Secretary.'

By this point, T1 and T2 had been analysing the intelligence the service shared with MPSB long enough to identify more current PIRA suspects on the mainland, such as Sean McNulty.[41] Since the intelligence linking them to PIRA's mainland campaign was more recent than the intelligence in the MPSB warrants – and T2 had finite resources – it seemed obvious that MI5 should

[40] Home Office Warrant.
[41] See Chapter 4, Operation BROOM, background, and Chapter 5, Operation BROOM, T2A goes 'live'.

devote its full resources to the more recent suspects. However, T2 management insisted that desk officers spent days, if not weeks, re-researching and drafting old warrants which had already been used to investigate suspects but without results.

This clearly tied up hard-pressed officers trying to get on top of a new target. It diverted resources from where they needed to be – targeted against terrorists who at that time were planting bombs in London, almost at will. For example, in October 1992, a PIRA operative whom MI5 assessed to be Rab Fryers[42] hijacked a taxi – without wearing a mask – and ordered the driver to take a bomb to Downing Street. As a parting shot, he told the driver to get a good look at his face so that he could give the police a proper description. This suggests that PIRA was hardly living in fear of imminent detection at the time.

The T2 officers all thought the revalidation of old warrants was a terrible waste of time, especially when they were told that it was designed to spare MPSB's embarrassment at having so little current intelligence about the IRA threat.[43] Nevertheless, officers were forced to go ahead with the out-of-date applications.

As HOWs are only supposed to be used when 'necessary in a democracy' – sparing the Met's blushes does not fall within this category – T2 desk officers felt strongly that these taps were illegal and took resources away from the real targets. A group of around ten officers met to discuss the issue, including David. Linda Harman,[44] the most senior of the group, agreed to take the concerns to T2 management. But Canute brushed aside their concerns, stating that they were to renew the Met warrants. Any officer troubled by this was to see the staff counsellor. Afterwards, David suggested that officers take their concerns *en masse* to the counsellor, but desk officers strenuously warned him off this course of action, stating that the service would hold it against those who complained, making them less

---

[42] Fryers was subsequently convicted for terrorist offences. See also McNulty chapter.
[43] This again fails the 'necessary in a democracy' test of the HRA.
[44] T2A/3. Again, a fictitious name.

likely to get promotion. As David had been in the service less than a year, he accepted their view.

The vast majority of the renewed Met warrants were cancelled at the two-month review or the six-month review. David comments:

'The whole exercise was a monumental waste of the time and resources of desk officers, management and transcribers, which set back T2's progress against the IRA. This ultimately enabled the IRA to continue to carry out attacks like Bishopsgate, in which a press photographer died, and Warrington, in which two young boys died.'

Routine problems with telephone tap warrants

This process was further complicated by MI5's general approach to warrantry. During the Cold War, MI5 found it very easy to deal with the allocation of resources because, generally speaking, the targets were static. MI5 tapped the phones of hostile embassies and the HQs of subversive organisations and put permanent static surveillance posts outside them. Managing these resources meant renewing the warrants at six-monthly intervals. Since the targets were not terrorists, officers could at their leisure apply for and renew warrants without thinking that the lives of the general public were in danger.

The authorities have tried to claim that David objected to procedures protecting civil liberties. However, the truth is that MI5 management were incapable of following procedures enshrined in the 1985 Interception of Communications Act (IOCA) and subsequently the 2000 Regulation of Investigatory Powers Act (RIPA). Management never asked, for example, whether officers had made enquiries of publicly available material.[45] Senior

---

[45] To make them lawful under IOCA/RIPA and the HRA. It cannot be necessary in a democracy to tap an individual's phone to obtain information which might be available from public sources.

T2 officers like Steve Canute never disputed the actual intelligence case or the validity of the HOW application, as it was usually obvious to desk officers and group leaders which terrorists posed the most dangerous and current threat. Many of the more senior managers of the day had largely cut their intelligence teeth when counter-subversion and espionage were the order of the day, not terrorism. It was not as if they could draw on vital desk experience in this area that the desk officer might not have.

On the other hand, T Branch management spent hours poring over stylistic points, a bureaucratic exercise designed to make it look like they were adding value, but which only served to slow the whole process down. Given that a warrant could take weeks to pass through all the layers of management, yo-yoing back and forth, this meant that there was a period when a suspected terrorist – about whom there was current security information – could run free while T2 management pored over the draft warrant. In the meantime, the target of the warrant could actually be carrying out terrorist acts and T2 would be none the wiser.

Because a warrant was not in place, we cannot know how often T2's bureaucracy meant that vital intelligence was lost, allowing otherwise avoidable PIRA attacks to happen.

For the record, the routine HOW went through the following officers:

T2A/11 – Desk officer who drafts the warrant and sends to secretary to type – in this case, David.

T2A/2 – Group leader checks and amends warrant, sending corrections back to the desk officer, who has to send it to his secretary for retyping. Very often these amendments are stylistic, like changing 'but' to 'however' or 'might' to 'may'.

T2/1 – Senior officer checks and amends amended warrant as above, but without seeing the original. On a number of occasions, the senior officer would redraft a warrant, returning it to the desk officer correcting the 'amendments' made by the group leader thus returning the warrant to its original version.

T2/0 – Assistant Director, as above with same caveats. The same process of amended amendments could happen at any time. Each correction would revert the warrant to the desk officer and then to the secretary again.

Dir T – Director, as above.

H1 – Secretariat. Drafts letter based on original warrant.

DDG – Deputy Director General signs letter including an intelligence summary on which the warrant application is based, but without the actual supporting material, and sends it to the Home Secretary for approval.

All this is the fault of MI5's Civil Service culture. Police and HMCE have to operate within the same legal framework, but manage to process HOWs in much less time. Of course, the warrants may not be quite as lovingly drafted, but as long as the case is accurate, a tap can be put in place and a crime prevented.

The services go to war

Turf battles between T2 and the Met

During this period, there was also intense and ongoing hostility between MI5 and the Met, as the latter were piqued that MI5 had taken primacy away from them. Although MPSB insisted on having every document copied to them, not once did an officer ever get in contact with T2 staff to propose even a simple idea to move forward an investigation. As MI5's primacy was to be reviewed after a year, some MPSB officers took it on themselves deliberately not to share information in the hope of embarrassing the service. In any circumstance, this would be bad enough but, in the context of security, this meant that lives were being put at unnecessary and intolerable risk.

A good example of the failure of the services to work together effectively at a time of the greatest rate of PIRA attacks on the mainland is the experience of a MPSB officer seconded to MI5 in early 1993 to work specifically with T2A. As part of his MI5 induction process, the detective sergeant went to spend a day with MI6. On his return, the group leader, Wendy Probit, T2A/2, told him off loudly in the middle of the T2 long room for having attended without specifically seeking her permission. As this officer's secondment was designed to build bridges with the Met this was clearly an awful way to deal with an individual, designed to humiliate him in front of his peers. Unlike MI5 officers, the detective sergeant had the benefit of his union. He went to the Police Federation and complained. Representations were successfully made on his behalf; his secondment was abruptly brought to an end; and he was taken back to MPSB because he had been put in an unworkable situation.

Relations between MI5 and local SBs on the one hand, and MPSB on the other were so bad at this time that, when MI5 officers and local forces met for drinks, a frequent toast was made to the common enemy: 'To MPSB and its abolition.' It always raised a laugh.

Turf battles between T2 and T5

Director F eventually allowed me to move to my second posting in August 1993, where my new STAR designation (job title) was T5E/2. This was an unusual post within T Branch as it had a roving brief to investigate and counter the logistics of Irish terrorism, both Republican and Loyalist, anywhere in the world. This involved working with all sections of T Branch, as well as liaising with external agencies such as Special Branch, government departments in Whitehall, and acting as T Branch's liaison with HMCE. The latter was a particularly delicate but productive relationship for MI5.

My predecessor *en poste* had dipped into operations in an ad hoc and arbitrary manner, on the basis of what tickled his fancy rather than which targets posed the greatest threat. As a result, there was a dearth of information about the methods Irish terrorist groups, particularly PIRA, used to procure arms and ammunition, and no coherent database of suspects who might be involved. My support staff and I put a great deal of effort into:

- Researching PIRA logistics.
- Compiling an organised database.
- Visiting SB and HMCE to co-ordinate their support.
- Providing feedback on the intelligence provided to T5E, once they realised MI5 was interested.
- Ensuring intelligence was shared and properly exploited.

After a year, the systems were in place and working so well that we – my support staff and I – received performance-related bonuses for our work. We got results. This was why I had joined MI5 in the first place. Then, just as we began to make a real difference, the dead hand of senior T Branch management came down on us, as we were caught up in a turf war. T2/0 Nick Kent, the head of T2, had for some time been casting covetous glances at the database and the relationships developed

71

by T5E. His opposite number in T5 – Peter Clarke – did not, of course, want to lose a section developed under his supervision. Over the following months, there was a bitter tug of war. When PIRA called its ceasefire in 1994, T2 saw its opportunity. T Branch broke up T5E, allocating its responsibilities amongst different desks within T2, disrupting relationships with local SBs and HMCE and undermining its effectiveness. By the time the ceasefire broke down, T5E's expertise had been squandered.

As I had a proven track record of being able to build good working relationships with SBs and HMCE around the country, my Assistant Director recommended me for a new liaison post with the National Criminal Intelligence Service (NCIS), looking at organised crime. This was a new, challenging and high-profile post and I was keen to take it on. However, a year before, a female MI5 officer had buckled under pressure while working with MPSB. MI5 management therefore decided that working in a police environment was no job for a woman, whatever her experience and expertise. As I had no employment rights and no staff federation to turn to, I could not challenge this blatant sex discrimination. The job went to a far less experienced male colleague.

I was offered instead the only other posting free at that time – coordinating briefs for senior management and Whitehall for a year in a section called G3A.

The failure of MI5's cover story

Before I take a detailed look at Operation BROOM, the investigation into a PIRA member in the north-east of England, it is worth mentioning an incident which demonstrated that MI5's concern for its staff security – usually used to justify the draconian nature of the OSA and a whole variety of injunctions against the media – was in fact less than adequate when tested. David takes up the story:

'In Spring 1993, I was trawling through addresses of suspected IRA members on Durbar [Irish section computerised records] when I saw my own address, Clapham Court, come up on screen. Durbar referred to no. 21. At the time, I lived at no. 4, next door. I quickly scrolled to the top of the record only to find that the target living at the address was Donna Grew. I already knew she came from a well-known Republican family. Her brother Dessie had famously been killed on active service for the IRA a couple of years before.'

Donna Grew had previously come to David's attention when he worked in C3/Vetting. A stunningly attractive brunette, she had gone out with two civil servants, one from the Home Office and one from the Central Information Office, within months of each other. C3 had been looking at her because it suspected her of using the civil servants either to steal or take copies of their security passes, enabling PIRA terrorists to enter government buildings undetected.

'As Clapham Court was two sets of twelve flats with one residents' committee,' David explains, 'I was horrified to think that I could have met Donna Grew at such a meeting without having any knowledge of who she was. Although I would have been under MoD cover at that meeting, she would no doubt have seen me as a target, in the same way as she had targeted the Home Office and Central Information Office civil servants. Of course, if she had then had me followed, it would soon have been clear that I was not working in the MoD building on Whitehall, but in the famous MI5 building at Curzon Street, just off Piccadilly [officially at the time a state secret but well-known to cab drivers and bus tour reps, who pointed it out to their passengers over a loud-hailer]. As an MI5 officer, I would have been a prime target of the IRA.

'I was appalled that B2, MI5's personnel section, and

B1C, internal security, had clearly not bothered to look up my address in the service records to check that the address was safe. After all, MI5 checks all flatmates and partners of officers against its records to ensure that they are no security threat. As it is much more likely that a terrorist will live next door rather than be one of your friends or flatmates, it seemed highly remiss that neither B1C nor B2 had performed this simple security check as a matter of form.'

When David raised the issue with his line management in T2, their first response was: 'Do you have a window with a direct line of sight of her front door?' (He didn't.) When he went to seek further security advice, B1C more or less told him to keep his head down and simply avoid Donna Grew. There were no offers to help him find temporary accommodation or to make a permanent move away from a real and actual threat to his personal security. Instead, he had to live in perpetual fear that a member of the residents' committee – which he no longer attended – would in his absence innocently mention that he worked for the MoD.

Given Donna Grew's record of relationships with public servants working in Whitehall, she could have begun to research his movements and habits without David's knowledge. Once she had established where he worked, PIRA could quite easily have kidnapped or murdered him. This was the time when PIRA was enjoying its greatest ever period of activity on the British mainland.

When David was under a genuine threat the service provided no real help to him, even though PIRA might have come after him. Despite its claims to the contrary, MI5 has no real interest in the security of its officers, especially where this might involve action or expense on the part of the service.

This episode also rather neatly illustrates the inadequacy of the MI5 cover story at that time. Officers are told to tell associates they work for the MoD in a research job they can't say much about. It is difficult to see how this rather flimsy 'legend', as it is known in the spying game, would fool (or in fact fail to interest) the terrorists or their sympathisers. It is one further example of the flabby thinking that pervades MI5.

Despite this, David was still keen to get on with stopping PIRA atrocities. In late 1992, he took over the investigation into Sean McNulty, who had originally come to the attention of the services in January 1992 after meeting Phelim Hamill, the co-ordinator of PIRA's mainland campaign.

Chapter 4

Operation BROOM, Background

In summary

Operation BROOM[46] was the investigation into Sean McNulty, a PIRA member who had been born and brought up in the north-east of England. He came to attention as an associate of Phelim Hamill, then the co-ordinator of PIRA's mainland campaign,[47] and was responsible for two PIRA attacks on volatile gas and oil plants in the North East in June 1993.

David took over as the McNulty desk officer in late 1992. Chapters 4 and 5 are his own account of how:

- T2 failed to put in place procedures which would adequately protect national security.
- McNulty nearly got away with it because of cock-ups on the part of the security forces.

The bombs go off

10 June 1993 started as any normal day in T2A. I had arrived at work just before 10 am only to realise that PIRA had let off yet another bomb on the British mainland, this time just

---

[46] Codeword changed on orders of MI5.
[47] Later sentenced to 25 years in prison for terrorist offences.

before midnight at an Esso oil plant in Wallsend, Tyneside. At that point, one of my less rewarding responsibilities was writing briefs on mainland activity for the DG herself. The day before had also been busy for me, as there had been a bombing just after midnight at a gas station in the North Shields area – not far from the Esso plant. So I had spent 9 June and the morning of 10 June:

- Phoning the Metropolitan Police to get the details of the attack out of them (without success because they resented giving any information to MI5).
- Checking details of the attack on Ceefax, which usually came up with the goods in a more timely and accurate fashion than the Met.
- Drafting and re-drafting the simple facts of the attack and how this affected our assessment of PIRA's mainland campaign. (This was done at the request of my group leader who seemed to have no idea that the purpose of the brief was to give the DG a simple and timely record of events.)

For the previous 18 months, MI5 had been investigating Sean McNulty, a suspected PIRA targeting officer, who lived in North Shields, within a few miles of the two latest bombings. At this point, there was no information to link him to either attack, but unusually for PIRA mainland activity in those days, there was at least a prime suspect, in the form of McNulty. We had to tread carefully though. Although we had been conducting an *intelligence* investigation into McNulty, there was absolutely no *evidence* of him being implicated in illegal activity. Up until that point, we assessed that he did little more than play a support role for PIRA, which may have included targeting sites for his fellow operatives to attack or perhaps even tending weapons hides and so on. Although these activities were illegal, they were extremely difficult to detect and prove in court. That afternoon the situation changed – almost by accident.

The surveillance photo of McNulty arrives late

It happened when I got up to go to the toilet. As I passed my group leader's desk, I noticed a pile of photographs on it. I knew they had come from CCTV coverage of a target building as:

- They had the date and time recorded on them in the bottom right-hand corner.
- They had the usual slightly blurred and scratchy quality to them.
- They were in black and white.

The top photograph showed a burly figure walking down the path of a well-tended suburban garden. It caught his face almost full-on. I recognised the distinctive, thick, pointed eyebrows. Without a shadow of a doubt, they belonged to Sean McNulty. I asked my group leader where they were taken. She told me they had been taken outside Hugh Jack's house in Sauchie. Jack's house was near Alloa in central Scotland. At that point, it was the focus of PIRA's mainland campaign. Rab 'Fat Neck' Fryers, a member of Belfast battalion with an intelligence record as long as your arm, had met Phelim Hamill, the chief co-ordinator of the mainland campaign. McNulty's presence at the house indicated he was taking tasking from PIRA's northern command via Hamill and Fryers. The photographs were date-lined '29 May 1993'. I pointed out to Wendy Probit that the pictures showed my target, McNulty. I asked how long she had them and she told me since that morning. If they were on her desk then, that meant they had arrived in the service the morning before, a good 12 hours before the second attack on 9 June.

The pictures of McNulty arriving at Jack's house had therefore been taken 12 days previously. If the service had received them even a day or two earlier, T2 could have taken steps against McNulty. At this point, we did not know whether he was

79

involved in these recent attacks. If we had received the photos earlier though, he would certainly have been under round-the-clock surveillance and have been caught in the act. In fact, even if we had received the photos the day before, T2 would still have had an opportunity to have prevented McNulty from carrying out the attack on the Esso oil installation, the evening before.

As I had written the DG's brief on the two recent attacks, I knew how close the residential streets in the vicinity had come to major devastation. The bomber had put the device – or IED[48] as MI5 called it – next to the two pipes which did not contain highly flammable fuel, but only by a fluke. If the bomb had been placed a yard nearer the other five pipes, the whole plant would have gone up, maiming and killing nearby residents, wrecking vital fuel supplies and closing roads in the area. The images of the blazing night skyline and the huddled occupants of the nearby houses had already given PIRA an enormous publicity coup.

I already knew that 29 May 1993 was significant in Operation BROOM. That day, Linen (or a telephone tap) had reported McNulty's family discussing his strange behaviour that very morning, particularly his evasiveness and secrecy. For the first time, McNulty had taken his mother's car rather than his own because, we presumed, he (quite rightly) suspected it had been fitted with a tracking device. By coincidence, A4, the surveillance section of MI5, had been in Newcastle to carry out some routine surveillance of McNulty or Ice Cube, as he was nicknamed, that very day. After being passed that Linen material, they had been unable to locate McNulty at any of his local haunts.

---

[48] Improvised Explosive Device. A VBIED is a vehicle-borne IED. A PBIED is a person-borne IED.

The implications of missed intelligence

If the CCTV photograph of McNulty outside Jack's house had been passed on 29 May or shortly after, A4 would have covered McNulty on his return to Newcastle. By the end of the investigation, we had become convinced that during that very visit to Fryers and Jack on 29 May 1993 he learnt where the explosives and other bomb-making equipment – later used in the two attacks – were stored. The chances are he would have picked them up that day and then taken them to a hide or cache nearer Newcastle in preparation for the attacks. A4, being in the area, would have followed McNulty to the hide along with members of Northumbria SB. He would have been caught red-handed. In addition to preventing the attacks, this would have:

- Saved the time and effort involved in a long court case as a conviction would have been easier to secure.
- Saved the costs of the two-week surveillance operation which followed (see below).
- Meant that the authorities would have taken possession of the explosives and weapons so they could have:
  - Prevented other PIRA members using them.
  - Forensicated them, possibly producing further leads to PIRA members or further evidence against them in court.
- Probably led to Fryers and Jack being arrested more quickly.

In other words, the failure to pass on the photos cost the authorities dearly. And this is not a case of being wise after the event. It is highly foreseeable that taking 12 days to pass intelligence about the chief suspects in the mainland campaign from the target address to T2 in London will inevitably allow the IRA to carry out attacks and avoid detection. Remember that at the time this was T2's most important operation as Fryers was already suspected of the Downing Street bombing around six months before.

81

First operational steps

The afternoon of 10 June 1993 was frantic, even by MI5 standards. As soon as Wendy and I had agreed that the figure in the photograph was McNulty, I briefly spoke to the HSB[49] in Northumbria. MI5 officers are given strict instructions not to reveal operational information over an open telephone line (although I'm not quite sure who they thought had the capability to listen in after the demise of the Soviet Union. The NSA[50] perhaps?) Trying not to sound overly dramatic, I told him we had intelligence which led us to assess that McNulty was playing a much more significant role in the mainland campaign than we had previously thought. I asked him to deploy surveillance on McNulty at his end as quickly as possible while I would send him an immediate telegram to explain what had happened in more detail.

Once I had got the telegram off, I phoned A4 to tell them that we had an urgent requirement for their services. They agreed that they could reallocate resources in order to assist Northumbria SB. After that, I rushed up to the A2A live transcribers on the fifth floor of Curzon Street, W1 – an imposing but shabby 1930s building; T2 was on the second floor – and filled them in on the latest intelligence. I told them they had to alert me immediately to any indication whatsoever that McNulty was going to be AWOL or was preparing to move anything even remotely suspicious. Both A2A and A4 wanted an update in writing so I had to spend a couple of hours drafting separate briefs by hand for the live monitors and the mobile surveillance teams.[51]

---

[49] Head of Special Branch.

[50] National Security Agency, the US equivalent of GCHQ.

[51] At this point in the service's IT development, MI5 officers had to hand draft briefs on green paper, send them to the secretary for typing and then wait for the typed draft to come back (also on green paper) before correcting the typos and sending it back again. Eventually, the officer would sign off the final version, which was printed on white paper and copied to the relevant officers. An organisation devoted to the gathering, analysis and dissemination of information really should have had better IT communications by 1993. The work of desk officers was inevitably impeded by antediluvian business processes, which made it harder to stop terrorists in fast moving operations.

By the end of Thursday 10 June 1993, it had become clear that Steve Canute, T2/1 the deputy section head; Paul Jenkins, T2B/1 the regional liaison officer, and I were to fly to Newcastle the following Monday (14 June). We were to discuss with the local SB how we were going to advance the operation against McNulty.

Background to the IRA's modern mainland campaign

In 1988, PIRA had restarted its mainland campaign. It had realised that every minor bomb which exploded on the British mainland created headlines in British newspapers and on television, whereas even large scale attacks in Northern Ireland barely made more than a paragraph in the British press. At this point, PIRA had become much more sophisticated than in the 1970s and early 1980s, when it had still been possible for the police to investigate bomb attacks and find the perpetrators through dedicated but routine post-incident police work, like forensics and questioning witnesses. By the early 1990s, it was virtually impossible to bring PIRA terrorists in Britain to justice using these methods. It was therefore more important than ever that MPSB should make every effort to obtain prior intelligence about PIRA's operational planning. MPSB, though, were struggling to cope with the new wave of large-scale attacks, which included a mortar attack on Downing Street in 1991 that very nearly killed the British Cabinet. Shortly after that, a leak to the press had made it clear that the Met had little or no intelligence about the resumed mainland campaign.

The problem lay largely with the Met's culture. Although it saw itself as the elite police force (and had been famously called into South Yorkshire to solve the Yorkshire Ripper case a decade earlier), it seemed unwilling to learn new methods in the face of a modern threat. Put simply, it had little idea of what was happening in the mainland campaign because it had not recruited any controlled agents[52] from within the ranks of PIRA.

At the time, the Met was also a victim of its own arrogance. As less than one in five PIRA attacks took place outside London, it believed that visiting local SBs was a waste of time. In fact, prejudice often informed the Met's assessment of individual terrorist targets outside the capital. All too often, it dismissed cases which warranted further investigation and let crucial leads fall by the wayside, simply because it could not be bothered to send its officers out of the capital.

Even by the Met's own figures, one in five PIRA attacks still took place outside London. More importantly, the work of T2 had established that many of the attacks in London were planned and executed by PIRA ASUs[53] based in the provinces.

In short, the Met's strategy at the time consisted of:

- Waiting for the RUC to pass on intelligence about mainland activity it had gathered from its network of sources in Northern Ireland.
- Vainly waiting for telephone intercept to come up with hot intelligence, even if the intelligence case to support the operation had long since ceased to be relevant or was founded on inaccuracies in the first place.
- Following a target around for days or even weeks on the off-chance that they might plant a device or carry out another terrorist attack. This was all very well and good for police overtime but was a very blunt, ineffective and expensive weapon to use against an organisation like PIRA. You could after all follow a terrorist for weeks then lose him as he deployed anti-surveillance to put down the bomb.

---

[52] The term used for a target in for example a terrorist organisation who is turned and gives intelligence to the security services. In the US, they are known as 'assets'. In the UK, 'agent' is never used by the intelligence agencies to denote an intelligence officer.

[53] Active Service Unit, a cell of around three or four PIRA operatives who plan and execute an attack.

Then, in January 1992, the Met's S Squad and MI5's A4 picked Hamill up on his latest visit to London. To their surprise, Hamill – nicknamed ███████████[54] – left London and got off at Newcastle. There, he met a tall, powerfully built, dark-haired local in Yates's Wine Lodge, just off the station concourse. It was quite obvious to the surveillance teams that the bespectacled, slight figure of Hamill, an academic by profession, had little in common with the scruffy labourer he had met for only half an hour before catching another train which took him back to Northern Ireland. The local lad was alert as he left the meeting, adopting a number of anti-surveillance measures: he left the station and took a Metro to the end of the line, jumping off and then climbing back into the next Metro into town at the last moment. Despite this, surveillance officers *housed*[55] him at 152 Vine Street, Wallsend. Enquiries with local records identified him as Sean McNulty, born in North Shields, on 13 October 1967.

RUC information

Enquiries with the RUC established that in the late 1980s, McNulty had been spotted on two or three occasions by soldiers in the Dungannon area in the company of well-known members of the local PIRA battalion, including at one point Brian Arthurs, the OC.[56] In June 1990, McNulty had been detained under the PTA[57] at Luton airport coming into the UK with a relative who was also a PIRA operative. The Luton Special Branch (SB) report had gone to the SB in McNulty's home area of Newcastle. It had in turn made enquiries with MPSB, who had told the local SB that there was not enough to justify MPSB's interest in McNulty. Interestingly, a personal diary belonging to McNulty

---

[54] Hamill's nickname, removed on orders of MI5.
[55] A technical term used by MI5 to indicate that a target was seen entering a house using a key rather than just visiting.
[56] Operational Commander.
[57] The Prevention of Terrorism Act.

had been photocopied during the airport check but no one had at the time bothered to run the names and addresses inside against security records. McNulty was released after a couple of hours.

It was not until many years later that anyone came to check his movements against the history of PIRA attacks on the mainland. When I took over the McNulty case in late 1992, I established that there had been two PIRA attacks not far from where McNulty had been working. Although this obviously wasn't proof of McNulty's involvement, it would have been a useful investigative lead, if the various SBs had followed it up at the time.

McNulty next came to attention in April 1991 when he was stopped at Stranraer, returning to Dungannon in the company of another PIRA member. Some months later, the diligent and highly efficient Newcastle SB established that McNulty had returned to the Newcastle area. By this time, MI5 was supporting MPSB on the British mainland in its attempts to tackle PIRA. Part of this role was to identify possible recruitment targets, that is potential agents whom it might not be worth investigating as terrorists but who might be persuaded to infiltrate PIRA and report back. Towards the end of 1991, MI5 was desperately trying to get MPSB's permission to begin a recruitment operation against McNulty. As usual, MPSB played down his role and didn't even bother to visit Newcastle SB to discuss the lead further.

Then, on 29 January 1992, Sean McNulty met Phelim Hamill at Newcastle Railway Station.

The investigation

Although the Met still led enquiries into PIRA activities in Britain at the time, its resources were stretched following up other operational leads in London. (These operations were eventually to lead to the arrest and conviction of James Canning, a PIRA quartermaster who lived in South London.) For the first time in its battle against PIRA, A4 moved *en masse* outside London to set up camp in a local constabulary area. Unlike in the movies, surveillance does not consist of one or two people following a target around on foot or parking outside a target's house to pull off in pursuit as the target leaves his drive. A4 took up in the region of 70 officers – so it could run more than one eight-hour shift a day – and a whole load of encrypted, secure comms[58] equipment – so surveillance operatives could communicate over enormous distances via a receiver installed at Northumbria Constabulary HQ. (A4 can operate freely up to the boundaries of the M25 around London as comms are relayed through their HQ at Euston Tower.)

There, A4 – ably supported by Northumbria SB with its specialist local knowledge and a mutual hatred of the Met – began to trail McNulty 16 to 24 hours a day. Coverage was set up on 152 Vine Street and McNulty's parents' house at 90 Falmouth Road, West Churton Industrial Estate, where Sean often stayed. Both locations posed significant problems to the surveillance teams, as they were both on rundown estates where strange vehicles attracted the attention of local criminals.

Over the next few months, the surveillance teams built up a picture of McNulty's life. He was a regular visitor to the Tyneside Irish Centre, played football, womanised and got drunk.[59] Although he was not seen to meet anyone of interest to the intelligence services, he did on a number of occasions take off in his battered and rusty S-reg, red Capri and use crude but effective anti-surveillance methods. These included:

- Driving very fast then very slowly to see if any other cars followed the same pattern.
- Driving around roundabouts four or five times to spot other cars as they came onto the roundabout.
- Driving down *cul de sacs* to wait for any pursuer.

---

[58] Communication systems.

[59] He was also a big Newcastle FC fan, prompting some in MI5 to joke that David was more motivated by putting a rival fan behind bars than by catching a suspected terrorist.

The anti-surveillance led MI5 and Northumbria SB to assess that McNulty was carrying out some kind of support work for PIRA. On one occasion, he had even stopped by a series of lock-up garages – although it was not clear if he had used them, as surveillance could not maintain *eyeball*[60] on him. At one point, the RAF was called in to help track him. (Rather bizarrely, this attracted the attention of a local planespotter who reported the aircraft's unusual deployment to a specialist magazine.)

At the time, MI5 was supposedly developing the technology to cope with this sort of target. Their plan, like that seen in endless spy movies like *Enemy of the State*, was to record a target's movements via satellite, even if the target wasn't being tracked by a surveillance team at the time. In that film, satellites were able to pinpoint a vehicle's movements to an actual house on any street. In practice, the system was never used while I was still in MI5.

By this time, James Canning, like McNulty an associate of Hamill, had been arrested in South London in charge of a bomb factory. Although there was little evidence against McNulty, those around him were involved enough to maintain the interest of MI5 and, begrudgingly, MPSB. In April 1992, though, he returned to Northern Ireland. RUC enquiries established that he was staying with his aunt in Dungannon. It was not clear what he was up to, but the RUC did report that he was meeting local PIRA members. Around the same time, Linen on Sean's parents' home telephone indicated that he was thinking of going OTR[61] to the Republic. There was speculation that this meant McNulty had noticed surveillance and wasn't going to hang around in the UK, waiting to be arrested.

---

[60] Term used to indicate whether a surveillance team has actual sight of a target as opposed to merely having him under control in an area where he cannot be seen.
[61] On the run.

PIRA member with a Geordie accent

Sean McNulty was unusual by PIRA standards. The early work of T2 had established that nearly all PIRA operatives on the mainland – whether they were terrorists, routine criminals or *clean skins*[62] used to fox the authorities – were originally from Ireland. PIRA did not seem to trust those born outside those shores, even though this meant its operatives on the British mainland were readily identifiable by their Irish or Ulster accents. But McNulty was different. His father, Bernard, came from the Dungannon area in Co. Tyrone, long known as a hot-bed of PIRA recruitment, but had left the area when he was in his twenties, before the current civil war had begun. He had no traces[63] in connection with Irish Republicanism. He had not even come to attention on a Republican parade or singing Republican songs in his cups. When Bernard came to the North East of England, he settled and married Sean's mother, Dorothy, a working class Geordie woman.

Significantly though, Sean began to visit relatives in Co. Tyrone in his teens, often spending a whole summer holiday there. By this time, the modern conflict had taken a grip on the area. At an impressionable age, Sean was exposed to the deprivations and injustices that Catholics in Northern Ireland faced – on a daily basis. Enquiries with the RUC established that most of McNulty's relatives at least had Republican sympathies or, worse, were actively involved in PIRA. Of course, Sean's Geordie accent and Newcastle address meant he could operate on the mainland without the suspicion attracted by his cousins and uncles.

---

[62] Term used to describe a PIRA member, whom PIRA believes to be unknown to the security forces.
[63] Individual mentions within security records.

89

Suggested recruitment

By the time that he went missing on 29 May 1993, MI5, MPSB and Northumbria SB had probably devoted more resources to McNulty's case than any other individual before or since. By his constant movement from address to address, he had caused me many headaches not least because I had been responsible for keeping the warrantry[64] up to date. Although consorting with PIRA members is an offence under the Prevention of Terrorism Act (PTA), the authorities often turn a blind eye to potential prosecutions, not for civil liberties reasons but for fear of embarrassment, should a suspect be acquitted.

After McNulty returned from Northern Ireland in April 1993, I had tried to identify potential agents who might have been able to report on him. It was, I reasoned, the only way we could properly keep track of McNulty and was much less expensive than round-the-clock surveillance. But as usual I could not get anybody to look at the work I had done, let alone act on it. Then one day in early May, my boss came out of *group leaders*[65] with a brilliant new idea: why not try to recruit Sean himself as an agent?

This was desperation on the part of T2 management, who had no idea how to advance the operation. If they had consulted me – the officer who knew the case inside out – they would have realised that there was no point in even trying to approach McNulty. There was no carrot or stick to induce him to work for MI5. He had no conflict of conscience with the cause; no personal gripes with other personalities in PIRA; no particular need for money; no problems in which MI5 could help him with a view to securing his co-operation. In fact, there were many other reasons why, even if he had been recruited, he would never have made a particularly reliable source. He was a drinker, a womaniser and a bigmouth who had been arrested

---

[64] The legal authority, signed by the Home Secretary, which allows MI5 to tap telephones.
[65] The name given to the Monday morning meeting of the head of section, his deputy and the heads of the subsections.

by uniformed bobbies on several occasions for drink driving, beating up his girlfriend and smashing up a flat.

He was the sort of character who, if recruited, would have boasted of his MI5 connections to uniformed police to avoid arrest and/or a night in the cells or, worse, a conviction. And, even if all this hadn't counted against him, there was one good reason why he simply wouldn't agree to be recruited by MI5: being a native-born Englishman, he had fought hard to win the trust of the RA.[66] For an unemployed Geordie, membership of PIRA was probably one of the few areas of life where he could command any respect from his peers. He was not going to blow his only prestige in life by abusing the trust of those close to him.

So I quickly wrote a Loose Minute, which I sent to Wendy recommending that we did not even begin a recruitment operation as we risked jeopardising all the good work we had already done. If approached, I argued, he would most likely turn down our offer, lay low for six months to a year then strike when he was sure we had lost interest in him. I copied my Loose Minute to T2 management and the recruitment idea was quietly dropped.

---

[66] Pronounced rah. Short for Republican Army and the name PIRA calls itself.

Chapter 5

Operation BROOM, T2A Goes 'Live'

The way forward for Operation BROOM

Constabulary HQ buildings are usually dark, brooding 1960s edifices built on the outskirts of the county town that force covers. Northumbria Police HQ is very different. It is located about 10 miles outside Newcastle in a small village called Ponteland. As a former residential training college, it has a series of dormitory houses in a circle around a kind of village green (in addition to the pre-fabs and add-ons). As the green is usually deserted during the day, it gives the whole set-up a slightly eerie air. When you pass the security control at the gate, it is as if you have just entered Midwich, the village of the damned, or have found yourself in an episode of the Avengers. Being clandestine even to other police officers, the Branch is based in one of the houses that surround the green. Unlike the other buildings, the entrance is security-coded to prevent unwelcome nosy parkers.[67]

Steve, Paul Jenkins, the T2B liaison officer, and I represented the Service at the meeting to discuss McNulty. Northumbria SB was represented by:

- Kelvin, the Detective Superintendent and Head of SB (HSB). He had what is referred to in the *Dilbert* cartoons as

---

[67]The building also contained the paperwork from the Stephens Enquiry.

'management hair'. In other words, he boasted a thick head of distinguished silver-grey hair, parted at the side. He always wore a not-too-expensive, off the peg suit. SB was, to him, another box to tick on his CV, more evidence of the breadth of his experience within what he would no doubt call the police 'service'. He was, though, an effective officer, who was going all the way to the top.

- John, the Detective Chief Inspector and deputy head of the SB. He was a hard-bitten, long-serving officer of the old school who had seen it all. A big bear of a man with a pink face, he was cynical about SB work, believing it wasn't 'real' police work as it seldom involved collaring villains. I once played five-a-side football against him and was impressed by his aggressive leadership of his team. As a Sunderland fan, he often used to try to wind me up about my team, Middlesbrough, even though we were, and still are, better than them.

- Denzil, the Detective Inspector responsible for Irish matters in the SB. He was a slightly balding, kindly bloke nearing the end of his police career and a lifelong fan of Newcastle Utd. He bought a square yard of the pitch at St James's Park when they replanted it in 1994. John, the DCI, used to wind him up mercilessly about anything ranging from Newcastle's latest defeat to his section's performance indicators.

- John, the Chief Superintendent and head of operations for Northumbria Police, who was understandably worried that more bombs might go off on his patch.

As usual, SB officers below the rank of DI were excluded from the meeting with Box.[68] MPSB had declined our invitation despite the fact that they still in theory maintained a national role in intelligence gathering against PIRA but in support of the Service rather than in the lead. At this time, MI5 and local

---

[68] MI5's name in Whitehall and the police, taken from its former postal address of Box 500.

SBs shared a mutual dislike of the Met, which they saw as arrogant, lazy and unhelpful. As usual, this feeling helped ease us into the meeting[69] and was one of the reasons that the local SB did not make more of the 12-day delay surrounding the CCTV stills. That and the attitude of Kelvin the HSB, who knew that many high-flying police officers had fallen to earth, after being stitched up by Box. If the DCI had been in charge, I doubt we would have got away with it so easily. Even as I protested that we were being completely open with his SB, I felt convinced that the DCI suspected that we were not telling him everything about the delay. 'Cock-up is more likely than conspiracy in my book. After all, you have to organise a conspiracy and that is clearly beyond the management capabilities of the Service,' I pointed out to him.

The main purpose of the meeting was to discuss whether we had enough information to arrest McNulty. The DCI was firmly of the opinion that 'coincidences like this don't happen outside television'. He felt we should strike while the iron was hot. The problem was that we had no *evidence* of McNulty's involvement, apart from his visit to the Jack house in Scotland. But you can't just arrest a suspect for going to another suspect's house. At the same time, this information couldn't have been used in court without blowing the ongoing operation into Jack and Fryers. In fact, all we had to show for investigating McNulty for 18 months were associations and suspicions. Although it is very easy to obtain search warrants under PTA, we felt we would be in a stronger position if we had further information we could use to convince a judge. Of course, while McNulty remained at large, we risked:

- Losing him – Linen suggested that he had disappeared to the Irish Republic in June 1992, precisely because he thought he had been rumbled in the UK.

---

[69] I started off by solemnly stating that this was no time for egos; we had to unite in the face of the common enemy then paused and said: 'The Met'.

- Him letting off another bomb and making us look stupid, if it ever got out that we had suspected him but not acted quickly enough.

We had checked the CCTV coverage of his parents' house. There was no sighting of him around the time the bomb would have been put down – about an hour before it exploded. PIRA usually used an hour fuse and explosives experts had confirmed that the devices used to blow up the fuel stations bore those hallmarks. It was tempting to presume that McNulty was guilty but there had been another attack in the Newcastle area in April 1993. At the time, McNulty had been living and working down in Portsmouth. Rather than alert our suspicions to McNulty being the bomber, this had supported our assessment that he targeted installations and sites for other operatives to put down the actual bombs. Although in theory, he could have been charged with conspiracy (if we could have established that he had researched the targets for the attack in April 1993 or June 1993), in practice, it would have been extremely difficult to prove in court. And then there was the embarrassment factor. Unlike other PIRA operatives, McNulty had never even been formally arrested in connection with PIRA activity, let alone been convicted. If we had sent in SO13[70] and it had revealed nothing, the Service and the police would have been open to charges from some commentators of persecuting McNulty on account of his Irish descent.

However, there was one other good reason for not going in then. For the first time since January 1992, we had clear evidence that McNulty was at the heart of the mainland campaign, in the form of his visit to Hugh Jack's house in Scotland. I argued that we should therefore devote more resources to Operation BROOM in order to uncover the extent of McNulty's role. After all, we had followed him around on and off without

---

[70] The anti-terrorist squad of the Metropolitan Police. They have a national role and carry out arrests on behalf of MI5.

success for 18 months so what difference would another two or three months make. Now, we really had everything to gain. He could potentially lead us to weapons caches and other PIRA active service units (ASUs). In short, we stood to learn far more about PIRA's mainland campaign than ever before.

As usual, we decided to take the middle route, more out of resource concerns than bold rationale. A4 were already pre-occupied by the investigation into Fryers and Jack in Scotland, so it was difficult to know if they were going to have the capacity to follow McNulty in the long term, as well. We reasoned that if we had McNulty under surveillance 24 hours a day, we would be able to prevent him from setting off any more bombs. So we decided to put him under surveillance until the end of the week (Sunday 20 June) in the hope that:

- He would be caught red-handed about to let off another device, or:
- He would lead us to his arms cache where he could again caught in the act, or:
- He would lead us to other PIRA operatives on the mainland.

A couple of A4 teams were on their way up to help the surveillance-trained officers of Northumbria SB, particularly as they had the only cars fitted with radar equipment to track the device placed in McNulty's red Capri the April before. This tracker only worked in conjunction with the surveillance cars following a target.

When we got on the plane back to London that night, I thought I would be controlling the operation from MI5 HQ in Curzon Street. On the plane, Steve and I agreed that I would be best placed if I were based in Northumbria. I dreaded having to tell Annie that I was going to be away for the next week, as we had only just started going out.

En poste, back in the North East

Steve also decided that it would be better if there were two officers to cope with all the work that might be produced. Paul Jenkins, the usual T2B regional liaison officer, was due to go on holiday so William[71] Perkins, who normally liaised with southern forces, was sent up with me. He looked much older than his age, 38, as he was almost totally bald on top and had a Zapata moustache, which also dated him. Like many others, he had joined MI5 in the 1970s, after completing a research degree, in his case zoology, and had made the most of the *Buggins' turn* promotion policy to reach GI2, the vast middle management grade in MI5 which made the structural diagram of MI5's management look heavily pregnant. He was an affable bloke who realised that staying at his grade provided him with fairly stimulating, not badly paid, secure employment. In short, he was a bit of an ex-hippy.

I barely knew him before we went to Newcastle but I grew to like his irreverent sense of humour while we were there. In fact, about twelve months later, he was the subject of one of the biggest *faux pas* I've ever heard. During a drinks party, the head of section, T2/0, got up to 'say a few words', like 'sterling effort', 'everyone pulled together', 'couldn't do it without your contribution', 'great success blah, blah, blah'. In the week before the drinks party, two major events had happened in Bill's life: he had found out he was to be posted to Northern Ireland and he had broken his right wrist. Commiserating with him for this unfortunate double whammy, T2/0 uttered the immortal words:

'And what can we say about Bill? He has had to suffer the double misfortune of being posted to Northern Ireland without his wife and of having broken his right wrist.'

Not many laughed at that. But I just couldn't resist.

When we arrived at Northumbria HQ that Tuesday afternoon

---

[71] Fictional name we used changed on orders of MI5.

(15 June), we went into the makeshift Ops Room that A4 had set up in the SB house. As usual, it all looked very impressive, full of strange black boxes with mysterious glowing dials and even more mysterious wires protruding all over the place. But at least it looked like an Ops Room. The enormous amount of encryption and comms equipment meant there wasn't room for Bill and me, so we had to re-locate to a small back room which had once been used as a store cupboard but was in the process of being renovated.

It was early days as far as operations outside MI5 HQ were concerned. The Service had plenty of experience of operating from home but had little knowledge of what it was like to operate long term in another force area. To say we were unprepared would be an understatement. The room had only one desk, which we had to share. There was no stationery, no telephone; a computer was clearly out of the question. As I knew the SB pretty well, I went down to the Detective Sergeant and Detective Constable's room in the block. There, I bumped into Ian the DS, a tall and refined type whom I had met a number of times since I had joined MI5.

'So what's going on, then?' He asked almost immediately.

'Don't you know?' I replied, amazed.

'No one ever tells us anything. I mean, given the fuss something must be up.'

'I shouldn't tell you this but...'

His management had charged him with the responsibility for drawing up the operational rota and plan but had not seen fit to tell him why everyone was suddenly on alert. Why? Did they think he was going to leak the information, damaging the reputation of the Branch and letting McNulty off the hook? It was clearly not in his interests: a successful operation would count towards his promotion prospects. In all my experience of intelligence work, I always found the local constabulary SBs to be the least leaky and most reliable officers, no matter what their grade. I briefed Ian the DS who was, once again, grateful to me for providing the relevant information.

We go operational

After Bill and I had gone out and bought pens, paper, rulers, staplers, paperclips and the like and had the phone installed in our 'cell', we were ready. Surveillance proper started that day, Tuesday 15 June. I opened the operational log – designed to record all conversations between the SB and us; A4 and us; and MI5 HQ and us, just in case there was any disagreement or witch-hunt in the event of the operation going toes up. Then ... nothing happened.

Ice Cube came home from work then went out for a few drinks. There was no anti-surveillance, no suspicious meetings or phone calls, no furtive, guilty behaviour. In fact, nothing happened at all. Talk about boredom. Spywatchers, particularly some journalists who should know better, imagine the world of spooks is all hanging around on street corners anxiously awaiting a brush contact or trying to lose enemy surveillance before attending to a dead letter-box with the latest vital intelligence from Morocco Mole or Deep Plant. But it's not.

Operational activity can be both the most exciting and the most frustrating aspect of intelligence work. Later in my MI5 career, I was involved in a live operation into Phelim Hamill (yes, the same one). I was on duty in the MI5 Ops Room on the 18th floor of NSY[72] when Hamill arrived at a service station to pick up a Nissan loaded with explosives. Here we go, I thought, this should be an interesting shift. But when Hamill arrived, he seemed incapable of locating the target vehicle. He wandered around for a couple of hours or so then got a bus back to Preston. Once was bad enough but Eye Liner[73] did the

---

[72] New Scotland Yard, the HQ of the Metropolitan Police.
[73] Hamill's nickname changed on orders of MI5.

same thing again and again. And I always seemed to be on duty when it happened.

Anyway, Bill and I sat there in the tiny, scruffy office with the tiny, streaked window, regaling each other with office gossip and rumours to pass the time. To start with, we didn't even have a clock, which made the passing of each interminable minute of the 12–14-hour shifts intolerable. Occasionally, A4 would phone up from their Ops Room downstairs just to tell us that Ice Cube had left work or had moved from one pub to another. Otherwise it was desperate. In normal operational circumstances, we would both have been passing by secure telegram or fax the addresses of McNulty's contacts to MI5 head office so they could be checked against:

- MI5 records in R2, the main file registry.
- MI5 temporary records in R10.
- DURBAR, an IT database of terrorist targets.
- The Met's records.

If it had been a larger scale operation, T2 would have set up a cell in COBRA, the Cabinet Office Briefing Room. It had been designed before the days when MI5 studied PIRA so it had generally been used as an Ops Room during hostage situations and the like. As its name suggests, it had a secure hotline to the Cabinet Office where the PM and other members of the Cabinet would be waiting for the latest intelligence and assessment from MI5 before deciding how to proceed. But as Operation BROOM only involved McNulty, COBRA was empty. It was left to T2A/9 Jane, one of my colleagues in the T2A/Northern group, to carry out any enquiries at MI5 HQ.

As A2A, the transcribers of telephone taps communicated directly with A4, warning the surveillance of any prior intelligence about Ice Cube's movements, Bill and I were not even in this loop. Occasionally, we received transcribed material by secure fax, mainly so I could check it against my expert knowledge of the case, but the McNulty family was not using the phone much at that time. After a day or two of this, Bill and I decided to split the shifts with him doing early – 06:00 to 14:00 – and me doing late – 14:00 to 22:00. If anything happened outside the shifts, it was up to A4 or A2A to contact us in our hotel rooms.

During one shift handover, we devised a cunning plan to flush him out. According to our scheme, someone with an Irish accent would phone McNulty's parents, pretending to be Phelim Hamill. Our anonymous caller would pass on a message along the lines of: 'Move the weapons'. McNulty would then, we hoped, make his way to his arms cache, where we would arrest him. At the time, it seemed brilliant but that was probably because we were bored witless. In the end, the Met advised us against it as we would have to disclose it in court and it might somehow be interpreted as entrapment.

On the Friday afternoon (18 June), I arrived in the cubby-hole to find the balloon had gone up. A2A had reported that McNulty's parents had discussed a 'gu-' on the phone in the context of Sean's increasingly strange behaviour at the time. As McNulty's mother spoke broad Geordie and his father spoke unintelligible Ulster, the A2A transcriber hadn't been sure whether they were talking about a gun.

Bill had decided that he wanted to return home for the weekend so my boss Wendy was at that moment heading north on a speeding Intercity train, with the actual tape of the offending conversation in a secure briefcase. When she arrived that evening, we all crowded around a tape machine in the HSB's office to listen to its contents. Northumbria SB had suggested that they might be able to shed some light on the accent, but it was McNulty's father, an Irishman, not his mother, a Geordie, who had said 'gu-'. None of us could be sure that he had actually said 'gun', given the thickness of his brogue. Fortunately, there was a transcriber on secondment to A2A from the army in Northern Ireland. He was able to near-as-damn-it confirm that Bernard had said it.

It added to our profile of Sean, but we still risked looking like idiots if we were to raid his parents' home and find nothing. After all, there was no indication in his parents' conversation that the gun had ever been in the McNulty home.

That evening, we agreed to let the operation run until Monday (21 June). If McNulty was not seen to do anything incriminating, we would have to take the risk of having him arrested, turning over his parents' place and not finding any evidence to implicate him. I would have liked to have seen the operation run longer but practicalities took over – A4 were required to cover Fryers and Jack the following week.

But as I literally walked out of the door of Northumbria SB that Monday evening, everything changed. An SB officer who had been reviewing footage from CCTV cameras in the Tyne Tunnel, shopping centres and elsewhere excitedly called me back. He replayed a video on the screen in front of him from a service station near the scene of the second attack. It showed a burly figure filling up his red Capri with petrol. It was McNulty and his car. The date on the footage read: '09.06.93'. The time was an hour or so before the attack that night. Allowing for the hour timer, it put McNulty in exactly the right place at exactly the right time to have planted the bomb. With that, I left for London, in the full knowledge that we were going to hand over to the Met to take executive action.

On the morning of 24 June 1994, SO13 arrested Sean McNulty and his family under the PTA.

The unjustified arrest of the McNulty family

While I thought we had good information about Sean, I was less convinced it was right to arrest and interview his family. Under caution, his sister – I think her name was Annette – recounted how she had seen Sean actually take a gun and the materials to build a bomb, including Semtex – she described it as a ball of orange plasticine – from a holdall in his bedroom. She then related how she had seen him construct the bomb and had pleaded with him not to endanger lives. Later that day, she learnt from the news that one of the fuel terminals had been blown up. The judge presiding over the McNulty trial ruled that this was inadmissible evidence.

MI5 knew from the telephone taps that McNulty's parents had also tried to prevent Sean from carrying out terrorist attacks on the British mainland. They confirmed this under interview and were charged with withholding information about terrorism under s.18 of the PTA and held on remand in a high-security prison prior to trial.

MI5 knew that the family were alarmed and upset by Sean's suspected activities. When faced with a terrible dilemma – shop their son to the authorities or allow him to engage in acts of terrorism – they froze. They turned a blind eye to their son's activities rather than help send him to prison for 20-odd years, the standard sentence for terrorism on the British mainland. Sean's father, Brian McNulty, an innocent man, died on remand from a heart attack, just like Giuseppe Conlon in *The Name of the Father*, the film about the wrongful convictions of the Guildford 4 and the Maguire 7.[74]

The Crown Prosecution Service (CPS) dropped the charges on the morning of the trial, after the McNulty family had been in custody for the best part of a year. It was quite clear from MI5's investigation of McNulty that his family were utterly opposed to terrorism. Under police caution, they had described Sean's suspicious activities in the belief that they were helping the authorities. There was no moral reason to use the full weight of a highly controversial section of a highly controversial Act of Parliament against them. This all remains relevant today as the clause is part of the Terrorism Act 2000. The arrest and trial of relatives of Al Qaeda convicts is hardly likely to secure the co-operation of the Muslim community in informing on Islamic extremist activities in Britain.

---

[74] Our solicitor, Gareth Peirce, is played by Emma Thompson in the film.

Vital evidence lost in the McNulty prosecution

Although McNulty was prosecuted after Fryers and Jack had been arrested in connection with terrorist offences, the photo of 10 June 1993 was never brought before a jury.

Once back at MI5 HQ, I established the reason for the 12-day delay in sending the pictures. Although Central Scotland SB regularly monitored the video CCTV coverage of Hugh Jack's house, taking stills of any visitors, they had no secure way of passing the stills to MI5 HQ in London. As a result, the product[75] had to be included in Central's secure bag. This was picked up by a van, which used to visit all the Scottish SBs collecting their secure material about once every two weeks. In the age of the Internet and digital encryption, MI5 has no excuse for not ensuring that intelligence, even where it takes the form of photographs, is disseminated promptly.

And I am not benefiting from hindsight. Anyone with half a brain could foresee that a 12-day delay in passing CCTV stills from the OP to MI5 HQ was likely to lead to vital intelligence being received too late to act on. This is a clear example of how MI5 failed to adapt its methods to a fast-moving target like PIRA and instead used methods more appropriate to the long-term investigation of spies and subversives. In these cases, time is not of the essence because spies and subversives do not put down bombs which threaten life and limb. But PIRA did.[76] The same thing happened when the authorities failed to react to specific intelligence which revealed that Jimmy 'Cyril' McGuinness, an IRA member with a long security history, was to launch a spectacular on the weekend of 23–25 April 1993.

When I visited Northumbria SB for a two-week secondment in 1994, I also learnt there had been another key failure regarding evidence in the McNulty investigation. Newcastle SB told me

---

[75]The generic name for the intelligence, information or evidence from a human or technical source.
[76]The delay was so heinous, it may well represent a breach of Article 2, the right to life, which puts a responsibility on the state to protect the lives of its citizens.

that they had recovered a pair of McNulty's chino trousers, which forensics had established were covered in extensive traces of Semtex. The trousers had been sent to the Met for the court case but had been lost. On my return from secondment, I raised this matter with Steve Canute. He told me that the Met were claiming that Northumbria police had lost them. I suggested that there must be some way to establish who was at fault but Canute just shrugged his shoulders, indicating that we should let sleeping dogs lie.

MI5 covers up mistake in brief to ministers and Whitehall

Some weeks after McNulty was arrested, I discovered that Steve Canute and others had covered up its honest, if eminently foreseeable, mistake over the 12-day delay in passing the photos back to MI5 HQ.

In summer 1993, I wrote a short summary of the investigation to be included in the Operational Report, a summary of all the operations that MI5 had carried out that year. Each recipient received a numbered copy with No. 1 going to HMQ (or the Queen as she is more usually known); No. 2 going to the PM; and No. 3 to the Home Secretary.[77] As I had contributed to the report, I also received a copy of it. When I turned to my piece, I was horrified to find that the chronology of the McNulty case had been bowdlerised. The report gave the impression that the CCTV stills of McNulty at Hugh Jack's house had been *taken* the day they arrived on T2A/2's desk – 10 June 1993 – that is the day after the attacks, not 12 days before.

At first, I thought I might have misled T2/1 but I checked my version and found that I had clearly referred to the 12-day delay. When I approached Canute to point out the problem, he raised his finger to his lips, clearly indicating that I should

[77] The original version of my report will be on the McNulty file, PF356326, and also on my "letterbook", the record of all the documents I created in MI5.

106

keep quiet about this. As I've said, mistakes can happen. They are, though, less likely to happen in the first place if you have a staff confident enough to bring problems and, possibly, solutions to the attention of management. But here was clear evidence that MI5 had lied about a problem rather than bringing it to the attention of its masters in Downing Street and Whitehall.

I let it drop there. I already knew that I would only get more hassle if I rocked the boat again.

In July 1994, a jury convicted Sean McNulty of conspiracy to cause terrorist offences but only by the slenderest margin allowed to uphold a conviction, 10–2. He was sentenced to 22 years in prison. I was proud to be the first MI5 case officer to see his investigation lead to an IRA conviction, after T2 took over from MPSB. At the same time, I once again found myself ashamed to be British over the treatment of the McNulty family. In 2000, Sean McNulty was released under the Good Friday agreement.

Chapter 6

The IRA: More Abuses of Power by MI5

The following is an account of other matters which arose during my posting to T5 and David's posting to T2. They reflect our concerns at MI5's inability to work within the law. They are all issues which arose through formal channels and cannot therefore be called 'bar-room gossip', one of the lies the authorities have used to try to undermine David's disclosures, without ever of course hearing his evidence.

Innocent man kept locked up, despite the evidence

In the case of McNulty's family, T2 could at least argue that it was merely following the law, no matter how unjust that law was. The service could not use those arguments in the case of Patrick Murphy, who was arrested and charged with hijacking a minicab, which exploded at Downing Street in October 1992. T2 management demonstrated that it would rather ignore the concerns of desk officers, even where these involved the freedom of an individual and a possible miscarriage of justice, than do the right thing and alert ministers to the unlawful detention of an innocent man.

From the description given by the hijacked taxi driver, and other relevant intelligence, T2 desk officers had quickly identified Rab Fryers as almost certainly the culprit for the Downing Street taxi bomb. However, on the basis of some spurious physical resemblance to Fryers, Murphy was arrested, charged and held on remand for the offence. However, MI5 did not intervene with the Anti-Terrorist Squad or the CPS to draw their attention to its identification of the person responsible. (T2/1, Steve Canute, may have raised the issue on an ad hoc basis as part of his role liasing with the Anti-Terrorist Squad but representations should have been made on a formal basis.) I am quite sure that MI5 would have let the prosecution of Murphy proceed to trial and conviction without intervening with its information indicating Murphy's innocence. Fortunately, Murphy was released after his solicitors were able to call on a number of reliable alibi witnesses who swore that he had been at a meeting of Alcoholics Anonymous at the time of the attack.

Again, this demonstrates that MI5 does not understand that it has a duty not just to help catch terrorists with a view to putting them on trial but also to ensure that human rights are observed. To allow a suspect to continue to be falsely imprisoned is a clear violation of human rights.[78] I seriously doubt whether ministers even have the appropriate information to ensure that MI5 is performing its duties correctly in this area. In fact, if I were not including this account here, no one would know that MI5 was complicit in the unlawful detention of a suspect.

Illegal spying on the Garda

During David's prosecution, the state argued that an intelligence officer had a lifelong duty of confidentiality. But what are we to make of a situation in which MI5 itself violates this principle with a friendly power's security and intelligence information? It is a convention that friendly countries do not run undeclared – or unavowed, to use the intelligence services' jargon – agents in each other's countries. In addition, there are formal procedures for sharing intelligence, which carry certain 'caveats' or warnings

---

[78] HRA, Article 5, ECHR, which is designed to prevent arbitrary and unlawful detention.

about its handling. One of these caveats states that the recipient of any intelligence cannot act upon it or pass it on without the permission of the originator.

In spring 1994, David came across a source report containing information about suspected terrorists in the Irish Republic which was relevant to the targets he was investigating in the north-east of England. The report was marked: 'Do not disseminate without reference to T8,' indicating that the material was not to be shared with the Garda. As David needed to share the intelligence with UK police, he went to see the relevant person in T8 to ask why he couldn't mention it to the Garda, when requesting further security traces. The agent runner explained that the report came from a Garda officer whom T8 were running as an undeclared agent. He clearly knew that this was a violation of procedure and the laws of the Republic of Ireland as he insisted that David did not mention the existence of the agent to his colleagues in T2.

There are, of course, official channels for MI5 and the Garda to share relevant intelligence about IRA suspects in the Republic. For legitimate reasons of national security, the Garda has a right to know what happens to its intelligence. What would happen if, for example, the material had to be used to help prevent an attack in Britain? The original agent run by the Garda could then have been compromised to the IRA in the Republic, undermining Garda investigations and possibly leading to the execution of an informer. MI5's tasking of an undeclared agent in the Garda could therefore lead to the national security of the Irish Republic being undermined. In addition, MI5 was guilty of aiding and abetting treachery, in this case, the unauthorised dissemination of Republic of Ireland state secrets to a foreign power.

In other words, T8 encouraged an Irish public servant to betray his colleagues, his employers and the Irish people to a foreign power.

From the context of David's conversation with the T8 officer, he gathered that this was a long-term operation rather than a one-off. As such, it represented strategic and conscious flouting of the law, and the conventions which govern intelligence work. Although David knew this was illegal, what was he to do? It was clear that MI5 management were complicit in the recruitment and running of the Garda agent, yet the current oversight arrangements mean that he could not raise this issue with independent officials outside the service.

Illegal tapping of phones ███████████████[79]

If MI5 wanted to tap a telephone outside the UK, there was no warranty system, and therefore no democratic oversight of the procedure – at all. The relevant MI5 officer would simply task GCHQ ████████████████████[79] to intercept communications to the number, without a warrant to govern the invasion of privacy of the target and without informing ministers who oversee the services. The privacy of UK citizens was also unlawfully compromised when an intercepted call was made to or from the UK because the individual involved could not complain that the tap was unlawful.[80]

Interception of client/counsel conversations

In June 1992, Michael O'Brien, at the time an innocent Irishman who had been arrested and charged with terrorist-related offences,

---

[79] Blacked out on orders of MI5

[80] This represents a violation of HRA, Article 8, ECHR and Article 13, the right to redress, because the subjects of the telephone tapping and the ministers responsible for the legal interception of communications have no way of establishing whether the interference of their privacy is legitimate under the Convention. In Malone v. UK (1984) 7 EHRR 14, the European Court of Human Rights (ECtHR) found that the UK was not acting in accordance with Convention law because it did not have statutory procedures for monitoring the phone calls of private citizens. 'To that extent,' the Court concluded, 'the minimum degree of legal protection to which citizens are entitled under the rule of law in a democratic society is lacking.' As a result, the British government was obliged to introduce the Interception of Communications Act, which became law in 1985.

asked to see Gareth Peirce, the solicitor who overturned the wrongful convictions of the Guildford Four and the Birmingham Six. (She is also the holder of an MI5 PF and our solicitor.) At the time, O'Brien was being held on remand at HMP Belmarsh, the high security prison. At his first meeting with Peirce, she asked him to recount what he had been doing in North Yorkshire just before his arrest. O'Brien gave a full account of himself. How do I know this? Because the Metropolitan Police Special Branch (MPSB) recorded the conversation, even though client–counsel discussions are privileged. Not only did the police record the conversation, they also decided to listen to it. A senior MPSB officer heard a great deal of the tape, although not, I'm told, all of it.

Wendy Probit, David's MI5 line manager, officially briefed her group about this case. Charles Conaught,[81] MI5's legal adviser, even gave his opinion on the matter. At the time, the recording of counsel–client conversations was not actually illegal under English law because we had no written Bill of Rights.[82]

This is not some dry, abstract and arbitrary article of a declaration of human rights. It is there to prevent the law enforcement agencies from gaining an advantage at trial via their prior knowledge of an accused person's defence. At the briefing in the T2 long room in 1992, David heard that the tape had indeed been destroyed (but only after MPSB had listened to it) removing any evidence of an obvious human rights violation. Of course, due to the excessive secrecy which surrounds the work of MI5 and its executive arm, Special Branch, this fact was never divulged either to the trial judge or the defence at O'Brien's trial. As such, we have to ask whether that trial was fair.

But this issue has greater repercussions. Why was there a recording device in the room where Peirce met O'Brien, in the

---

[81] Name changed on orders of MI5.

[82] Anyone seeking redress for this abuse of democratic rights would have had to go to the European Court as it is a clear breach of Article 6, ECHR, the right to a fair trial. Thank God for the HRA.

first place? Presumably, that room was used for other client–counsel conversations. We therefore have to ask ourselves whether SB listened to and recorded other conversations between innocent remand prisoners and their lawyers. Prison visiting rooms can be legally bugged without the permission of ministers if the property belongs to the Prison Service, and it consents to the interference with its property to install an eavesdropping device or bug. There is no need for a property warrant. This means that there is no ministerial oversight of a process which – as demonstrated here – can lead to unlawful behaviour and human rights abuses on the part of the authorities.

Since Gareth Peirce is also our lawyer, we know that she wrote to Jack Straw, then Home Secretary, asking for details of this operation. She has confirmed that the contents David was made aware of at the briefing – and other T2 officers briefed me about – were indeed a summary of their encounter. *The details could and should have only been known to her and her client, O'Brien*. Straw wrote back, saying that he was not aware of any such recording.

But none of that represents an excuse for Straw simply to turn a blind eye to it. At the very least, Straw's admission confirms that the services do not readily admit their mistakes to government as no minister has been made aware that SB came to be in possession of at least one legally privileged conversation. If ministers are not made aware of human rights abuses on the part of the services, they are in no position to know whether the services are breaking the law.[83] In this case, it is made worse because the Home Secretary shows no interest in investigating a disclosure indicating that the services used their secret powers and techniques not to protect national security but to undermine an individual who was at the time an innocent man seeking confidential legal advice, his right in any fair trial process.

---

[83] Under the HRA, the common law and specific legislation which makes them responsible and accountable for the activities of the law enforcement and intelligence agencies.

Further illegal enquiries: the L744 file series

The following case may seem like nitpicking. But MI5 prides itself not on stopping terrorism but on its slavish adherence to bureaucratic procedure. This example demonstrates that the service is not much good at that either.

In 1993, David became aware that one of the filing systems used by the section failed to comply with human rights legislation. Although the brighter officers often discussed the problem, none of them dared to raise it with T2 management for fear that they would somehow be black-marked for drawing the failure to their attention – such was the culture in which we worked. As a result, the ensuing illegal enquiries went on for much longer than they should have, around 12–18 months, and concerned many hundreds of individuals.

Before T2 took over Irish Republican primacy from MPSB, Wendy Probit was tasked to create a working file system to record communications with each separate police constabulary and to collect general details of Irish Republican activity in that force area, including correspondence relating to low-level suspects who did not have their own PFs. It was called the List 744 series, with each force having a unique reference number, for example L744–1 for Avon and Somerset SB. Under the European Convention and the 1989 Security Service Act, every enquiry and investigation must be centrally retrievable from the MI5 archives so that, if there is a complaint, the Security Service Commissioner can access all the relevant information to assess whether MI5 behaved lawfully or the complainant has a case for compensation. In normal circumstances, a target has a PF which holds all the details of the investigation. It is retrievable via the STAR system, which archives MI5 files.

But the L744 series were only recorded on STAR as List files. The central computer did not record the identities of individuals investigated using this file system. If the individuals concerned complained to the Commissioner, their names would have come up 'no trace' or 'no record of the individual'. The Commissioner would then be obliged to come to the conclusion that MI5 had not interfered with the complainant's privacy because MI5 had never investigated him, when in fact the details of the illegal investigation were held on a L744 file.

To make enquiries filed on a L744 file centrally retrievable and therefore lawful, the desk officer had to create a Green Durbar record, named after MI5's database of terrorist suspects. But there was no indication on the L744 that this was necessary for MI5 to comply with legislation. Steve Canute tried to blame the whole fiasco on R25 (later T25), T branch's dedicated clerical support section. The whole affair caused outrage throughout T Branch and the Registry. As far as I am aware no action was taken against Wendy Probit. In addition, clerical staff were taken away from their routine duties to study the papers the L744s had collected in that year and identify which of them needed to be cross-referred to a Green Durbar record.

I stress that this did not come about because MI5 was dealing with a new area of work. It came about because partly as a result of the abortive 'Palace Revolution': MI5 bosses had created a culture in which any idea or criticism might be treated as dissent. In those circumstances, officers were rather more inclined to turn a blind eye to unlawful activities than risk a black mark for asking awkward questions. Even where officers had the courage to raise issues of illegality or ethical questions, they would generally be ignored on the grounds that they were of a lower service grade than management or that their boss would brand them as a troublemaker. As far as I am aware the matter was never raised with ministers, the Commissioner or the victims of this unlawful invasion of privacy.

PIRA escape justice due to inadmissibility of phone tap

In 1991, when MPSB still led investigations into the Provisional IRA on the British mainland, William and Siobhan O'Kane had

116

been under investigation for their support of terrorism. In 1991, they were arrested and charged with terrorist offences after telephone intercept had reported that they had knowingly moved a car with weapons and explosives in the boot on behalf of the IRA. At trial, they denied any knowledge of the ammunition in the car, claiming that they had agreed to move it for a friend. As telephone intercept is not admissible as evidence, the jury believed the two and acquitted them. Rather than reform the law to allow telephone taps to be used in evidence, the security services were more concerned with maintaining the secrecy of their operations.

This obsession with secrecy is founded on the erroneous belief on the part of MI5 that telephone tapping is still such a sensitive technique that the man on the street has not heard of it. As a result, telephone intercept remains inadmissible. Wouldn't it be a terrible tragedy if suspected Al Qaeda terrorists were allowed to go free because evidence obtained by telephone tap continues to be inadmissible? In fact, it hardly seems a proportionate response to Al Qaeda to imprison suspected terrorists without trial before making telephone intercept admissible.

T2 and the ceasefire

Eventually, T2 Branch scored some notable successes against the IRA but this was usually as a result of the endeavours of hard-working desk officers, *in spite of* not because of management. Of course, the ceasefire had implications for T2 as well. Many of the founding members of staff had come to the end of their two-year posting and were moved to new sections. By the time a massive bomb in Canary Wharf shattered the ceasefire in February 1996, T2's experienced staff had been scattered throughout the service and their replacements had yet to experience 'live' counter-IRA operations. However, the other directors refused to allow the experienced officers to return to T2 as it would diminish their staff numbers and authority. Once again PIRA had to be countered by untried officers struggling to get up to speed. Once again, the egos of senior management prevented the British people from being properly protected from the evil of terrorism.

With exquisite timing, David was posted to the Libyan desk in G Branch in October 1994, a month after the IRA ceasefire had begun. Despite what he had seen in T2, he was prepared to give the service the benefit of the doubt. He preferred to think incompetent managers had caused the operational and administrative failures in T2.

Like everyone else, David had read the conspiracy theories about the Lockerbie attack. He wanted to know the truth for himself.

Chapter 7

Lockerbie, Lawson and Misinformation

ORBAT

Director G	Head of Branch. Responsible for the investigation of all terrorism except Irish
G9/0	Paul Mitchell, Assistant Director, head of G9, MI5's section dealing with Middle Eastern terrorism
G9/1	Andrew Knight, Deputy Assistant Director for G9
G9A/1	Jerry Mahoney (replaced in December 1995 by Paul Slim) head of MI5's G9A section dealing with threats from Iraq and Libya among others
G9A/5	David Shayler, head of the Libyan subsection
G9A/15	Jane Thomas (replaced by Jackie Barker in spring 1995), Libyan desk officer
G9A/17	Jonathan Beaver (replaced by Phil Brown), administrative support worker
R/ME/C	James Worthing, MI6 intelligence requirements, Middle East, Libya
PT16	Richard Bartlett, head of MI6's agent targeting and handling section for the Middle East
PT16/B	David Watson, head of MI6's Libyan subsection

David's role

In addition to being responsible for MI5's effort to resolve the Lockerbie impasse and ensure that the evidence was not undermined, David's responsibilities as G9A/5 initially included:

- Investigating overseas Libyan activity.
- Providing threat assessments to Whitehall and providing briefs to service management. Part of the job involved representing the service at committee meetings in Whitehall, like the CIG, the Central Intelligence Group, which collated and assessed intelligence from a variety of sources like MI5, GCHQ, MI6 and Special Branch for the Joint Intelligence Committee or JIC, comprised of the heads of service.
- Overseeing initiatives to bring the Lockerbie Two, Abdulbasset Al Megrahi and Lamin Fhimah, to trial and defending the evidence against the Two, as it was being undermined in the media. David was trusted to represent the service to high-level meetings with the FBI, the US Secret Service, the CIA and the Chief Constable of Dumfries and Galloway police. As part of this work, he succeeded in engineering the first official meeting between the British government and the Libyan regime to attempt to resolve the impasse over bringing the two suspects to trial, in January 1996.

In summer 1995, he was made head of the Libyan sub-group, overseeing counter-terrorist operations against Libya in the UK. It was here that he took over the investigation into *The Guardian* journalist, Victoria Brittain, which he tried to bring to an end on the grounds that it was illegal and bore no relation to the actual intelligence. He also took on management responsibility for another officer and a clerical worker. As part of this work, he mentored an A2A transcriber who had temporarily transferred to the 'officer class' and an officer new to the service while developing the skills of two clerical workers so that they could take on more intelligence work, during a period of intense activity on the part of Libyan intelligence, including an attempt to launch what the Libyans hoped would be the 'biggest terrorist attack in history'. He also co-ordinated the expulsion of the Libyan chargé d'affaires, Khalifa Bazelya.

As part of his work with MI6, David was responsible for day-to-day liaison with MI6's Libyan group, PT16, headed by PT16/B, David Watson. In order to ensure G9 was making progress towards its section targets, he instituted a regular tri-monthly meeting to discuss matters of mutual interest, including the recruitment of sources with better access (as he did with G9A's other major provider of intelligence, GCHQ). These took place in addition to other ad hoc meetings to discuss specific matters which had to be dealt with as they arose. I mention this to demonstrate the laxity and ineptitude of MI5 management. Had no one in the previous years ever thought that MI5, MI6 and GCHQ could make better progress towards mutual targets simply by sitting down and:

- Discussing developments.
- Creating and reviewing 'action' plans and objectives.
- Prioritising the work.
- Not stepping on each other's toes.[84]

That failure on the part of the service pales into insignificance, when seen against the strategic attempts of certain elements of the state to undermine the Lockerbie evidence, which had been painstakingly gathered by police and security services across

---

[84] The most disastrous example of the agencies stepping on each other's toes was the Matrix-Churchill 'arms to Iraq' case in the 1980s. Paul Henderson was working for MI6 but was arrested by Customs. Rather than admit to his MI6 role, the service persuaded Tory ministers to sign gagging orders to ensure documents confirming Henderson's relationship with MI6 were not placed before a court. Without them, he could have been prosecuted with no defence. It is this kind of behaviour that puts off potential agents, not whistleblowers exposing MI5 and MI6 corruption, in the media. By the arguments of the services, MI6 once again 'damaged' national security.

the world. With its death toll of 270, Lockerbie was the biggest terrorist attack in history in terms of fatalities, until 9/11.

Lockerbie, Libya, the British media and MI6

The British media's attempts to pin the blame for Lockerbie on Iran, Syria and/or Palestinian groups have been extensive and desperate. But before we look at the misinformation surrounding Lockerbie, let me just say that David and I are absolutely convinced that the Libyan regime was responsible for the attack on flight PA103 in December 1988. When David originally went on the record in August 1997, it would have been very easy for him falsely to confirm the conspiracy theories that had dogged the investigation from the outset.

As the expert on the case, he could have had newspaper headlines across the world, proclaiming that an MI5 officer had confirmed Libya was not responsible for Lockerbie. The Libyans would then have claimed to have good grounds to refuse to hand over the two suspects, Abdulbasset Megrahi and Lamin Fhimah, for trial. But David did not choose that route. Nor did he keep quiet about the issue. Instead he went out and championed the case against the two Libyan intelligence officers.

'I got very involved in the Lockerbie case,' says David. 'I kept thinking what it must have been like to be on that plane, when the bomb went off at 30,000 ft and the cockpit came away from the fuselage. Although you lose consciousness at first, you regain it at about 18,000 feet. Contrary to popular belief, you are conscious when you hit the ground, some minutes later. I used to try to imagine what it felt like.

'The attack on flight PA103 was one of the most cold-blooded and despicable acts of terrorism ever uncovered. If the Libyans had done their homework better, the bomb would have gone off over the Atlantic and no one would have been any the wiser. I was determined that those responsible should face justice for their actions.'

In fact, when Libyan intelligence approached David in December 1998 after his release from prison in Paris, they offered him millions to speak out against the evidence and campaign against the indictment of the Lockerbie Two but he turned them down.

In addition to the evidence which led to the conviction in March 2001 of Megrahi, there is an abundance of evidence to implicate members of the regime, which was never put before the court for fear of complicating the case. For example, documentary evidence has established that a member of the Libyan intelligence services technical department placed the order, while the ministry of transport was responsible for taking possession of a batch of timers exactly like the one used to explode the bomb over Lockerbie. If anyone is still in any doubt, then I point them to Colonel Gaddafi's agreement in 2003 to compensate the relatives of the victims to the tune of £2.7 billion. However, there was absolutely no evidence to implicate Gaddafi himself.

The operation remains a testament to excellent co-operation between MI5 and Dumfries and Galloway police, and other national law enforcement agencies. At the same time, the history of UK/US and Libyan relations is a blueprint of how not to deal with the terrorism of rogue states. It is proof that using violence to fight violence always results in more not fewer deaths of innocent people, from both sides of any given conflict.

UK/US relations with Libya

Britain repeatedly takes steps such as locking up 'suspected' terrorists without trial or taking violent action against them – as happened when the US bombed Tripoli in 1986. The truth is, these measures simply do not work. Whether it is the internment of so-called IRA suspects in Northern Ireland in the

123

early 1970s; the current internment of so-called Al Qaeda members in HMP Belmarsh; or the bombing and invasion of Afghanistan and Iraq, these initiatives only increase sympathy and support for the groups in question and create the kind of instability in which terrorism can flourish, putting British lives at greater risk.

Up until 1984, relations between Libya and the UK had hardly been cordial but the authorities in Britain had used the laws of the land and diplomacy to either imprison or expel Libyan terrorists. But that year saw the murder of WPC Fletcher during a demonstration by Libyan oppositionists outside the Libyan People's Bureau in London. Two years later, a US serviceman and two others were killed in a terrorist bombing at La Belle Disco, West Berlin. ████████[85] quickly established that Libya was responsible for the attack. (Although this assessment caused some concern among left-wing campaigners at the time, a German court found two Libyans guilty of the attack in 2001.)

A couple of months later, the US president Ronald Reagan ordered the bombing of the Libyan capital Tripoli in revenge for the La Belle Disco attack. Gaddafi was the target. Also anxious for revenge for the shooting of WPC Fletcher, Margaret Thatcher allowed the F111s to take off from British soil. She was the only European leader to support the American decision to bomb Gaddafi, even though a hefty majority of the British people opposed it. The attack failed to kill its intended target. Instead, Gaddafi's two-year-old adopted daughter was killed in the attack, along with many other Libyan civilians, who had no control over their government.

In her autobiography, Margaret Thatcher claimed that the bombing of Tripoli put an end to Colonel's Gaddafi's terrorism, proving once and for all, she alleged, that you can fight terror with terror. Yet, the events which followed clearly undermined her argument. 270 innocent people were murdered, many of

---

[85] Redacted on orders of MI5.

them US and British citizens homeward-bound for Christmas, when the Libyan External Security Organisation carried out the Lockerbie attack.

By the time David joined G9, the two Libyans had been indicted for their part in the attack. One of MI6's main objectives was to get them to Britain for trial. Having failed to come anywhere near a diplomatic solution, MI6 embarked on its own state sponsorship of terrorism, when it funded the Al Qaeda plot to assassinate Colonel Gaddafi. MI6 hoped that Tunworth, their agent among the coup plotters, would hand the two Libyan suspects to the British authorities, on seizing power. When the actual attack took place, Gaddafi survived but the grenades and guns bought with British taxpayer's money ended up being used to murder innocent Libyan civilians.

How they got it wrong about Lockerbie

The British media's attempts to blame anyone but Libya began less than a month after the attack, perhaps because journalists had been so briefed to deflect attention from the UK/US provocation of Libya. The press reported that Khaled Jafaar, a US citizen of Lebanese descent, had taken the bomb onto the plane in his luggage. They continued with books by journalists like David Leppard of *The Sunday Times*. He 'revealed' that the Iranians had backed a PFLP-GC[86] cell in Frankfurt to carry out the attack on flight PA103, fingering Marwan Khreeshat, a member of the group as the bombmaker. However, just before the book was published in late 1992, the two Libyans, Abdulbasset Megrahi and Lamin Fhimah, were indicted. Leppard still brought the book out, modifying his thesis. In the amended version, Khreeshat still made the bomb, but gave it to the two Libyans to carry out the attack. However, forensic tests established that the timer used to explode the Lockerbie bomb was a

---

[86] Popular Front for the Liberation of Palestine – General Command.

straightforward device which is set for the time of the explosion. Khreesat's bombs were made with barometric timers, which work very differently.

Even as late as 1995, British newspapers leapt on a US Air Force Intelligence report, released under the US Freedom of Information Act. It indicated that the Iranian foreign minister Ayatollah Montashemi had paid an unnamed group $10 million to carry out the attack. But the information came from an untried agent quoting second and third hand sources. It was therefore virtually worthless in intelligence terms – far weaker even than the controversial 45-minute claim used to justify the invasion of Iraq.

Of course, the majority of these articles, books and reports did not appear by accident. They appeared as a result of the Libyan regime's strategic efforts to undermine the evidence against it. As part of this initiative, the former Liberal leader, David Steel, was invited to Libya in June 1995 to be briefed by Gaddafi on Lockerbie. Meanwhile, a lobby company called GJW, run by Andrew Gifford, Steel's former parliamentary private secretary, was awarded a £4 million PR contract with the Libyan government.[87] As part of an earlier initiative, the regime had persuaded businessman Tiny Rowland to fund a documentary about Lockerbie called the *Maltese Double Cross*. Shown on Channel 4 in Spring 1995, it attempted to blame just about everybody except the Libyans but was too long and too confusing to make any real impact.

During this same period, officers in the PT14 section of MI6 – it targets and investigates Iranians – would occasionally file a report indicating that Iran was responsible for Lockerbie. As a result, David researched all the material indicating that the Iranians might have been responsible.

'There was no evidence to support this theory,' says David.

---

[87]Although £1.5 million was paid to Khalifa Bazelya while GJW International carried out the work.

126

'By that, I mean there was no information which could have been used in a court of law to convict any member of the Iranian regime. There was, though, some *intelligence* but it either came from sources with no history of reliable reporting or it was hearsay and rumour. Not one MI6 source could provide any details which might demonstrate that they had the sort of access required to know about the planning, logistics or execution of the attack.

'I shared my findings with PT14 at MI6. I expected that to be that. But MI6 kept trying to undermine our findings and the evidence on which they were based. MI6 intelligence reports went from PT14 section to Whitehall getting the government in a flutter, only to create more work for us in MI5 as we had to refute our sister service's claims by putting out comments on the reports to the same addressees.'

Eventually, PT14 accepted MI5's evidence and stopped circulating its less than reliable information.

Conservative government not interested in bringing Lockerbie suspects to trial

It would also be true to say that the Conservative government showed no interest whatsoever in bringing the Lockerbie two to trial or in protecting the evidence from one-sided scrutiny in the press. Although David repeatedly asked to present the Lockerbie evidence to the UK families of the deceased, in order to set their minds at some rest and to convince them the police had identified the right men, G9 management claimed *they could not allow this as it might infringe the rules of sub judice*. This of course ignored the fact that sub judice only applies once a suspect has been charged. At this time, the two Libyans had only been indicted for their part in the attack. The FBI did in fact brief the US relatives with the same material. As a result, the US relatives of the deceased accepted Libyan responsibility while the UK families were left to chase shadows as a result of misinformation in the British media. This continues to this day and in no way assuages their grief or gives them a sense that justice has been done.

Sub judice is anyway a nonsense argument in this instance. If the case had gone to trial by jury in the UK, then the relatives would obviously have been barred as jurors as a result of personal involvement. In the absence of such briefings, the British relatives had to get their information from the press, which was being influenced by the Libyans and other sinister off-the-record sources.

So why were the Conservatives so loathe to get to grips with the issue? In MI5, we used to joke that the Tory Party was the political wing of MI6 and *The Sunday Telegraph* was the in-house newspaper. Based on reporting from a couple of its sources (one very well-placed), senior MI6 officers had early on in the Lockerbie investigation convinced ministers that Iran had sponsored the PFLP-GC to carry out the attack. Although MI6 does not formally assess its own intelligence, it can lobby Whitehall and ministers through informal channels – usually the old boy networks of old school tie or Oxbridge college – to take certain CX reports more seriously than others.

Although the idea of a trial in a neutral country had been floated, ministers in John Major's Cabinet insisted that this was impractical, as it would require the establishment of a special court in The Hague to hear evidence under Scottish rules. Since there was no precedent for special trials, David and I were at the time inclined to believe the government. However, a third country trial was clearly not beyond the wit of politicians and diplomats. Within two years of the new Labour government taking office, the arrangements for a third-country trial in The Hague had been put in place.

Although David was not allowed to brief the relatives, he was determined that the Libyan regime should not get away with mass murder simply because the government had been unduly influenced by MI6 intelligence. This is not the same thing as evidence, which comes from accountable witnesses who can be cross-examined. He therefore systematically refuted the central allegations of the *Maltese Double Cross* along with the claims made in many newspapers. As this concerned information already in the public domain, his report was unclassified and could therefore be made available to the media and the public. He was not though allowed to use the actual evidence police had gathered against the regime. Although David did not personally carry out the briefings, he was pleased that the other side of the story had been put.

The effect was almost immediate. The press stopped repeating the refuted information. And the Libyan-backed campaign was brought to a halt – apart from in one publication.

Further Lockerbie misinformation

In 1995, a concerned MI6 officer confided to David that he suspected that either MI6's Intelligence Operations section (IOPs) or one of the officers in PT14, MI6's counter-Iranian section, was briefing *The Sunday Telegraph* that Iran was responsible for the Lockerbie attack. At the time, David thought nothing of it. After we left MI5, a former *Sunday Telegraph* journalist ventured to us, out of the blue, that Con Coughlin – the author of the Lockerbie articles – was getting his information directly from MI6 sources. From these briefings he produced a series of articles which all cast doubt on the case against the two Libyans and fingered Iran for the Lockerbie attack, even after MI5 had issued a refutation of Iranian or Syrian involvement. Generally, the articles drew attention to the fact that the Ayatollah Montashemi, a leading member of the Iranian regime, had called for reprisals after the USS *Vincennes* shot down an Iranian commercial airliner in summer 1988.

Even as late as the trial, the BBC's veteran foreign correspondent, John Simpson, wrote in *The Sunday Telegraph*:

'There has, however, already been a rumble of incredulity at the judges' suggestion that the attack originated in Libya and that there was no evidence of any other country's involvement.'[88]

Two years later, long after Megrahi had been convicted and his appeal had failed, *The Sunday Telegraph* continued to produce stories indicating that Iran was responsible:

'There is overwhelming evidence that both the Syrian and Iranian governments were directly involved in commissioning and planning the attack. ... The Iranians also paid Ahmed Jibril [the head of the PFLP-GC] $6m for his involvement in the bombing.'[89]

The claim that Jibril was paid $6 million is a misreporting of the unsubstantiated claim in the US Air Force Intelligence document. As well as stating that Montashemi had paid $10 million – at the time around £6 million – to an unnamed group for the Lockerbie attack, the US report stated that he had also paid $10 million to the PPSF, the Palestinian Popular Struggle Front to carry out other unknown operations. Once again, British journalists were incapable of accurately copying information from a published report. They claimed the report had mentioned payments to the PFLP-GC, when it had not.

These articles clearly harmed the national interest on two levels. Firstly, they indicated that the British government's view of Lockerbie was wrong and that it was using the issue to persecute Libya for political reasons. Secondly, since David and I – in my capacity as editor of briefing papers for Whitehall – had to spend time refuting these articles at the expense of actually investigating terrorists, they clearly harmed the national interest in that respect as well. The whole episode is also a

[88]*The Sunday Telegraph*, 4 February 2001.
[89]*The Sunday Telegraph*, 17 August 2003.

waste and an abuse of taxpayers' money since MI6 is working to its own ends rather than government policy or the interests of democracy and justice. However, this is not the only example of MI6 using *The Sunday Telegraph* to put out propaganda on its own behalf.

MI6's Information Operations and *The Sunday Telegraph*

In November 1995, David read an article in *The Sunday Telegraph* alleging that Saif Al Islam, one of Colonel Gaddafi's sons, was involved in forging Iranian money. MI6 claimed that Gaddafi's son was authorised by his father to enter into a money-laundering deal with Iranian middlemen. The elaborate scheme involved the movement of a 'clean' $8 billion out of banks in Egypt through a Swiss bank. In return the Libyans agreed to transfer to the Egyptians the same sum in Libyan dinars for a massive commission. But one of the middlemen – not Gaddafi's son – intended to use the deal to pass off a huge quantity of fake Iranian currency.

Al Islam did not have any security traces at that time. He was the subject of a MI5 temporary file or GEN, which had been made in response to his interest in coming into the country. It had only two or three serials, or separate reports in it. None of them indicated that Saif had any role in the intelligence or security services. In fact, MI5's information indicated exactly the opposite. Colonel Gaddafi was exasperated by his son's total lack of interest in the regime.

At a meeting in room 4.07 in Thames House shortly after the article in question appeared, David raised the matters in it with PT16/B David Watson, his MI6 counterpart, because the article concerned relations between Iran and Libya. The two countries had traditionally opposed the UK and the West in general, using terrorism and sponsorship of terrorist groups, but had never been friendly with one another. In early 1995, G9 received intelligence to indicate that the Libyan and Iranian regimes were beginning to co-operate in their armed response. Although the two regimes only planned to work together in the war zone of the Occupied Territories, the prospect of them forming an alliance filled the UK authorities with dread.

As *The Sunday Telegraph* article concerned possible counterfeiting and money laundering, which is associated with terrorist funding, David asked David Watson[90] if he had any intelligence to support the article. He said he did not because IOPs had made up the story, primarily to discredit Saif Al Islam who had expressed an interest in coming to the UK. The FCO wanted to keep Al Islam out because it did not want the embarrassment of a son of one of Britain's enemies living the high life here. There was though no security information against Al Islam which could be used as a reason to refuse him a visa. MI5 checks individuals from Libya against its records and in conjunction with the FCO decides whether or not to refuse them entry.

Sometimes the system didn't work. At one point, the son of Abdulsalem Jalloud, Colonel Gaddafi's former second in command, entered the UK with a visa after being cleared by an MI5 clerical worker who did not realise the significance of the family name.

Although the UK can refuse a visa to any foreign national, government policy is to refuse Libyan nationals who pose a threat to UK security through their connections with hostile intelligence services or whose presence is 'unconducive to the public good'. In the absence of any real intelligence information, FCO officials could use *The Sunday Telegraph* article as a reason for refusing Al Islam entry to the UK without looking like the decision was arbitrary.

---

[90] See also the MI6/Al Qaeda conspiracy.

How the story appeared

David was so concerned that MI6 could simply make up information, which was then processed uncritically by journalists to become fact, that he briefed Mark Hollingsworth, the investigative journalist who had helped break David's original story. His enquiries established that Malcolm Rifkind, then Conservative Foreign Secretary, two senior diplomats and several *Sunday Telegraph* journalists, had attended a discreet lunch on 19 October 1995. Rifkind told the group that WMD proliferation was funded by clandestine schemes to obtain hard currency, usually US dollars.

Con Coughlin, chief foreign correspondent of *The Sunday Telegraph*, then set up two lengthy briefings – on October 25 and October 31 – with a senior MI6 officer with whom he had dealt for several years. The intelligence officer informed him that an Austrian company was raising hard currency for Iran to fund its weapons programme by selling oil on the black market. In November 1995, Con Coughlin was put in touch with a second MI6 officer who explained there was a Gaddafi connection to the currency operations they had been discussing. According to papers obtained by Hollingsworth:

'On 21 November 1995 Mr Coughlin had a private luncheon meeting with Source A, who introduced him to another senior security official (Source B) whom he described as having expertise in Middle East banking and finance, and as possessing particular knowledge of Egypt. In the course of this meeting Source B explained the plaintiff's connection with ... the failed money-laundering plan ... Source B made these disclosures under the guarantee from Mr Coughlin of complete confidentiality.'

Coughlin tried to obtain hard evidence for the story. According to Hollingsworth, on Thursday 23 November 1995, the two intelligence officers showed Coughlin photocopies of what purported to be banking records proving Saif Al Islam's business links with one of the Iranian middleman. But the MI6 men refused to allow him to make copies, which was hardly surprising as the documents were themselves forgeries.

Three days later, *The Sunday Telegraph* published the story under the headline: '[Gaddafi's] Son Linked to Sting on Iran'. The article made no mention of MI6 being the source of the story, nor did it indicate that Coughlin had carried out any independent enquiries to check the story. It did, though, include a quote from 'a British banking official' who was in fact a senior MI6 officer with expertise in Middle Eastern finance.

IOPs' role is to place stories in the world media which present Britain in a good light, support its foreign policy and discredit Britain's enemies. In practice, this means, *MI6's* 'enemies'. That service does not see any difference between protecting *its* interests and protecting the interests of the country and its democracy, even where these are directly in conflict. Sometimes MI6's briefings to the media are based on fact, although IOPs is reluctant to use real intelligence information for fear of compromising sensitive agents who may have provided the original intelligence. They find it much more acceptable to give the media invented stories – which cannot by definition damage national security. If the information about Gaddafi's son were true, it would be difficult to see how MI6 could put it into the public domain without compromising the original and sensitive source of the intelligence.

In March 2000, the editor of *The Sunday Telegraph*, Dominic Lawson, told *The Guardian*: 'We stand by the story which appeared in *The Sunday Telegraph*,' despite the fact that he (and Coughlin) knew his sources were MI6 officers, not 'a British banking official'. Less than a month later, Lawson was forced to apologise to Saif Al-Islam for the original article and another story, which accused Gaddafi's son of having sought to lure Coughlin to Tripoli to meet a sinister fate. In settling the action, which was also taken against *The Sunday Times* for making the same allegations, Lawson was forced to make a grovelling apology, which admitted that the documents were forgeries:

> '*The Sunday Telegraph* accepts *not only that there is no truth* in these allegations, but that *there is no evidence to suggest that there is any truth in them.* We sincerely apologise to Mr Gaddafi.'

Legal experts have estimated that *The Sunday Telegraph* ran up around £1 million in lawyers' fees trying to defend facts made up by MI6.

Dominic Lawson: MI6 agent of influence?

In December 1998, Labour MP Brian Sedgemore named the editor of *The Sunday Telegraph* in Parliament as an agent of MI6, after receiving the information from former MI6 officer Richard Tomlinson. Labour MP George Galloway told the house:

> 'I am greatly disturbed by the news that Mr Dominic Lawson ... has for a period of time served as an asset of the British secret service who paid him large sums of money ... for services he rendered under the guise of a journalist.'

The Guardian also reported that Lawson had published two articles in *The Spectator* magazine, of which he was then editor, in 1994, designed to influence public opinion on the Bosnia conflict under the pen name of Ken Roberts. Lawson did not tell his readers that Roberts was in fact an MI6 officer, later claiming it was 'news' to him.[91] The paper also pointed out that, while editor of the magazine, Lawson had also commissioned articles from Alan Judd aka Alan Petty, an MI6 officer. Again, Judd's MI6 role was not revealed to readers.

---

[91] *The Guardian*, 17 December 1998.

Although Lawson has denied the claims that he was a paid agent of MI6, we do know that he regularly and uncritically reproduces stories from MI6 sources in *The Sunday Telegraph* (see above and below).

Black propaganda in *The Sunday Telegraph*

As editor of *The Sunday Telegraph*, Dominic Lawson has also published a number of defamatory and wholly untrue articles about David, which have clearly worked in the interests of the services at the expense of democratic accountability and human rights. On no occasion did a *Sunday Telegraph* journalist contact David or myself to check the facts of any of the articles which appeared. In fact, in 2001, when David's mother, Anne, phoned David Bamber, a *Sunday Telegraph* reporter after he had written yet another misleading article about her son, he admitted to not checking his facts and apologised for getting it wrong. Anne wrote to the paper to point out the inaccuracies but her letter was not published. She then phoned Coughlin in his capacity as one of the paper's editors to discuss an apology. He simply hung up on her. When David phoned Coughlin because he was angry that he hung up on his mother, Coughlin hung up on him and refused to take his calls. I cannot imagine any other business dealing with complaints from customers in this way.

To compare David to Kim Philby and George Blake, who between them were responsible for the deaths of over 50 British agents through their betrayal of our country to the Russians – as *The Sunday Telegraph* did in 1998, when David was in prison in France – is clearly libellous and no reflection of the facts of his case. Not even David's opponents in the authorities have tried to claim that he gave information to a foreign power or that he betrayed his country. If that had been the case, David would have been charged under the 1911 Official Secrets Act, or with treason and would have faced at least 14 years in prison.

136

In June 1999, David wrote to Dominic Lawson to set the record straight, enclosing a copy of *Secrets and Lies*, a document David had prepared on his case. Despite this, *The Sunday Telegraph* continued to publish stories about him without ever bothering to check the facts, even though *Secrets and Lies* demonstrated that the authorities were using crude propaganda to discredit him. When an MI6 document later appeared on the Internet confirming that MI6 had a source involved in a plot to assassinate Colonel Gaddafi in a coup, *The Sunday Telegraph*, unlike the other broadsheets, did not cover it.

Chapter 8

MI5 and MI6 Undermine National Security

The investigation of Khalifa Bazelya

From June 1993 to December 1995 the British intelligence services spent millions of pounds keeping tabs on Khalifa Bazelya, a member of the Libyan External Security Organisation (ESO), whom they had let into the country with a view to recruitment. The ESO was responsible for the Lockerbie attack, in which 270 people were killed, and the attack on a French plane, UTA 772, which killed another 171 people over Africa in 1989.[92] It also has a long history of funding terrorist groups like that of Abu Nidal, which attack Western interests, and of persecuting Libyan dissidents who have sought refuge in the West. As such, Libya was at this time a JIC Priority 1 threat. HMG policy is to prevent members of the ESO from entering the UK because of the threat they pose to public safety and national security.

In Bazelya's case, ministers made an exception purely because MI6 convinced them it could recruit him, even though the services already had reliable intelligence from separate sources indicating that he had contacts with Sinn Fein and the IRA.[93]

---

[92] In France, members of the Libyan regime have been found guilty of this attack *in absentia*.

[93] We really have to ask why the real James Bonds who are trained to operate abroad couldn't simply carry out any recruitment operation in another country. That way, when they failed, at least the British taxpayer wouldn't have had to foot the bill for Bazelya's surveillance or have their security put at unnecessary risk.

139

At the time, the MI5 desk officer for this area, Jane Thomas, advised G9 management that MI6 had virtually no chance of recruiting him. However, when the Assistant Director, G9/0 Paul Mitchell, wrote to the Foreign Office to ask for Bazelya's expulsion, he stated:

> '[Bazelya] was granted a visa to come to the UK as it was assessed at the time that the potential intelligence dividends of recruiting him outweighed the likely threat he would pose to the security of the UK.'

Thomas turned out to be right. MI6 got nowhere near recruiting Bazelya and failed to gain any significant intelligence from him. As neither service made any progress with the recruitment, MI5 was obliged to divert resources from investigations into other threats to the security of the UK. In the end, MI5 and MI6 put national security at intolerable risk for no benefit to the nation.

Bazelya's record before he was allowed into the UK

Bazelya had first come to the attention of MI5 during his first posting to the UK in the 1970s, when he was reported to be one of Gaddafi's agents, responsible for liaison with Libyan-backed extremist groups in the UK. Separate sources reported that during this period Bazelya had links with Sinn Fein in the Republic of Ireland. After leaving the UK, he was posted to Ethiopia in March 1981, where separate sources reported that he was heavily involved in activities on behalf of Libyan intelligence throughout the 1980s. In January 1992 the FBI reported it had reliable source information linking Bazelya with PIRA. He was also reportedly in regular contact with the Irish–Arab Society in Dublin, then suspected of having close links to the IRA.

Even before Bazelya arrived in Britain in July 1993, a source had indicated that he was not the Libyan MFA[94] choice for chargé d'affaires in the UK. It was therefore assumed that he had most likely obtained the post through intelligence connections. Shortly after he arrived in London, a reliable MI6 agent provided corroboration of Bazelya's intelligence role. The agent reported that Bazelya was close to leading members of the regime, including the then *de facto* head of the ESO in 1993, Abdullah Senussi and later his successor, Musa Kusa. The two are still wanted by the French authorities for their role in the bombing of Flight UTA 772 in 1989.

Bazelya's activities within the UK

MI5 can hardly claim that it didn't know what it was getting with Bazelya. Once in the UK, he proceeded to use his position to lead MI5 and MI6 a merry dance for the next two years, using his contact with MI6 to raise his profile within the regime. He promoted 'a Libyan PR campaign aimed at persuading the British public that the Libyans were not responsible for the bombing of Pan Am 103 over Lockerbie'. Bazelya also quickly set about co-ordinating ESO activities in the UK. Four Libyan intelligence officers (IOs) – Mohammed Marwan, Yousef Shakona, Bulghasem Massoud and Abdelsalem Radwan – working under student cover, reported to him on a regular basis. In addition, Bazelya illegally ran Libyan agents to report on Libyan dissidents based in the UK, personally threatening the dissidents when they did not co-operate. These were no empty threats. In June 1993, around the time Bazelya was posted to the UK, Libyan intelligence had kidnapped Khaled Mansour, a prominent dissident, in Cairo and smuggled him out of the country in the boot of a car. He had been taken back to Tripoli and tortured.

In 1995, a reliable and trusted agent reported that Bazelya

---

[94]Ministry of Foreign Affairs.

had had detailed discussions with Dr Abdul Majid Abdulrahman, a Libyan researcher in High Energy Physics at the Rutherford Appleton Laboratory, about setting up a Libyan Scientific Centre. According to source, in May 1995 the head of Libyan intelligence approved the project on Bazelya's recommendation. The centre was to have an 'unattributable' name, implying that it was to be used as cover for 'technology transfer' to Libya. In other words, Bazelya's time in the UK courtesy of MI5 and MI6 also aided Libya's attempts to gather the requisite technology to make nuclear, chemical and biological weapons.

In late 1995, intelligence indicated that Bazelya had sent the ESO a list of Libyans who had not attended the Libyan National Day celebrations in the UK. Non-attendees were reportedly recalled to Libya, where they could be dealt with, or were denied travel documents to return to the UK. This disrupted the activities of MI6 agents, a matter MI5 was again forced to admit in the letter recommending Bazelya's expulsion:

'The SIS Libyan agent runner, has pointed out that three of the individuals named are important SIS sources. He voiced great concern that Bazelya's actions may disrupt these sources' reporting by affecting their ability to travel between the UK and Libya. HMG therefore stands to lose a great deal of important political intelligence.'

MI6 agents also provide security intelligence so their disruption potentially damaged national security as they were unable to provide MI6 with their vital information about Libyan intelligence.

Eventually, MI5's mistake in letting Bazelya into the country came home to roost. On two occasions in 1995, the Libyan Intelligence Services (LIS) overruled Bazelya, insisting that he continue to support those suspected of involvement in terrorism, all of which created more work for busy MI5 desk officers:

'In October 1995 telecheck and source 1 reported that Bazelya was initially unhappy about extending the student status of Muhammad Warrad, a hardline revolutionary student suspected of having links with PIRA during the 1980s. However, Bazelya quickly changed his mind on the receipt of a fax from Kusa ordering Warrad's studentship to continue. Similarly, Bazelya, though not happy with the arrangement, is obeying Kusa's instructions to subsidise another revolutionary student, Muhammad Marwan, a suspected Libyan intelligence officer, out of LIS[95] funds to enable him to stay in the UK.'

A reliable source also reported that:

- Bazelya had in the past provided munitions to the Muslim-backed Eritrean Liberation Front for several years, some of which were reportedly used to assassinate an Ethiopian minister during the civil war.
- In 1984 the Revolutionary Committee in Libya, of which Bazelya was a prominent member, was directly responsible for ordering the hanging of 13 anti-regime student activists at Al Fatah University in Tripoli.

The service also became aware that Bazelya had been expelled after the Ethiopian authorities discovered a consignment of guns in his diplomatic bag. By this point, it had become absolutely clear that Bazelya was the 'puppet' or 'right hand man', of the head of Libyan intelligence, working to the brief of an organisation with one of the world's worst records for terrorism.

Bazelya's expulsion

In December 1995, acting on strong representations from David and his Libyan team, Paul Mitchell, the head of the Middle

---

[95]In this context, Libyan Interests Section, based at the Saudi Embassy in the absence of proper diplomatic relations. LIS is also used as an abbreviation for the Libyan Intelligence Services.

143

Eastern section, was forced to admit to the Foreign Office that Bazelya's presence in the UK '[posed] a *direct threat* to the national security of the United Kingdom'. By way of clarification, his letter added:

'What is clear is that, should the Libyan regime wish to resume its violent activities, it has a pool of individuals in the UK, headed by Bazelya, who would be willing to participate, and an established structure for coordinating these activities.'

Later that month, David succeeded in having Bazelya declared *persona non grata* and expelled from the UK. Even though he had gone, his activities meant that the Libyans had a ready-made network to launch terrorist attacks in the UK. In spring 1995, G9 received intelligence to indicate that it had sent five terrorists to the UK to launch the biggest terrorist attack in history. MI5 and MI6's decision to allow Bazelya into the UK had laid the groundwork for a Libyan terrorist operation. Bazelya's period in the UK also coincided with the IRA's greatest rate of attacks on the British mainland. MI5 had to devote resources to covering a threat of its own making in Bazelya, while the IRA ran amok. At least the Bazelya operation was justified. He had a record of terrorism. The same cannot be said of Victoria Brittain, a *Guardian* journalist who posed no threat to national security but was in essence persecuted by MI5 for over a year.

Coda

In February 2000, MI5's letter to the Foreign Office recommending Bazelya's expulsion was leaked and appeared on the Internet. Although David oversaw the production of the document and drafted large parts of it when in the service, this was years after he had left MI5 and he could certainly not have accessed

144

it and put it on a website. In fact, he was being filmed for a documentary when he first became aware that the document had been put on the net. His astonishment – and his condemnation – is there for anyone to see. In addition, he has far greater respect for national security than that. However, this has not prevented shadowy anonymous sources trying to pin the blame for it on him.

Chapter 9

Operation SHADOWER, the Investigation into a Guardian Journalist

Background

At the same time that MI5 had to deploy valuable resources to monitor Khalifa Bazelya, they were also devoting considerable funds to investigating Victoria Brittain, a *Guardian* journalist. Codeworded Operation SHADOWER, MI5 tapped Brittain's home phone for over a year, beginning in early 1995. Although she was suspected of money laundering and financing terrorism, the service established that the funds were being used to finance a libel action on the part of Kojo Tsikata, a former official of Ghana. Not even MI5 would now argue that Brittain had ever posed a recognisable threat to national security.

At one point in the investigation, Director G, International Terrorism Branch, told officers that this was the most important investigation on the Libyan desk in ten years. David pointed out the incongruity of this statement. The bombing of flight PA103 over Lockerbie had taken place only six years previously. At the time, an extensive police and MI5 operation had led to the indictment of two Libyan intelligence officers for the attack. However, to a senior manager who had cut his teeth investigating left-wing 'subversives', targeting a *Guardian* journalist must have felt like a return to the good old days.

Early problems with the investigation

Victoria Brittain first came to the attention of G9 in late 1994 when the Service learnt that she had received two payments into her bank account from two separate Libyan accounts based in London. A junior desk officer, Jane Thomas, G9A/15, had carried out the initial investigation. She had little experience of intelligence work as she had entered the GD[96] as a GD6, after transferring from the secretarial pool. At the time, Jerry Mahoney, G9A/1 and group leader for G9A, was also an inexperienced officer, who had been in the service less than two years. When David took the case over in April 1995, Thomas had warned him that she had tried to raise her reservations about the investigation with G9 management but had been ignored. I mention this because it demonstrates how management could push around junior desk officers, particularly if they had not been recruited as part of the 'officer class'.

In this case, Home Secretary Michael Howard had already granted the HOW, which governs telephone intercept or tapping *before David took the case over*. I mention this as off-the-record briefings have claimed that David began the investigation. It then became his responsibility to renew the HOW every six months.[97] Again, renewal requires rigorous justification in strictly defined circumstances.

When David came to examine the warrant, he found it was inaccurate. Some of the transfers of funds had gone through several of Brittain's accounts, although the original flow diagram did not reflect this. David explains:

'As a result, some movements of the funds had been counted twice or even three times as further payments into her account when in fact, they were the same funds moving between Brittain's different accounts. One of the first tasks

---

[96] General Duties group. The General Intelligence Duties group, or the 'officer class', and the admin group were merged at around this time. Grade GI6 became GD6 etc.
[97] In accordance with the 1985 Interception of Communications Act.

I performed was to trace and clarify the movement of funds through all her accounts. This established that the amount in question was rather nearer £200,000 than the figure used to justify the warrant, around £500,000.'

Reasons for investigating Victoria Brittain

MI5 uses 'recording categories' or definitions that a target must fall within before MI5 can actively investigate them. Brittain already had a PF because she had previously come to the attention of the service as a 'contact of a hostile intelligence agency' in 1991 after she met a Cuban at an embassy function as part of her work on the foreign news section of *The Guardian*. Although the Cuban was an intelligence officer working under diplomatic cover, there was certainly no indication that she knew of the Cuban associate's intelligence role.

For the purposes of the SHADOWER investigation, Brittain was recorded as 'the suspected contact of a suspected contact of the Libyan intelligence service', although there was no intelligence on her file to indicate that she had any connections with Libya at all – other than the payments to her bank accounts. Although Tsikata was also recorded as a suspected contact of the LIS, there was little or no hard intelligence to indicate that he was actually working for the Libyans. MI5 certainly had no record of him being involved in hostile intelligence or terrorism against UK interests.

In fact, when Kojo Tsikata had stayed in London in summer 1994, itemised billing information on the telephone in his hotel room established that it had been used to contact Brittain's home phone. Although her subscriber details – V Brittain, 57 Gibson Square, London NW3 – had been checked against service records, Jane Thomas had failed to match them with Victoria Brittain, 57 Gibson Square, London NW3, the subject of an MI5 file. It was only when MI5 actively began to investigate Brittain and Tsikata some six months later that this missed contact was found on *his* file. David comments:

'When officers came to apply for the Home Office Warrant in late 1994, they justified the investigation on the grounds that Brittain was either:

- Laundering money on behalf of the Libyans.
- Helping the funding of terrorism in the UK.

'However, I stress there was no specific intelligence to support either proposition.'

Defects in the case and delays in taking action

Some will think that payments from Libyan accounts to Brittain would be enough to justify at least beginning an investigation into Brittain, even in the absence of specific intelligence stating that she was money laundering. However, there were a number of fundamental defects in the case which were not addressed in the warrant and therefore not communicated to the Home Secretary who authorises the tap. The payments into her account clearly came from two official Libyan accounts, one in the name of Khalifa Bazelya, the chargé d'affaires at the Libyan Interests Section, and the other in the name of the Libyan Interests Section in London. Given that the Libyans believe that the British intelligence services are as pervasive in Britain as the LIS is in Libya, it was risible to suggest that the overt passage of money from official accounts was sufficient reason to suspect money laundering or terrorist funding.

'If I had been the case officer when MPSB had provided the original intelligence about the movement of funds in summer 1994,' David explains, 'I would have recommended that they interviewed her. There would have been nothing unusual about this.'

Brittain had first come to the attention of MPSB after it had received a routine financial notification under the PTA. This legislation requires banks to notify the police of any deposit of more than £10,000. Under the PTA, SB officers could have asked Brittain directly or served her with an Explanation Order requiring her to justify the funds. This overt method of enquiry was never undertaken although senior MI5 officers did contemplate it some months into the investigation but dismissed it. It would have saved a lengthy investigation and unnecessary, expensive telephone tapping and mobile surveillance on the part of MI5, which drained the service's resources to the tune of around £750,000.

Where laundered money has to be moved through accounts, at least some of it moves on quickly so that it can get to its destination before being intercepted by the law enforcement agencies. G9A first reacted to the existence of the funds only towards the end of 1994, well over a year after the first payment from Bazelya's account in September 1993 and around five months after the second payment in July 1994. Ironically, if the money had been intended for the funding of terrorism, it would have been long gone before MI5 had even started to investigate the matter.

Some will argue that I am benefiting from hindsight. I dispute this. When David took over the investigation, he tried to persuade those involved, including the City of London SB, that the payments were innocent. By this time, the telephone tap on Brittain's phone had reported that she was discussing 'the case' and 'the money' with Kojo Tsikata and the lawyer Geoffrey Bindman. It was therefore very clear from very early on that the money in question was being used to fund a legal action. Although MI5 should never have begun to tap her phone, it was even more inexcusable that it continued the operation, even when all the intelligence indicated that the funds in question were payment for some kind of legal action on Tsikata's part. It wasn't as if Brittain and Tsikata didn't have good enough reasons for their relationship. As she was the deputy foreign editor of *The Guardian*, with a history of writing on Africa,

151

and Tsikata's native Ghana in particular, and he was a former official of the state, the two had obvious legitimate reasons to know each other.

The failure to follow procedure

In this case there can be no dispute about MI5's failure to follow legally enshrined procedure designed to ensure that the services do not abuse human rights. Intelligence organisations must use overt, non-intrusive methods to resolve an enquiry before invading anyone's privacy as a last resort. It cannot be 'necessary in a democratic society'[98] to invade an individual's privacy to obtain information that could be obtained openly. The failure on the part of the services to first check open sources led directly to a human rights abuse, unnecessary invasion of privacy, and an unlawful operation.

In order to maintain the legality of its warrants, MI5 officers use a 'tick box' pro forma to ensure they have complied with all procedure. One box reminds officers to insert a line to the effect that they have exhausted overt methods of enquiry before applying for a warrant. There is though no box to tick off the actual enquiries carried out. In effect, the officer ticks the checklist to indicate that he has included in any warrant the line regarding the exhaustion of overt enquiries – without actually doing any enquiries. Although MI5 management assert that they play a valid role in the processing of warrants, they never ask whether – or which – enquiries have been carried out to make the warrants legal.

---

[98] Article 8(2) of the ECHR states, 'There shall be no interference by a public authority with the exercise of this right except such as *in accordance with the law* and *is necessary in a democratic society.*'

152

Failure to access public databases

Given that Brittain was a *Guardian* journalist, MI5 could have checked public records, such as newspaper archives, now held on the Lexis-Nexis database, or in the computerised archives at the British Museum. This would have shown Brittain's and Tsikata's activities and interests. David takes up the story:

'When I took over the case around spring 1995, I remarked to my bosses that I was surprised that no overt enquiry had taken place, particularly in this sensitive operation. I even suggested interrogating a newspaper database to my direct boss and the head of G9.[99]

'I had also mentioned this very early on to Jane Thomas, who was responsible for the investigation before I took it over. Given that Ms Brittain was a journalist, any interrogation of a commercially available newspaper database might shed light on her actions. I stress, up to this point, the only intelligence against Brittain was that she had received money from the Libyan regime through traceable and routine transfer between bank accounts, hardly a secure method of laundering money.

'As the service had no access in-house to commercial databases, I specifically offered to go to a library to "bottom" – or resolve – the case. Remember at this time, G9 was devoting considerable resources to following Khalifa Bazelya, the Libyan chargé. As MI5 only has finite resources, it was clear even at the time that the SHADOWER investigation was detracting from the proper investigation of an individual with an established history of aiding terrorism.'

But David's suggestion was not authorised. He did think about

---

[99] G9/0, the head of G9, Counter-Middle Eastern Terrorism. He also took the stand as witness C in David's court case but Judge Moses refused to let David cross-examine him about the legality of the intercept.

carrying out the public enquiries in his own time but he knew that any initiative would count against him with MI5 bosses, even if he were proved right.

In fact, the service did eventually research publicly available material. Jonathan Beaver, a clerical officer, spent many days in the MI5 library looking through copies of *The Guardian* for articles by Victoria Brittain. But by this point, the Home Secretary had already signed the warrant, believing that overt enquiries had already been exhausted. Details of the true purpose of the funds were more likely to have emerged from coverage in *The Independent* newspaper, which was the target of the libel action for which Ms Brittain was receiving funds. Either way, poring over page after page of *The Guardian* hardly constituted an efficient use of a clerical officer's time, when Brittain's name could be checked in seconds using a newspaper database.

As a result, David was also prevented from using a commercial database to check the names of journalists which came up once the telephone was tapped. David explains:

'I can clearly recall that during one intercepted conversation, the name of Richard Dowden was mentioned. He was no trace in the service's records but we have since learnt that he worked for *The Independent* newspaper and was involved in opposing Tsikata's libel action. It is also a principle of phone tapping that it should continue no longer than is necessary.[100] Again, I maintain that if I had been allowed to research openly available material, we would have more quickly established that the money was of no concern to MI5. G9 would have therefore have been obliged to cancel the warrant sooner, restoring Brittain's right to privacy.'

---

[100]The 'necessary in a democracy' test under HRA, Article 8, ECHR.

Illegality upon illegality

However, instead of cancelling the already illegal telephone intercept, MI5's internal appetite grew. It obtained a property warrant from the Home Secretary to legally 'effect a covert entry' into Brittain's home to search and copy her papers or to install an eavesdropping device – or bug. As covert entry is otherwise known as breaking and entering or burglary, it represented an even greater invasion of Brittain's privacy than tapping her phone.

But the property warrant was based on the same flawed case as the HOW, so it represented illegality mounted on illegality.[101] Under the 1989 Security Service Act, MI5 is only supposed to break into private homes to protect national security or prevent serious crime and then only where there is a strong intelligence case. Secret searches of an individual's home – 'sneak and peak', as it is known in the US legislation proposing this kind of invasion of privacy – are banned in the vast majority of democracies.

At one point in a formal discussion with the Assistant Director, Paul Mitchell, the possibility of tapping the lawyer Geoffrey Bindman's home phone was raised. The senior MI5 legal adviser, Richard Woods,[102] rejected the idea on the grounds that there had to be 'a more direct threat to national security' before the phone of a lawyer could be tapped. This was of course a tacit admission from a legal expert that the case against Brittain was ill-founded. In a later discussion when the SHADOWER investigation was over, the legal adviser denied that he had made any such claim, even though it had been included in the minutes of the meeting and he had not complained when he had received a copy of the minutes. Instead, he claimed that he had given advice as to the undesirability of tapping the phone of a lawyer,

---

[101] The 1989 Security Service Act contains the same caveat as the 1985 Interception of Communications Act. Other methods of enquiry must be exhausted before the service interferes with a target's property.
[102] Name changed on orders of MI5.

given that conversations between lawyers and clients are privileged.

Yet MI5 showed no ethical concerns when it recorded and transcribed conversations between Bindman and Brittain, even where they specifically mentioned 'the case' and might have covered privileged client–counsel discussions.[103] And, if MI5 really believed that the money was destined for terrorists, why should Bindman be given some sort of immunity just because he was a lawyer? The legal advisor's position was illogical. But it went from bad to worse.

The unlawful plan to arrest Brittain's daughter

Once a property warrant has been signed, the case officer sends his requirements to MI5's A1 section, which then 'recces'[104] the target address and comes up with an operational plan to plant the bug and carry out the search. ██████████████████ ███████████████████████████████[105] In this case, A1 hatched a plot to have Thea Sharrock – Brittain's daughter and a key holder of the Gibson Square flat – arrested on trumped-up charges, while she was holidaying in the US. The fact she was in the US should have counted as security enough. Even if she had suddenly decided to return home, her flight would have taken at the very least seven hours, more than enough time for A1 operatives to withdraw from the target premises.

David takes up the story:

'I complained in the most vociferous terms possible but was asked to create a file on Brittain's daughter. In the file, I recorded that I was doing it effectively under duress

[103] Now protected by the HRA, Article 6, ECHR, the right to a fair trial.
[104] Reconnaissance.
[105] Information removed on the orders of MI5, although it concerns official policy which hampers the operational effectiveness of MI5, not secret intelligence.

and that the file should be "destroyed" – removed from the MI5 indices rather than actually physically burnt – as soon as the relevant action had been taken to stop the collection of even more intrusive personal material in the MI5 archives.'

Evidence of the true purpose of the money

By spring 1995, MI5 had established that Brittain had received three further payments made in December 1994, January 1995 and February 1995 of around £35,000 each. As Brittain, Bindman and Tsikata discussed the matter quite openly on her home telephone, it became even more risible to suggest that the funds were destined for the support of terrorism. No trained terrorist in this day and age uses the phone, particularly not their own, to discuss any criminal activity. When David took over the investigation shortly after, he found no references that could in any way be construed as relating to money laundering or support for terrorism. The transcribers of the tap had not noted, for example, that any of the conversations were guarded or suspicious or that word 'case' could be code for more underhand activity.

Before David had even taken over Operation SHADOWER, financial enquiries had established that the funds were being placed in a client account at the law firm of Bindman and Partners. This appeared to be conclusive proof – if any were still needed – that the funds in question were being passed through Brittain's accounts to Geoffrey Bindman, the senior partner of the firm, to pay him for the unidentified legal 'case' in which he represented Tsikata. Yet the investigation went on for nearly a year more.

It also seemed to be lost on MI5 management that no solicitor with the profile and reputation of Geoffrey Bindman would willingly allow laundered or terrorist funds to pass through his client accounts. Although Bindman had a PF, he was recorded as a '?Communist sympathiser' – a category given to almost anyone who had communist friends, clients or colleagues in the 1960s and had not come to attention in a security context since then. There was certainly no indication on his file that he had any direct connection with terrorism, money laundering or Libya.

The failure of the Commissioner

When one of the Commissioners[106] came to the service in late 1995 or early 1996 to discuss the warrant against Brittain, G9/0 Mitchell refused to allow David to attend the meeting. Instead, David had to provide an anodyne brief on the investigation for Mitchell's meeting with the Commissioner. David was forbidden from telling the Commissioner that:

- Contrary to information included in the warrant, MI5 had not researched publicly available material on Brittain before tapping her phone.
- Even after David had raised the above with Mitchell, G9/0 still included the line about overt enquiries in the six monthly applications to renew the warrant.
- The intelligence was based on inaccurate and illegally obtained financial information.

As Mitchell had signed off the warrant application,[107] he was hardly likely to raise these issues with the Commissioner.

David couldn't legally take his concerns directly to ministers or the Commissioner about the Brittain warrants.[108] Even if he had been able to go to ministers, it is highly likely they would

---

[106] Under the Interceptions of Communications Act and the Security Service Act, Commissioners have a responsibility for ensuring that warrants are legally obtained.

[107] As warrant applications are not sworn under oath, MI5 officers can lie or misrepresent the truth in them without fear of perjuring themselves.

[108] A criminal offence under s.1 (and s.7(1)) of the 1989 Official Secrets Act.

have consulted the Commissioner, who would have told the Home Secretary that he had been to MI5 to discuss the warrant and had been assured that it was legal. Neither the Commissioner nor the Home Secretary could have known that Mitchell's claims in the warrant that procedures had been followed were not just false but were made by Mitchell in the full knowledge they were false.

Unlawful financial enquiries

Another matter also troubled David. The police and MI5's H1 section, which deals with external liaisons and 'delicate' enquiries, had acquired detailed financial information from Brittain's bank account without a court order.[109] David takes up the story:

'Although I raised the unlawful collection of financial material when I took over the case, MI5 did not make an application to a judge to invade Brittain's privacy in this regard, although a few of the police enquiries – carried out by City of London SB – may have been covered in this way. In fact, the conduct of the investigation was hindered because H1 and the police had difficulties obtaining the information from the banks concerned without the proper paperwork.

'H1 was well aware that his actions were unlawful. He insisted that Brittain's financial details were kept hidden on a separate file from Brittain's main PF. Ironically, if the money had been destined for the support of terrorism, illegal and slow procedures could have prevented us from either intercepting the money before it got to its intended targets or from bringing the culprits to justice, as the

---

[109] The PTA allows investigators to gather private financial information to prevent terrorism, but a judge must grant a formal court order for the authorities to gather this material under the Act. Again, this procedure is designed to protect the right to a private life, in this case, with regard to the privacy of an honest individual's financial affairs.

information was not obtained under evidential procedures.[110] This is further proof that the service itself did not really believe the central claim of the warrant; that the funds were destined for the support of terrorism

'As far as I am aware, neither the IOCA Commissioner, who notionally oversaw the telephone intercept and specifically came to the service to discuss the case, nor the Home Secretary, ever asked whether the financial information was legally collected, even though they knew private financial information had been gathered to support the warrants.

'The individual in the bank who gave out Brittain's private financial information should be investigated by the police for violating banking law. Their name will be on one of H1's files with evidence of the information passed.'

The rest of the operation

Having made his protest where and when he could, like any other MI5 officer, David had to then 'follow orders' or resign. Although he personally disagreed with the situation, professionalism dictated – for the time being at least – that he did the job to the best of his ability by revalidating the warrant and continuing to co-ordinate the investigation. I shudder to imagine what would have happened to him had he told his bosses that he was refusing on ethical grounds. At this point – autumn 1995 – despite many reservations, David still saw himself pursuing a career in MI5. David explains:

'If I wanted to continue working in MI5 and effect change from within, I was not able to question the judgment of my bosses without being labelled as someone who "rocked

---

[110] In this day and age, MI5 does use evidential procedures in its investigations into genuine terrorism.

the boat". Yet I desperately wanted to change MI5 so that it performed a useful job well and lawfully, but I did not then feel that I would have been able to do that either from outside the organisation or from a lower level job. In every potential situation, I therefore came up against a dead end. To complain would mark you out as a troublemaker.[111] To leave took you outside any potential ability to alter things.'

The former DG, Stella Rimington, has confirmed just how little room was given to protest within the service: 'But I soon realised that people regarded you with suspicion if you asked too many questions, so I learned to keep quiet...' I knew that open protest was not likely to be successful. If one got a reputation as a revolutionary, one would be regarded as suspect and written off.'[112] However, unlike Stella Rimington, who 'whiled away the time reading Dornford Yates novels under the desk', David did not let serious illegality on the part of the service pass unchallenged. He did what he could while still in the service.

When it became clear by the end of that year that no one in MI5 management was prepared to end an investigation based on flouted procedures and inaccurate information, he began to think that he had no option but to resign. As we left Thames House to begin Christmas leave, David confided to me that he had had enough, not only because of the Brittain investigation but also because, shockingly, he had just learnt that MI6 had paid money to Al Qaeda associates to assassinate Colonel Gaddafi of Libya.

MI5 did not remove the tap on Brittain's home phone until early 1996 when it reported her and Bindman discussing 'the money [for the] *legal* case'.

---

[111] True to form, MI5 did brief against David saying just that.
[112] *Open Secret*, pp. 98, 121.

Conclusions

Given that David's disclosure of the Brittain case was used to prosecute him under the OSA, the following are the arguments – based on the above evidence – he would have put before the jury had he been allowed to argue in his defence that his disclosures were in the public interest. Given the strength of the arguments, it is hard to see how a jury would have been able to convict him, had he been allowed a defence:

- **The telephone tap and the financial investigation were illegal**: the warrant was illegal because procedure designed to prevent illegal or criminal invasion of privacy had not been followed. The financial investigation was illegal because MI5 did not obtain a court order under the PTA.
- **Deliberate flouting of the law**: in the Brittain operation MI5 management knowingly continued to violate the law, even when officers brought this to their attention.
- **Political expediency over legality**: the service simply did not dare inform the Home Secretary that it had obtained a warrant and started an intrusive investigation on the back of a warrant application based on untruths.
- **MI5 paranoia**: senior MI5 officers who had cut their intelligence teeth in an era obsessed with 'reds under the bed', were still preoccupied with *Guardian* journalists and libertarian lawyers. If Victoria Brittain had been a housewife living in East Cheam, I do not believe MI5 would have launched such an extensive and intrusive investigation into her and her family. Her real crime was to be a *Guardian* journalist with unusual friends.
- **Sexed up and flawed intelligence case**: even if procedure had been followed, there was still no real basis for investigating Brittain. She and the Libyan intelligence services would hardly have been likely to use official Libyan accounts in London to launder or move money to fund terrorist activity in the UK. Even then MI5 got its sums wrong.

- **Operational ineffectiveness**: ironically, MI5 was so slow to start the investigation that, if the funds had been destined for terrorists, they would have been long gone before the service began its investigation.
- **Bad judgement**: Operation SHADOWER was a waste of MI5's time and effort, as resources needed to prevent actual terrorist planning and attacks were taken away from those areas, putting the public at greater but unnecessary risk. MI5's budget would have been better spent on other targets which posed a clearer and more direct threat to national security.
- **Lack of on-going justification**: nothing emerged from the year-long telephone tap to show that Victoria Brittain was involved in money laundering or any other illegal activity. In fact, Brittain was exonerated by the telephone intercept very early in the investigation when it provided intelligence about 'the case' and 'the money'.
- **Justification for whistleblowing**: even MI5 now accepts that her actions were entirely legitimate. If David had not gone on the record, she would never have known that her privacy had been unlawfully invaded and her daughter nearly been arrested on trumped-up charges so that MI5 could plant a bug in her house.
- **Deliberate misrepresentation of the truth**: the investigation clearly demonstrates that MI5 management can quite easily mislead ministers and Commissioners. As there is no need for MI5 to swear its case to the Home Secretary under oath, it can misrepresent or use facts selectively or simply lie to government, without sanction.

Chapter 10

The MI6/Al Qaeda Conspiracy, Part 1

The MI6-funding of Islamic extremists and Al Qaeda members to assassinate Colonel Gaddafi is the main reason why David finally left the service. It is the real 'case that made [him] quit'. To quote David:

'Although I knew about the plot before making my decision to leave – I believed at the time that it was more MI6 *"Boy's Own"* stuff – I was nevertheless physically sickened by the fact that MI6 wanted to sponsor Islamic extremists to carry out terrorism. At around the time I was debating whether to leave because of the Victoria Brittain investigation, MI6's David Watson told me he had in fact supplied his agent with $40,000 to buy weapons to execute the operation to assassinate Gaddafi.[113]

'I joined the service to stop terrorism and prevent the deaths of innocent people, not to get involved in these despicable and cowardly acts. I still cannot believe that the Prime Minister has refused to take my evidence or investigate this matter as this decision has sent out a clear message to the intelligence services that they can fund terrorism; conspire to murder people with impunity; and take enormous risks with our security.

---

[113] The actual attempt on Gaddafi's life – which went wrong, killing innocent civilians – occurred when David was beginning to take steps to leave MI5. The Gaddafi plot caused him to apply for new jobs with greater zeal.

'After all, would you give an individual you hardly know – who has admitted to connections with Al Qaeda – an enormous sum to carry out a terrorist attack, when you know the group he is leading is opposed to the values of Western society? It is difficult to imagine a greater disregard and contempt for the lives and security of the British people.'

Key points

The following issues arise from David's whistleblowing about MI6 support for Al Qaeda:

- Contrary to misinformation published in some newspapers, the following account was not 'bar-room gossip'. David's MI6 counterpart, PT16/B David Watson, briefed him officially on the plot as it unfolded. As MI5 officers, both David and I knew the serious threat the funding of Al Qaeda posed at the time.
- Despite the then Foreign Secretary Robin Cook's denials in 1998, I have now found out that intelligence officer ██████████████[114] was MI6's man Tunworth. He is a member of the Islamic Fighting Group (IFG) aka the Militant Islamic Group, an Al Qaeda affiliate based in Libya.
- French intelligence has also established that leading members of the IFG like Tunworth are also *members* of Al Qaeda.
- The MI6 agent Tunworth admitted his connections with Islamic extremists and Al Qaeda members during a debrief with his MI6 handler, David Watson, in late 1995 so MI6 cannot deny it did not know what it was entering into.
- At the very least, MI6 failed to realise that it had prior intelligence about an Al Qaeda coup in Libya. If successful, MI6 would have allowed Al Qaeda to take over an oil-

[114] MI5 and MI6 censorship still prevents me from naming Tunworth.

166

rich state in North Africa, putting the lives of British and US citizens, in particular, at far greater risk.

- By the time MI6 paid the money, Osama Bin Laden's organisation was already known to be responsible for the 1993 World Trade Centre bombing and MI5 had set up G9C, a section dedicated to the task of defeating Bin Laden and his affiliates.
- Under the 1994 Intelligence Services Act, the real James Bonds do have a licence to kill or immunity for criminal acts carried out abroad in the course of their work, provided they gain the permission of the Foreign Secretary. But without that permission they are breaking the law, should they become involved in a conspiracy to murder and to cause terrorism. In this case, they did not even seek that permission.
- MI6 gave money to individuals who posed a greater threat to our lives and security – Al Qaeda – to assassinate an individual who posed a lesser threat, Colonel Gaddafi. It just doesn't make any logical sense. In fact, it demonstrates that MI6 was motivated by revenge on Gaddafi, rather than any desire to protect British lives and national security, because he nationalised the Libyan oil industry in 1976, at the expense of BP.[115]

How David was briefed on the conspiracy

In summer 1995, at the height of the illegal investigation into Victoria Brittain, David was first briefed on the plot. David Watson, David's counterpart in MI6, asked to meet to discuss an unusual case which he could not mention over the phone. At the subsequent meeting, PT16/B told David that:

---

[115] Revenge for Lockerbie may have been one of Watson's motives as well. At the time, he was one of the few MI6 officers who accepted that Libya was responsible, as he had talked at length with David about it. We must also remember that Lockerbie was a revenge attack for the UK/US bombing of Tripoli.

167

- A senior member of the Libyan military intelligence service had walked into the British embassy in Tunis and asked to meet the resident MI6 officer.
- The Libyan 'walk-in' had asked for funds to lead a group of Islamic extremists in an attempted coup, which would involve the assassination of Colonel Gaddafi, the head of the Libyan state.
- Although the Libyan military intelligence officer led the group, he had said he was not an Islamic extremist himself.
- The Libyan had a brief MI6 record, which PT16/B thought was enough to confirm that the Libyan did have the access to the regime that he claimed.

In exchange for MI6's support, the Libyan offered to hand over the two Lockerbie suspects after the coup. Getting them to the UK for trial had at the time been one of MI6's objectives for about three years but there is no guarantee that the coup plotters could have done this. It is debatable whether the coup plotters would have had either the resources or expertise required to track down the suspects after their planned coup. At first, David was sceptical to the point of *ennui*. After all, MI6 officers had often claimed that the Lockerbie two were about to be handed over or that Gaddafi was about to die or be toppled but nothing had come of this supposedly keen and reliable intelligence.

In the following weeks, PT16/B told David that the Libyan was codenamed Tunworth. At some point in the following weeks David briefly saw the printout of MI6's record of him. It contained around two or three separate mentions. They supported his claim to be a senior member of Libyan military intelligence but were not detailed. David checked the Libyan's name against Durbar and STAR, MI5's records, but the service had no trace of him. David did not make any effort to remember the name because he believed that the whole thing would come to nothing as other MI6 plots had done. Watson also issued at least two CX reports detailing intelligence provided by Tunworth at his meeting with the resident MI6 officer in

Tunis.[116] David remembers it concerned changes in personnel in the Libyan regime. MI5 had collateral for it so G9 assessed that Tunworth had some access to the regime. David takes up the story:

'Throughout this process, I briefed my line manager, G9A/1 – Jerry Mahoney until December 1995, Paul Slim after that – about these developments. As the operation was in its infancy when Mahoney left, I don't believe that I told him anything other than the bare basics. When briefing his successor, Paul Slim, I told him that this might be more *"Boy's Own* stuff" on the part of MI6 and that we shouldn't take it too seriously although we agreed to review this in the light of new information.

'It is inconceivable that G9A/1 did not think an MI6-funded plot to engineer a coup in Libya was worthy of mentioning to his line manager, G9/0, Paul Mitchell. In turn, it is unthinkable that Mitchell did not raise the matter with his line management who would have informed his boss until the DG herself had been made aware. I wonder if it was included in the first draft of Dame Stella's book and removed on the orders of the authorities.'

In December 1995, James Worthing,[117] R/ME/C at MI6, circulated CX95/ 53452[118] report to Whitehall and other addressees, warning of a potential coup in Libya. It confirmed that a member of the rebel group gave detailed intelligence to his MI6 handler in anticipation of help from Britain. The report clearly demonstrated that Watson knew that Tunworth was planning terrorism and his group had already been involved in attempts on Gaddafi's life:

---

[116] CX reports summarise MI6's key intelligence findings and are circulated to the Prime Minister, the Cabinet Office and JIC, which guides Britain's national security strategy.
[117] Fictitious name.
[118] CX is the code used for MI6 intelligence. It was this document that appeared on the Internet in February 2000. See Chapter 15.

'In late November 1995 *[Tunworth's identity removed]*[119] described plans, *in which he was involved*, to overthrow Colonel Gaddafi ... The coup is scheduled to start at around the time of the next General People's Congress on February 14, 1996. Coup will start with unrest in Tripoli, Misratah and Benghazi...

'The coup plotters were responsible for the death of [*blank – Names removed to protect security* ————— *blank*] was about to take up the position as head of Military Intelligence when he was forced off the Tripoli–Sirte road and was killed. The 2 coup plotters involved escaped unhurt. In August 1995, 3 army captains who were part of the coup plot attempted to kill Colonel Gaddafi.'

The report then listed Libyan installations that would be attacked and described supporters in Libya's principal cities and their occupations. The start of the coup was to be signalled through coded messages on television and radio. It also said that at least 250 British-made weapons were distributed among the plotters.

Tunworth also told his MI6 handler that:

'...plotters would have cars similar to those in Gaddafi's security entourage with fake security number plates. They would infiltrate themselves into the entourage in order to kill or arrest Gaddafi...

'One group of military personnel were being trained in the desert area near Kufra for the role of attacking Gaddafi and his entourage. The aim was to attack Gaddafi after the GPC [General People's Congress], but before he had returned to Sirte. One officer and 20 men were being trained for this attack.'[120]

---

[119] Apparently removed before the document appeared on the Internet.

[120] David later provided this information to Mark Urban of the BBC and *The Mail on Sunday* accurately from memory.

David also remembers another MI6 CX report being issued about the plot in early 1996. It was a shopping list of the group's requirements to carry out the coup, including the supply of weapons and basics like jeeps and tents.

Around the same time, Christmas 1995, Watson told David that he had met Tunworth in Geneva and paid him $40,000. Jackie Barker, who had replaced Jane Thomas as G9A/15, told him that Watson had told her the same information 'in confidence'. During routine G9/PT16 meetings around this time, officers occasionally mentioned the plot. Watson then met Tunworth on two further occasions early in 1996 in Geneva. David does not know of any further details except that Watson mentioned that he had paid 'similar sums' to Tunworth on each occasion. Although PT16/B never specifically mentioned it, it was tacitly understood that Watson was working with the approval of his direct line manager, PT16, Richard Bartlett.

Lack of government sanction

At some point – David can't be sure when exactly – Watson mentioned that the 'submission', MI6 jargon for the letter requesting permission from the Foreign Office for otherwise illegal operations, was going to go 'all the way to the top'. In about January 1996, Watson told him that the submission had been successful, indicating that the Foreign Secretary himself had signed the document permitting the operation.[121] When David briefed Paul Slim on the details of the plot, he specifically drew attention to the fact that the service only had Watson's word for this. He urged his boss to task senior MI5 management to raise the matter formally, to check that the operation was legal.

Then, in either February or March 1996, David read two,

---

[121] This claim is challenged by the findings of the *Panorama* investigation into the plot broadcast on BBC1 on Friday 7 August 1998. See Chapter 15, p.245. Malcolm Rifkind, Foreign Secretary at the time, has repeatedly denied authorising the operation.

possibly three intelligence reports quoting independent sources – the Egyptian and Moroccan intelligence services. They all stated that an attack had been made on Colonel Gaddafi in Sirte, Libya. Two of the reports indicated that the attackers had tried to assassinate Gaddafi when he was part of a motorcade but had failed as they had targeted the wrong car. As a result of the explosion and the ensuing chaos in which shots were fired, civilians and security police were maimed and killed.

'At a meeting shortly after, PT16/B ventured to me in a note of triumph that Tunworth had been responsible for the attack. "Yes that was our man. We did it," was how he put it. He regarded it, curiously, as a triumph even though the objective of the operation had not been met and reporting indicated there had been civilian casualties. Despite that, I very much got the impression that this was regarded as a coup for MI6 because it was playing up to the reputation that the real James Bonds wanted to have. I then promptly passed the information on to my line manager, G9A/1. Although initially reluctant, he said he would deal with the matter. I've no idea whether he did. In later months, I asked Watson several times what had happened to Tunworth, but was not given answers.'

By this time, David had already decided to leave the service and was actively looking for jobs in the private sector. As a result of MI6 funding Al Qaeda, on top of the general ineptitude and bungling I had witnessed, I also decided I no longer wanted to work for intelligence services who had ceased to protect democracy and instead funded our terrorist enemies. The services are supposed to protect us, not put our lives at greater risk from terrorist attack. It was time to leave.

Chapter 11

Bureaucracy Gone Mad, Our Final Months in the Service

In our final months in the service, we saw what can only be described as greater stupidity on the part of MI5 management. They only served to demonstrate that our decision to leave MI5 was the right one, and that the British public are not being properly protected by their secret servants.

Cancellation of intercept

In early 1996, after G9 had recommended Bazelya's expulsion, G9/0 Paul Mitchell told David to cancel one of the telephone lines on the Libyan omnibus warrant.[122] David protested because G9A had received indications that Bazelya was to be shortly replaced by another member of the Libyan ESO. In the meantime, David argued, it was likely that the phone would be used for intelligence activity. Mitchell tried to claim he was 'protecting civil liberties', even though the tap was legally constituted and had provided an abundance of information on Libyan intelligence activities. David takes up the story:

'Other officers in G Branch were appalled, including G6/0

---

[122] A warrant containing multiple telephone numbers for the same target.

Hugh Johnston, the Assistant Director of the Middle Eastern agent running section. Despite this, G9/0 made me draft an amendment to the warrant, more unnecessary work, which took me away from actually preventing terrorism.

'Before I could send out the amendment to the warrant, that particular line reported that the Libyans in the UK believed that they had identified an MI5 agent. Forewarned is forearmed. If that intelligence had emerged a day later, I would already have cancelled the tap on that line, meaning that this vital piece of information concerning the security of an agent would have been lost. In turn, that would have meant that G6 would have been unable to take preventative measures to protect the source.'

To David's and G6/0's relief, Mitchell had no choice but to concede that the line had to remain part of the warrant. In many cases, it is difficult to assess the damage done to national security by the incompetence, lack of judgement and inherent inefficiency of MI5 management because, if resources are not in place in time, we cannot know the nature and magnitude of the intelligence missed. In this case, we do know. We know that the source would in all probability have been compromised, had the tap been cancelled according to Mitchell's wishes. Who knows what would then have happened to the source? G9 could easily have lost the vital intelligence that the agent did provide about the Libyan threat to carry out 'the biggest terrorist attack in history'. Forewarned is forearmed. For want of common sense, the intercept was lost. For want of the intercept, the agent's life was lost. For want of the agent's life, the intelligence was lost. For want of the intelligence, civilian lives were lost.

The 'biggest terrorist attack in history'

In early 1996, shortly after the Brittain investigation had come to an end and the Gaddafi plot had come to fruition, David was faced with another MI5 debacle which confirmed to us that we had made the right decision about pursuing careers outside the service.

In this case, the service had received intelligence from separate sources with a proven history of reliable reporting indicating that the Libyans had sent five terrorists to Britain to launch 'the biggest terrorist attack in history'. MI5 took the intelligence so seriously it was included in a JIC paper which was circulated to Whitehall. As head of the Libyan subgroup, David was responsible for co-ordinating G9's response. It was a testament to the working practices he had put in place that G9 was able quickly to identify the potential culprits. One of them became the subject of a classic honey trap sting operation to recruit him.

The Libyan agents tasked with the attack were obviously very careful about how they communicated with Libya, particularly as Bazelya had been declared *persona non grata* as a result of his activities in support of the LIS while in the UK. G9 had received intelligence indicating that, in an attempt to mislead MI5, the Libyans were using the DHL courier service to send intelligence reports back to Tripoli. This sounded fanciful as it was hardly a secure route but the intelligence came from a very reliable source. Preliminary enquiries established that the Libyan interests section were indeed sending packages via DHL to Musa Kusa, the head of Libyan intelligence. Without a warrant though, MI5 was not entitled to open or otherwise interfere with the material.

In normal circumstances, a desk officer would have applied for a warrant to intercept communications under the 1985 Interception of Communications Act. However, that legislation only covered the intercept of calls made on the public telephone network or material sent via the Post Office.

'When I first approached an MI5 lawyer,' David told *The Mail on Sunday*, 'the first response was to say they were unsure if there was any legal way of intercepting the documents. Not surprisingly, I told them we were not dealing with a Sunday school but hardened Libyan terrorists. This had little effect.'[123]

Yet MI5 clearly had a rock-solid case to intercept any material in order to prevent the enormous loss of life and damage to property associated with a terrorist attack on the scale reported. Legal Adviser Richard Woods[124] advised that in this case, MI5 needed a property warrant to make its interference with the Libyan's private property legal. But rather than simply draft one warrant to cover any of the material, as you would under the usual legislation,[125] the lawyer insisted that a separate warrant be prepared for each separate piece of material, even though it was clearly the same (very strong) intelligence case. David told the paper:

'Sometimes we knew in advance that the material was being sent, but if for any reason the date was changed, we had to draw up a new warrant. It became farcical. I had to refer every warrant up the hierarchy. They would be handed backwards and forwards between lawyers, group leaders, assistant directors, right up to the highest level within the organisation. When I complained about this paper-shuffling exercise, they had the audacity to accuse me of failing to respect civil liberties.'

The arguments and the duplication deeply hindered MI5's attempts to get to grips with this Libyan threat. In fact, the interception did not begin until a couple of months after the intelligence was first received. Of course during that time, the packages were sent back without MI5 being able to read their contents. In the end, Richard Woods advised that the service

---

[123] *MoS*, 24 August 1997.
[124] Name changed on orders of MI5.
[125] The 1989 Security Service Act governs interference with private property. At the time, the 1985 IOCA dealt with intercepting mail but only that sent through the Post Office.

only needed a single warrant to cover the material, the position David had originally argued on the grounds of legality, efficiency and common sense. At the same time, David's group thwarted the planned attack by disrupting the five Libyan terrorists by other methods. Contrary to the strong intelligence, it turned out that the route was only being used to send back routine reports about the activities of Libyan students in the UK rather than about terrorism.

Some will see that as justification of the position of MI5 lawyers and management. However – at the time of the greatest threat – the intelligence, which came from a reliable source, strongly indicated that this route was being used to send possibly incriminating material back to Libya. For a period, intelligence – possibly warning of the precise target and or exact timing of 'the biggest terrorist attack in history' – could have slipped through MI5's fingers. It would have been an enormous tragedy if the LIS had succeeded because MI5 was obsessed with nitpicking bureaucracy, which had nothing to do with protecting civil liberties.

We know in this case it was because MI5 eventually adopted the one-warrant-fits-all approach, which David had argued for from the outset.

The MoD runs out of codewords

In the middle of all this, the investigation was nearly compromised by the MoD 'running out' of codewords. The MoD keeps a central database of words already used to denote a specific operation so that they cannot be duplicated across the different intelligence agencies. MI5 officers were not allowed to suggest a codeword. The MoD simply gave the desk officer the next one on the list. David needed several codewords for the different operations. For example, each of the five Libyan intelligence officers in the UK had one operational codeword for the investigation and one for the parallel recruitment operation

177

carried out by G6, the agent targeting section, in addition to the codeword for the overall operation to stop potentially the biggest terrorist attack in history.

David's conversation with the MoD official went something like this:

'I need some more codewords for our operations.'

'Didn't I give you four last week?'

'Yes but there have been developments. I need more.'

'There's a slight problem. (Pause.) We've run out.'

(David laughs.) 'Had a run on codewords, have we? It must be the time of year.'

'I'm serious. We don't have any new ones.'

'The English language has a greater vocabulary than any other language. We have 500,000 routine words plus another 500,000 technical and scientific words. Why don't you just open the *Concise OED* and put a pin in the page. If the nearest word is not in your database then you can use it. If it is there, then repeat the process with the pin until you find one that isn't.'

'I'm not sure I'm allowed to do that.'

'Well get back to me, when you've found some new ones.'

Although this all sounds comically bureaucratic, at one point it threatened to mess up G9's performance indicators, meaning that a number of ultimately successful disruption operations against the Libyans nearly counted for nothing with MI5 management and Whitehall.

Passing undisguised product to GCHQ

In spring 1996, David came across another example of the woolly-mindedness of MI5 management and its inability to deal with routine problems. At the time, David's G9A Libyan subgroup was passing intelligence product to GCHQ in disguised rather than raw form. Disguised intelligence uses phrases like 'a secret and reliable source has reported...' or 'a secret, reliable and well-placed source has indicated...' etc. and then summarises and paraphrases the intelligence the source has provided. Raw intelligence identifies a specific source using a codeword, like Linen for telephone intercept or Tunworth to denote a specific agent. It is usually a more detailed account of the intelligence than disguised reporting. It takes time to disguise intelligence, an issue made more difficult by the absence of office IT in G9A. This meant that staff had to write out the disguised brief in longhand, send it to their secretary for typing (then send it back for typos to be corrected) before getting it back to sign it off. When sharing raw product, an extra copy was made in the originating section which went straight to GCHQ without troubling G9A.

Q22A, David's opposite number on the Libyan desk in GCHQ, had been receiving disguised product as it concerned a target of mutual interest. In order to save time during a busy period for the Libyan sub-section, David decided to look into supplying Q22A with the raw product rather than the disguised version. There were no security issues because GCHQ was already receiving the disguised intelligence and knew the source that it originated from. In addition, its procedures for handling sensitive material were much more rigorous than within MI5 because it routinely dealt with caveated sigint.[126]

When David raised the idea in a Loose Minute addressed to G9A/1, G9/1, G9/0 and Director G, they all signed it off immediately. After all, it was a way of saving in the region of 40 manhours a month in a group of three officers (as well as saving time for the secretarial group). However, the Deputy Director General, Julian Hansen, turned down the request. David offered to go and talk to the DDG to explain the situation, but

---

[126] Signals intelligence, which carries various high-level warnings about how it is handled in the service.

G9 management refused to let him. At the time, David was furious because the DDG's decision meant taking staff away from investigating serious threats from Libyan terrorists – including the operation to prevent a potentially massive attack– in order to disguise material that patently did not need disguising.

But, as usual in MI5, the situation descended into farce. During a routine conversation with the Iraqi subgroup leader, G9A/4, Tom Potter, David learnt that the Iraqi desks were already sending undisguised product to GCHQ. This meant that there were clearly no reasonable reasons to refuse the same option to the Libyan subgroup. Again, David prepared a Loose Minute, which G Branch management approved up to director level. Again, the DDG simply refused to allow the Libyan subgroup to pass undisguised product to GCHQ. He did though allow the Iraqi subgroup to carry on passing their undisguised product from a very similar source, even though the Iraqi subgroup was not at that time involved in countering a specific terrorist threat.

Hansen did not justify his decision or resolve the issue to ensure that the service policy on passing this kind of product to GCHQ was at least consistent. He also did not appear to understand the pressing threat the Libyan target presented, because he did not seem to want to meet G9 officers to find out.

Hansen again demonstrated his talents when David put out a Security Service Report (SSR) to Whitehall, cleared by G Branch management, on the threat from the five Libyan IOs. On receiving his copy, he phoned David to ask him why he had included the actual number of Libyan officers sent to the UK.

'Because I wanted to give ministers an honest idea of the threat we are facing,' said David.
'Well, don't do it again,' said Hansen.

Of course there could be no security issue in passing the number of officers involved to government, as that number had come from the same source as the intelligence about the scale of the plot. However, imagine if there had not been a number included. MI5 could have said to the Prime Minister: 'Look, we've identified three intelligence officers and expelled them. What a success, Prime Minister,' when in fact there were still two terrorists on the loose, posing an enormous threat to the security of the country.

Before we pass on to other matters, I feel I must mention another tale about Hansen. As a keen jogger, he used to change in the same changing rooms which officers like David and Tom Potter used before and after squash matches. On one occasion, Potter had launched into one of his tirades against the service, oblivious to the fact that Hansen was behind him. As the other officers subtly tried to warn Potter, he took this as disagreement and therefore became even more vociferous in his condemnation of MI5. Although Potter went on for a good five minutes before realising that Hansen was there, the latter made no effort to ask him to discuss his valid criticisms of the service.

Potter was another promising officer who left the service disillusioned. David and I went to his leaving party in July 1997, where we met a number of friends and former colleagues of our generation. Without a single exception, they were all looking for new jobs. Natural wastage for officers at our grade was reckoned to be two or three a year. Between 1996 and 1997 *fourteen* officers at our old grade resigned. As David and I had already left MI5 and had new careers as management consultants we were frequently asked how to 'make the great escape'. MI5, of course, provided no help whatsoever to those wishing to leave and displayed no curiosity about why so many were doing so.

Open recruitment

Since so many experienced officers were leaving, MI5 decided to depart from tradition and begin recruiting through open adverts. Up until then, most recruits were found via a tap on the shoulder while sipping sherry in an Oxbridge college, through the Foreign Office exams, or in the early 1990s through oblique newspaper adverts, such as the one David applied to. In early 1996 I was selected to be trained as a recruiter, which involved assessing potential officers during the taxing two-day CSSB. This gave me a detailed insight into the progress of MI5's new open initiative.

As expected, MI5 received a deluge of applications from all those wannabe James Bonds out there. However, I think even they were taken aback when they received 20,000 CVs through the post. Once the B Branch recruiters had weeded through the applicants, the service realised that it had several stunningly good recruits on its hands. Not only did they have extremely good degrees, they also had exceptional interpersonal skills. Of course they were offered jobs and of course they accepted.

However, the trouble began even before the recruits had started work. No thought had been given by service senior management on how to train and motivate a large influx of new officers. The traditional mentoring system, whereby an experienced officer would take a recruit under their wing for six months, was time consuming. As so many of the good officers were leaving, it was difficult to find suitable places to put the probationers. B Branch repeatedly raised these concerns with senior management, but was repeatedly brushed aside. As the new generation of officers entered the service, they were placed in clerical rather than investigative desks, where they had little chance to learn the ropes. It was no surprise that many quickly became demotivated and disillusioned.

It is an expensive way to run an organisation – haemorrhaging good officers, retaining the less effective, and constantly having to recruit. The resignations lost the service years of operational experience and 'tribal knowledge' – the understanding and feel you build up for a target. Constantly having to recruit is an expensive process. The various selection stages, the prolonged vetting and all the attendant travel can mean that the recruitment of an intelligence officer can cost up to £10,000. That is a lot of money to spend if the new officer is demotivated within six months and resigns.

Incompetencies

Another management 'initiative' came to fruition in 1996. The identification of 'competency frameworks' had been a popular management practice in first the private sector and then the civil service over the preceding decade. Finally MI5 decided to jump on the bandwagon.

Competency frameworks are supposed to identify which personality traits are needed to enable an employee to perform their job to a satisfactory level or even excel. Competencies are distinct from traditional evaluation systems and try to identify types of behaviour which are required to do a job effectively. As MI5 had recently moved to a system of performance related pay, it had an urgent requirement for such a framework.

Once identified, these competencies can also be learnt. For example, the emotional intelligence skills, such as empathy, listening and personal authority, which are used to build working relationships, would register quite highly for an MI5 officer. The complexity of requirement would increase with responsibility, and would be particularly high for a senior manager, agent runner or liaison officer (you would think).

In an unprecedented move, MI5 brought in an external consultant to draw up a competency framework. The consultants involved as many staff as they could in focus groups. The exercise generated a lot of interest and enthusiasm, as staff finally felt they had some input into the way the office worked and that it was moving forward. In 1996 the consultants produced the draft framework. It was circulated for the staff to read, and the feedback was positive.

Then the senior managers added their comments. They had grown up in a service which looked primarily at 'reds under the bed' and espionage targets. They applied what they thought

183

were relevant comments to the framework with this in mind. Of course the nature of MI5's work had changed out of all recognition by this time – it was all fast-paced terrorism and organised crime targets, with a strong reliance on good relationships with outside agencies rather than just desk work. Despite all the time, expertise and money which had gone into this project, senior managers scratched out large swathes of the framework. More people left the service in disgust.

A year in G3

In 1995 my time in the Irish logistics department, T5E, was abruptly terminated when the section was split up after a predatory takeover by T2. I had been lucky for the bulk of my time in the section, as I had one of the few really good Group Leaders in the service. She was supportive, but hands off. I felt I was doing something worthwhile and my team was getting results. When the section was split up, my Assistant Director told me I was in line for a plum investigative and liaison post, working against organised crime on secondment to the National Criminal Intelligence Service (NCIS). He told me that my experience and track record were ideal for this job.

However, MI5 Personnel Section was worried. One female officer could not take the pressure when working on secondment at MPSB, and on those grounds alone they decided against sending another female officer to work in a police environment, no matter what her personal capabilities might be. My posting was therefore blocked. As I had signed away my employment rights on joining the service, I had no way of contesting this discrimination. The post went to a far less experienced male colleague.

The only other job available at the time was as G3A/2, a post responsible for the coordination of briefs to the DG, Directors and to Whitehall, G Branch's European liaison and the production of threat assessments for VIPs in the UK. The job offered no new challenges, but gave me an interesting overview of world terrorism and inter-agency politicking. However, it was one of the most unpopular postings in the service, as the job reported to G3/0, the mad Assistant Director, Terry Fawlty.

My predecessor *en poste* was overjoyed that she was escaping his tyranny. (I had the last laugh, as soon after I joined G3, Fawlty was posted to head her new section.) This man was renowned for his paranoia, obsessed with how his peer group was doing in the promotion stakes, and was one of the most demanding managers I have ever met. It would have been funny if he had not had so much power.

Terry was responsible for liaison policy with intelligence agencies in Europe. He was supposed to coordinate efforts on targets of mutual concern such as Al Qaeda and lobby for an effective working practice in various Euro committees. He was rabidly Eurosceptic – so an obvious choice for the job.

He also had a unique take on management theory. I was sitting in his office when a telephone call came through for him. He looked smug as he put the phone down and announced: 'Stephen Lander's the new DG. Good. He's *Stalinesque* [sic] and that's just what the office needs.'

Soon after Lander took over as DG in 1996, he toured Thames House meeting officers as a 'charm' offensive. Horror stories about his graceless behaviour began to precede him on his grand tour. However, I was still taken aback when he visited G3A. He spent the few minutes in my section swinging from side to side in the swivel chair. When we explained that our jobs involved tasking all the G Branch officers to produce briefs for him and coordinating them for him to use at innumerable meetings, he sniffed and said that he never bothered to read them. So much for motivating your staff.

SPIES, LIES AND WHISTLEBLOWERS

The report that never was

In March 1995, David completed a lengthy and detailed research and assessment paper on Libyan support for terrorism. It was timely because the Libyan regime had in recent years ceased to support the IRA and acted as a brake on terrorists groups to which it gave safe haven like Sabri Al Banna aka Abu Nidal. MI5 actually had very little reliable and up-to-date intelligence on the threat. Certainly, none of it was properly corroborated. Part of the problem was that MI5 and MI6 did not have good access to the principal Libyan intelligence service, the ESO.[127] In fact, the two services had never managed to fully recruit an ESO officer. In the assessment, David concluded that there was not enough information to make an informed analysis. He prepared an SSR[128] on the subject for ministers, the other agencies and Whitehall, including the JIC, which co-ordinates papers on the various threats Britain faces. G9/1 – G9/0's deputy – then asked David to be more robust in his assessment. The little intelligence G9 had on Libya did indicate support for Palestinian resistance groups in the Occupied Territories, but the sourcing for the material was not properly reliable. He asked David:

'Do you think Gaddafi is supporting terrorism?'
'I really can't say,' David replied. 'The intelligence isn't reliable enough and there is no collateral for the specific claims.'
'You seem to be saying that Gaddafi is supporting terrorism.'
'Only because we have some intelligence indicating that, but, as I say, it's not from wholly reliable sources and it's not detailed enough to make an informed assessment. I really can't say one way or the other.'
'I think we need to play up the difficulty of gathering

---

[127] External Security Organisation or the Amin Al Jahamirya.
[128] Security Service or Box 500 report, a less detailed version of the research destined for intelligence customers outside the service.

intelligence on the Libyan target and concentrate on the information we do have.'

'What does that mean in effect?'

'We take out the Key Point in the Executive Summary about the lack of intelligence as it should be self-evident from the paper.'

This was a clear case of what would now be called 'sexing up' by omission. David did as he was told and redrafted the SSR over the following months. It took time because he kept getting diverted by more pressing matters, like Libyan attempts to undermine the Lockerbie evidence and the Victoria Brittain investigation. He also had to incorporate new intelligence into the report, as the service received it. (None of the new intelligence really added any greater understanding to the issue but had to be included otherwise it would have looked like MI5 had missed it). Then the various branches of management sat on the report. After that, my boss in G3A – which co-ordinated reports to Whitehall – did the final edit before it finally went back to G9/0. By this time, over a year had passed since the report had been drafted. Ministers were no nearer to being informed about MI5's thinking on a JIC Category 1 Priority target.

Mitchell then restructured the whole thing so that the long executive summary was converted into the body of the report and the body became an annex. The executive summary was replaced by a couple of bland paragraphs saying that intelligence indicated that Gaddafi continued to support terrorist groups.

'At the time, I thought that Mitchell was doing his usual thing: messing about with drafts to make it look like he was busy,' says David. 'However, I have since come to the conclusion that this was a clever way of playing down the lack of hard, reliable intelligence in the report. Busy ministers were only going to read the key points and the body of the report, at most. They were not going to plough through an annex.'

Shortly before we left the service in September 1996, David approached Mitchell to ask what had finally happened to the SSR. Mitchell told him that it had gone out to Whitehall. David felt relieved that after an eighteen-month delay, ministers and officials finally had the information it needed to form policy on Libya. However, a couple of months after leaving MI5, David and I met Pete Gaskill, his former mentee, for a drink. Pete was still in G9, but was thinking of leaving the service after only a year. He told us that the report had still not gone out to Whitehall.

As far as we are aware, ministers never did learn about the dearth of intelligence on the Libyan target, which made it impossible to assess the true extent of Gaddafi's support for terrorism, if indeed there was any. The Libyan desire to launch a large-scale attack appeared to have been sabre rattling, prompted not by Gaddafi but by his head of intelligence, Kusa, who was frustrated by the lack of progress in the Lockerbie impasse and the expulsion of his protégé, Bazelya, from the UK.

For his work in G9, David received a performance-related bonus for consistently working above the standards expected of the grade, a matter confirmed in the prosecution witness statements against him: Witness B at David's trial – our old friend from F2 and T2, Steve Canute – begrudgingly admitted that David received 'an additional lump sum'. It rather undermined the claims of the shadowy sources, who briefed tame journalists that David left because he wasn't up to the job. Or the claims of Michael Mates, a member of the PM's ISC, who claimed that David had been sacked from the service.

On 27 September 1996, we both walked out of Thames House, sadder but wiser people, to take up jobs in separate management consultancies.

Chapter 12

Going on the Record

Why David and I felt the need to speak out

To recap, while David was thinking of leaving because of the Victoria Brittain investigation, MI6-funded Al Qaeda members made their attempt on Gaddafi's life. At the same time, G9 had seemed paralysed when faced with reported plans on the part of the Libyans to launch a spectacular terrorist attack. Although we had been prepared to live with the many abuses of power we witnessed during our first postings within the service, hoping that they were localised problems, these latest developments were of a different order. As I've said, we joined the services to stop terrorism, not become involved in it.

During early 1996, David and I discussed at length the pros and cons of going on the record and effectively taking on the secret state. I had had many reservations, mainly because such a decision would irrevocably dislocate our lives. It would inevitably lead to turmoil in our personal lives, frighten our families and friends, and put ourselves at risk of prosecution or possibly worse. Indeed, it would have been very easy to walk away as so many of our colleagues were doing. Contrary to the propaganda in some newspapers, we left MI5 to take up what many would see as prestigious new jobs, working as management consultants. It would have been easier to put everything we had seen behind us and get on with our new lives. David comments:

'After nearly five years working in these conditions – and after much soul-searching, discussion and many angry and frustrating sleepless nights – I decided that someone had to set the record straight about MI5 and its supposed new image. I knew that I might be sent to prison for my actions but that was a risk I was prepared to take.'

But what to do? While serving within MI5, we had raised our concerns wherever possible, even though small-minded MI5 managers watching their backs (*Rectum Defende*) had seen this as evidence that David at least was allegedly a 'troublemaker'. I was also increasingly vocal in my frustration at MI5's inability to learn from mistakes and change. A staff counsellor existed, but he was seen as a joke amongst MI5 staff, and officers who had consulted him were labelled at best 'unreliable' (Joe Hartley) or at worst 'mad' (Cathy Massiter). The staff counsellor also had no remit to investigate allegations of criminal activity. Our line management had also made it clear to us that there was no independent body with the power to investigate our concerns. Don't forget, David had been excluded from a meeting with the Commissioner who was supposed to oversee MI5 warrants because he had criticisms of the handling of the Victoria Brittain case. If there had been an independent route with a guarantee that the crimes reported would be investigated, David would have used it.

But to do nothing meant that the status quo would remain. The intelligence services would continue break the laws of the land, which they are now subject to. They would continue to abuse the rights of the innocent, while failing to protect the British public from terrorist attack. To be a citizen in a democracy brings with it certain rights – and certain responsibilities. It was part of our duty as British citizens to ensure that abuses of power were brought to the attention of the British people through the media.

Many have asked why we did not go directly to ministers, Parliament or the police with our disclosures. There are four principle reasons for this:

- We had been constantly told while still in the service that, under the 1989 OSA, any disclosure outside the service would have been illegal. This was confirmed by the document we signed when we left the service. When David took legal advice from the libertarian lawyer, Geoffrey Bindman, about blowing the whistle, he was again told that there was an absolute rule against disclosure. When finally given the opportunity to give evidence about the MI6/Al Qaeda conspiracy to British police in 2000, David needed the permission of MI5 to report that crime to the police. In other words, to go directly to the police, ministers or MPs without permission would itself have been a crime.
- There was no guarantee that any evidence we gave to ministers would be properly investigated. We already knew that MI5 officers simply lied to the government when faced with pertinent and constructive criticism after the twelve-day delay in the McNulty investigation was bowdlerised in the report to Whitehall. In the case of 'the report that never was' on the lack of intelligence on Libyan support for terrorism, MI5 just refused to send it to ministers.
- David has written many letters to ministers asking them to investigate our evidence but they have chosen not to, despite the glare of the media. What chance would there have been of our disclosures being properly investigated, had we chosen to approach them in private? I only have to look at what happened when I complied with the submission process for this book. I first submitted a draft in November 2003, then submitted another 8,000 words on 1 April 2004. By January 2005, parts of my submissions were still not cleared.
- On submission, the authorities could have injuncted us, preventing any discussion at all of our disclosures by the media and the British public. Again, our suspicions proved correct. Ministers did injunct David,[129] even though there

---

[129] The Order of Mr Justice Hooper, 5 September 1997.

191

was absolutely no evidence to indicate that there had been any damage to national security.

In order to ensure that there was public and Parliamentary awareness of the very serious nature of our disclosures, we decided that David had to go on the record in the media, while I would only make general supporting statements so that at least one of us would be certain to remain free to travel and argue the case. We expected to get a fair hearing. After all, Tony Blair's New Labour had just been elected by a landslide, on a platform of human rights, freedom of information and ethical foreign policy. At the time, he was riding on a wave of popular acclaim. If there was ever a time to make Britain's outdated and anti-democratic system – particularly with regard to the intelligence establishment – more open and accountable, this was it.

In fact, many ministers, including the PM, the Home Secretary, Jack Straw and the then Attorney General, John Morris, had voted against the removal of a public interest defence, when the OSA had been updated in 1989. I also expected that ministers would be outraged by the fact that the secret state had not only compiled files on them but also that it continued to hold private information.

When he was still DG of MI5, Stephen Lander admitted that he had not been entirely open in his dealings with the ISC in Parliament:

'I blanch at some of the things I declined to tell the committee early on,' he said. 'It hasn't always been comfortable. I could not claim to have agreed with all of Mr King's and his colleagues' judgements.'[130]

He seems to believe he should decide what our highly vetted, elected representatives on the ISC are allowed to hear. How

---

[130] *The Daily Telegraph*, 16 March 2001. I have to wonder if some of these early "omissions" were about David's case.

can the ISC then be expected to hold the services effectively to account? It is clear that even if David had risked prosecution by taking his disclosures to the ISC, the committee could not have relied on the DG of MI5 to give them full and frank answers. Under the 1994 Intelligence Services Act, the services can refuse to co-operate with the committee by withholding witnesses and documents. Nor do intelligence officers give evidence to the committee under oath. MI5 and MI6 witnesses can therefore lie with impunity under cross-examination.

I maintain that our assessment of the situation was exactly right. To this day, no government minister or member of the ISC has seen fit to hear our evidence. Considering that this concerns MI6 funding Al Qaeda terrorism, bombs going off needlessly on British streets, and MI5 wanting to lock up innocent individuals up on trumped-up charges, they are clearly failing to do their job. How can they claim that the services work within the rule of law, when they refuse to admit evidence that the services are breaking the law?

'Let's face it,' says David, 'there can be few greater abuses of power than the intelligence services operating outside government control and funding terrorists who are directly opposed to our way of life in an attack which kills and maims innocent people in Libya, which is a secular not an Islamic fundamentalist state. Who would argue that there should be greater sanction for those who talk about terrorism than for those who carry it out? Who would not want to know that their lives had been put at risk by terrorists, simply because the security services were wallowing in their own bureaucratic quagmire?'

But there is one further reason why we needed to go on the record: we were scared. We knew that MI6 officers had conspired to murder individuals in Libya. At the time, we were the only people outside the intelligence services who knew of the plot. In this case, publicity meant a certain level of protection.

193

Countdown to disclosure

In June 1996, David first made contact with the press, after tasking a close friend, Matthew Guarente,[131] to act as a 'cut out' or buffer. He rang around national newspapers offering them the chance to investigate David's disclosures about the service. He chose Nick Fielding of *The Mail on Sunday* (*MoS*) partly because the story would carry more weight if published by the Mail group and partly because Fielding had the time and resources to devote to the story. A few days later, David and Matt met Fielding in the Three Greyhounds pub in Soho. To gauge the reaction, David offered to do a story off-the-record about the files held on businessmen, politicians and celebrities as the counter-subversion section had been finally closed down a few months before. The *MoS* decided not to run the story.

Over the next few months, David continued to meet Fielding. As David began to trust him, he opened up about further breaches of human rights on the part of the services, including the SHADOWER investigation (without mentioning Victoria Brittain by name) and the funding of Islamic terrorists to assassinate Colonel Gaddafi of Libya. He gave only a flavour of the subject matter and did not include any detail. During this time, Fielding suggested that David take documents from MI5 to prove his *bona fides*. David followed his advice, but was careful to choose only documents which summarised intelligence and could not damage our national security. He kept them in a safe place until they were needed.

As there was no sign of progress with the *MoS*, Fielding discussed co-authoring a book, which would inevitably mean David going on the record. A couple of months later, David met Mark Hollingsworth, investigative journalist and author of *Blacklist*, the book David was given on his first day in C3, the vetting section – in yet another clandestine meeting. David then

---

[131] Guarente was one of David's referees.

194

prepared a treatment containing only very general information, which Hollingsworth could show to publishers. At the same time, Hollingsworth consulted Geoffrey Bindman – the lawyer whom MI5 investigated as part of the Brittain case – to seek legal advice on behalf of himself and David. As the treatment did not mention Brittain or Bindman by name, the latter could not know that he was the libertarian lawyer mentioned in it. As expected, the advice indicated that any disclosure by a former MI5 officer would be in breach of the 1989 OSA.

The three met a literary agent in February 1997. From that moment on, they adopted strict telephone security, just in case MI5 did have the phone tapped. The literary agent spent the following couple of months trying to interest publishers in the book, provisionally entitled *MI Farce: Five Years at the Heart of British Intelligence*. We could not simply circulate the proposal for fear that someone would tip off the authorities so the agent discreetly approached a couple of progressive publishers. Both were very interested but one rejected it on the grounds that MI5 would take out an injunction preventing sales; the other could not pay a small advance, which David needed to survive if he were to leave his new job to write the book full time.

As a result, in April 1997 Fielding was tasked to use the treatment to propose to the editor of the *MoS* that David should air his disclosures there. No progress was made over the following months. Hollingsworth then took over. In July 1997, he proposed to Jonathan Holborow, the *MoS* editor, that the newspaper do an exposé which would put pressure on MI5 and allow David to pull together his more serious allegations during the ensuing Parliamentary and media backlash against the services.

Throughout this long drawn-out process I had known these meetings were taking place, but I had stayed at arm's length. David and I had agreed that this would be safer. Even so, it had been a year of tension. Then some odd and apparently disconnected events cranked things up to screaming pitch.

Curious events

At this time in my new job as a management consultant I was doing a project on the application of competency frameworks in the civil service. This involved interviewing all the heads of personnel in the relevant government departments. As I knew all about MI5's problems in this area, I gained permission to visit my old employer.

My old boss, Steve Canute, was now B2/0, head of the personnel section. He had always cultivated the image of a progressive manager by strolling along the MI5 corridors with a management theory book under his arm. I spent an interesting hour discussing his frustration with MI5's lack of willingness to change. He described how the competency framework (eviscerated by senior managers) had finally been rolled out in 1997. However, the budget to support this had been slashed by the DG Stephen Lander and it had achieved minimal impact. Liaison committees between different grades had been abolished, and staff morale was at an all-time low. I was taken aback about how openly he criticised and complained about MI5 and particularly Stephen Lander.

David takes up the story:

'In the meantime, I continued to meet my old MI5 colleagues for drinks at the many leaving parties, which reflected the discontent within. In the best traditions of the spy, I developed a cover story: I told them I was writing a spy novel and actively looking for a publisher (which had some basis in truth as I was actually writing *The Organisation*, an off-the-wall thriller). I then had the ideal explanation if anyone questioned seeing me talking to publishers or other contacts in the media or if my phone was being tapped.

'It was just as well. From the last week in June to the middle of July, a series of strange incidents occurred, which I'm still convinced were connected. It started when I went to yet another farewell party for a capable officer, at the

196

Old Father Thames, a pub across the river from the offices of MI5. Like me, Tom Potter had entered the service as a former journalist and had tried to maintain his motivation and enthusiasm despite seeing incompetent time-servers in senior positions.[132] Like me, he had finally decided to leave after growing deeply disillusioned with the petty bureaucrats. (Incidentally, the vast majority of staff I met that night, even old hands, were either actively looking for jobs or thinking of leaving, factors which stiffened my resolve to go on the record about MI5 and its shortcomings.)

'Word had obviously got around about my novel, as I intended it to. Mitchell, my last senior boss in the service, quizzed me about it at some length. (He even tried to coax more information out of me by declaring that he too intended to write a novel, although when I pressed him about it, he wouldn't reveal details. Some cover story.)

'He was one of the old school with a face the colour and complexion of a cork freshly pulled from a bottle of heavy claret. I remember thinking at the time that it was ironic that he took far more interest in me that evening than he ever had when I was working under him. I then wondered whether top management in MI5 had tasked him to check whether the novel proposal was genuine.

'About ten days later, the Monday of the second week of July 1997, I tried to send a copy of my novel through the post to a long-time and trustworthy friend. On the Wednesday, he phoned to say that he had still not received it and on the Thursday I returned home to find a message on my answering machine from Steve Canute, now B2/0 and head of personnel. It came out of the blue and asked me to return the call. Rather sinisterly, he did not mention why he was phoning. I decided to play it cool and return the call the following week.

---

[132] Potter was told in an annual assessment that he was 'too enthusiastic'. When he complained, he was told to 'learn to curb his independent traits'.

'The next day, on the way to a wedding in Guernsey, Annie and I were stopped by Special Branch at Guernsey airport for no obvious reason other than to let me know they knew, if you see what I mean. The copy of the novel, on floppy disk, was never seen again.

'The following week, I returned the call to B2/0. Again, I was aware that the service had chosen an officer with whom I had worked extensively, whom it thought might be able to weed information out of me. He asked me if I was aware that I had to submit my "book" to them before publication. I quickly corrected him: "You mean my novel," I said and we discussed the mechanics of presentation

'At this point, he admitted MI5 did not have any procedures in place to deal with this situation. He was of course anxious that I submit any work about the service to him because he was personally implicated: he had lied to the authorities about the vital twelve-day delay in the McNulty operation. I told him I was happy to submit the novel before publication.[133]

'We then discussed some of the issues which staff had recently raised and even he attacked the service's management, particularly Stephen Lander, the DG, for its bureaucratic short-sightedness.

'None of these events made any sense. MI5 would not normally alert a target to its interest in such an obvious way. The only logical explanation was that they suspected me of writing a book but my cover story – and the copy of the novel they had presumably intercepted in the post – had convinced them that I was only interested in getting a novel published.

'Of course, I did not know this at the time, so these peculiar events made me more determined to get my disclosures published before MI5 closed in on me, and I became more cautious in my approach to the mechanics

---

[133] David did this in 1999 when he submitted the draft of *The Organisation*.

of that process. I still had to spend another frustrating month waiting, though, while others involved in our plan took their annual holidays around me. By the time Mark Hollingsworth phoned me in the middle of August to say there was good news, I was desperate to complete the task I had started over a year before.'

The early disclosures – *MoS*, 24 August 1997

Under the headline, the 'Truth that must not be hidden about MI5', David recounted mostly low-level information about how the service had wasted large amounts of taxpayers' money on unworthy targets; continued to be obsessed by reds under the bed at the expense of properly investigating terrorism; and was largely unaccountable to Whitehall, Parliament and the public.

I make no apologies for reproducing here a large part of what David told the paper, as it neatly summarises the contents and the thrust of this book. Anyone who has read up to here cannot, I believe, fail to conclude that David accurately reflects what we saw in the service. It is also worth remembering that David was convicted of a criminal offence under section one of the OSA and imprisoned merely for this work he did with the *MoS*:

'I firmly believe [the service] has to change. If it does not, MI5's effectiveness against terrorist organisations will be undermined. I soon discovered that MI5 was an inflexible bureaucracy, unable to shake off the outdated methods used for decades to investigate communism and foreign agents. I realised that while Rimington's profile as a moderniser was an astute tactic to ensure MI5 retained its huge – and unpublished budget – of some £200 million a year, behind the scenes the organisation was dangerously intransigent.

'The MI5 leadership of the 1990s had all cut their teeth under the old regime. Rimington had herself headed the counter-subversion section during the 1984 miners' strike. MI5 was obsessed with Arthur Scargill who even had his own classification – unaffiliated subversive'. ... Long serving officers, who in the real world, would have been sacked years ago, are allowed to serve out their time on pointless exercises, lost in a past when MI5 happily spent tens of thousands of pounds tapping the phones of left-wing activists.

'Ironically, I found that MI5 in the 1990s was a pale imitation of its old Stalinist enemies. Officers were only rewarded if they blindly followed "the party line". I felt new ideas were unwelcome, outmoded status-protecting orthodoxy being preferred. Within a year of joining, one of my closest colleagues – also part of the new intake – had been told to 'learn to curb his independent traits' and was accused of being 'too enthusiastic'. He has since left.

'During much of my time at MI5, the IRA was mounting an intensive terrorist campaign on the British mainland, which cost many innocent lives. As the bombs exploded, our Security Service remained obsessed with pedantic drafting of documents and I questioned whether time would be better spent investigating these terrorist targets.

'There is no doubt that MI5 has proved more effective than the Metropolitan Police in intelligence gathering against the IRA. However, there was always a feeling among the new intake that these successes were in spite of, rather than because of, our inflexible management.

'The IRA aside, I am still concerned about how I was instructed to carry out operations against tiny organisations and harmless individuals who posed no conceivable threat to national security...

'Finally I could take no more. Like half the intake that joined with me, I decided to leave. I could no longer bear the frustrations and pettiness. MI5 gave me a helpful reference to get a new job, so it is not an easy decision to go public with my concerns. During my time inside

MI5 I regularly raised issues with senior officers. But such is the obsession with secrecy my complaints were never taken seriously. The only forum is the Staff Consultative Group, which is filled with management stooges. MI5's official motto is *Regnum Defende* – Defence of the Realm. We always felt a more appropriate wording should be *Rectum Defende* – protect your backside...

'My concern is that MI5 should not remain trapped in a culture which is damaging the service and undermining national security at the expense of the taxpayer. Its obsessive secrecy means there is little or no public overview of its activities or the profligate waste of tens of millions of pounds... There has been for the past two years, a small measure of oversight of MI5. Even though the Parliamentary Security Committee has a limited remit I would be willing to appear before it – either in open session or camera – to disclose my experience of the service.

'Eventually I hope to record my experiences of working for MI5 in a book. I stress that this, like today's report in *The Mail on Sunday*, will not disclose operational details; discuss the precise methods by which MI5 achieves its goals; or compromise the security of MI5's personnel or its agents in the field...

'So a message to Tony Blair: Do not believe MI5 when it launches into its charm offensive to mislead you into believing that I am a troublemaker or my account of my time in MI5 is in some way misleading. I know how MI5 works, how it protects its image by resisting independent scrutiny, even from the rest of the Whitehall Establishment. Be sure to check out what I have revealed for yourself.

'And do not rely on those who have spied on members of your Cabinet to give you an accurate assessment of revelations or an honest account of their activities.'

Peter Mandelson

Under the headline 'MI5 bugged Mandelson', the *MoS* also recounted how MI5 had investigated the former minister without portfolio in the late 1970s when the then Labour government believed that industrial unrest was being fomented by the extreme left.

> 'I saw his file in the months leading up to the 1992 General Election,' David told the paper, 'and was appalled that the Service still had two thick volumes detailing Mandelson's phone conversations from more than a decade earlier. Had Labour won in 1992, a security assessment of Mandelson would have ended up on the desk of the incoming Labour Prime Minister. And it is likely that it was presented to Tony Blair last May when he took power [in 1997].'

David is prepared to admit where he made a mistake. He remembered that Mandelson had returned from a World Festival of Democratic Youth in South America some time in the late 1970s, but asked Fielding to check this fact from public records as it was not clear in his mind. Fielding failed to do so and wrote that Mandelson had come back from Chile in 1976, making him believe that the phone tap took place for three years. In fact, Mandelson actually went to Cuba in 1978. We now therefore believe that the tap took place for a year or so. Although Mandelson has denied that his phone was tapped, DG Stephen Lander told many journalists in non-attributable briefings that Mandelson's calls were certainly listened to.

According to the file, Mandelson had been a member of the Young Communist League in 1972, joining the Communist Party proper a year later. This was at the time the route taken by many into mainstream left-wing politics. But the Foreign Office took a rather different view of Mandelson's involvement in organising the British delegation to the World Federation of Democratic Youth in 1978. Whitehall saw these festivals as an opportunity for the Soviet Union to recruit fifth columnists to subvert the country from within. Indeed anyone who attended such an event, even though they were mainly concerned with cordial relations between the East and West, was considered to be politically suspect.

MI5 began to investigate Mandelson as a suspected 'sleeper', following the pattern of Kim Philby. In the 1930s, Philby's Soviet recruiters told him to play down his communist sympathies in order that he could better infiltrate the upper echelons and most secret recesses of the British state. The telephone tap on Mandelson revealed little of any relevance but did provide the authorities with abundant and detailed information about the activities of political activists and Mandelson's personal life. His file contained little that could be described objectively as subversion. In addition to his Communist Party membership card, it mainly contained photocopies of articles he had written and photographs of him at demonstrations, activities which could hardly be described as 'subversive'. These are the methods of legitimate political discourse and should therefore be of no interest to the security services.

When David assessed Mandelson, his file was still Amber even though there was no actual security information after about 1978. It is hard to fathom why the file was still open in 1992. Worse still, it continues to exist as a source of information which the security services could use to 'persuade' a minister into making decisions in their favour.

'The case that made me quit'

Although the *MoS* described the Libya/DHL courier fiasco as the 'case that made me quit', our decision to leave was part of a wider unease at illegal operations and an inability to stop terrorist attacks even when in possession of timely reporting from reliable sources. As already discussed, the service had received intelligence indicating that the Libyans had sent five terrorists to Britain to launch 'the biggest terrorist attack in history'. Out of respect for national security, David did not put the issue in that context, for fear of compromising the agents who had provided the original intelligence.

One of the five Libyans was disrupted by the classic honey trap sting operation, which G6 hoped would make him vulnerable to a recruitment approach. The article in the *MoS* recounted how an undercover SB officer took the Libyan to a brothel where he was secretly filmed *in flagrante* and smoking dope. Uniformed police then raided the premises. Acting as a concerned friend, the undercover SB officer offered to help the Libyan. He told him that he had a friend in the police who could get the prosecution dropped as long as the Libyan returned the favour. In this instance, he was asked to provide information about Libyan students involved in undesirable or illegal activities in the UK. Realising he had been caught in a trap, the IO confessed to his Libyan controllers who sent him back home.

Some have claimed that this aspect of the *MoS* story might have harmed national security because it revealed a 'sensitive' technique used by MI5. However, the honey trap is as well-known to intelligence services and their targets as an effective way of compromising – and thereby neutralising a target – as it is to those familiar with spy novels and thrillers. Details of such techniques can be found in any guide to espionage.

John Lennon and others

David also recounted to the *MoS* the story of MI5's record of John Lennon. Apart from containing a photograph of the hand-written lyrics of his song *Working Class Hero*, his PF was mainly concerned with problems between the FBI and MI5. When Lennon went to the US in the late 1960s, he applied for a visa to live there permanently. Already known as an activist for songs like *Give Peace a Chance*, Lennon was seen by the then US President Richard Nixon as a dangerous subversive for his opposition to the Vietnam War. Nixon therefore wanted to deny Lennon a visa but under the US Constitution needed a legitimate reason to justify this. The FBI asked MI5 for details of Lennon's 'subversive' activities.

The service already had intelligence indicating that Lennon had supplied funds and support to the Workers' Revolutionary Party and the Official IRA (which at the time was not violent, unlike the PIRA, which later split from it). However, much of the detail did not find its way to the FBI because MI5 had a very sensitive source reporting on the organisation. It feared that the source in the WRP might then be compromised if the FBI or Nixon used it to undermine Lennon in public. Under US freedom of information legislation, Lennon's entire file has been disclosed to the public – apart from the material sent by MI5.

Other matters

In the original article, the *MoS* also reported that:

- Victoria Brittain had been investigated for over a year on the basis of a flawed intelligence case.
- MI5 also held a file on Jack Straw, who was recorded as a '?communist; sympathiser' because of his involvement in left-wing politics when he was president of the National Union of Students from 1969 to 1971.
- MI5 also held a file on then Social Security Secretary Harriet Harman, simply because she was legal director of the NCCL (now Liberty) from 1978 to 1984.
- Charles Elwell, a former head of counter-subversion (who had already been publicly named), had been responsible for the decision to classify members of the executive of Liberty as communist sympathisers as he believed that it was a 'Communist front organisation'.
- In 1983, the service had stood up to requests for information from the then Defence Secretary Michael Heseltine to

undermine the activities of CND and the Greenham Women. Although the service had ten volumes on each, it argued that its intelligence was only concerned with communist penetration of these organisations. It therefore refused to hand over membership lists and details of their political activities.

- Gary Bushell, the *Sun* columnist, had a MI5 file for his membership of the extreme left SWP in the 1970s. He also came to attention for his connections to the extreme right-wing 'Oi!' music movement but the service concluded that he was not a fascist or Nazi sympathiser.

- MI5 opened a file called 'Subversion in contemporary music' to record the activities of bands like the Sex Pistols and UB40 in the 1970s.

- MI5 was badly affected by an endemic drinking culture, which saw one officer almost blow the cover of an operation against a suspected Czech IO and another regularly fall asleep at his desk after lunchtimes in the pub. This article also briefly recounted the story of Michael Bettany, the former MI5 officer who was sentenced to 24 years in prison for giving secrets to an enemy power. Although his drinking problems had been well known to his bosses, they had turned a blind eye and put agents' lives at risk as a result.

- David told the paper it was 'only a matter of time before history repeats itself' with regard to the culture of drunkenness.

The money

David agreed to go on the record with the *MoS*, and we decided to flee the country in August 1997. This would enable him to avoid certain arrest and imprisonment on remand for up to two years, and would give him a chance to ensure that his more serious allegations of crime were investigated by the newly-elected Labour government. Once it was confirmed that the story was going ahead, we had three days to give up our well-paid jobs, our life in London and leave our families and friends with no warning.

After David had agreed to go on the record, the *MoS* offered him £20,000 to help us survive abroad during this uncertain and difficult time. Two days after the story appeared, it was announced that MPSB had been sent in to investigate possible breaches of the OSA. The government's instinctive reaction was to shoot the messenger. Jonathan Holborow, the editor of the *MoS*, realised that the situation was turning nasty, and that we might have to spend more time abroad than we had thought. He then voluntarily offered me, not David, a further £20,000. Given our uncertain future and the fear under which we were living, I gratefully accepted it.

During subsequent negotiations with the authorities, David offered to give all the funds in question back, even the money we had spent surviving abroad, provided he could return to the UK and give his evidence to the government. On David's release from prison in Paris in 1998, when the British government's extradition attempt had failed, he turned down an offer of £20,000 from the *MoS* for his story, although the paper voluntarily made a contribution to his French lawyers for their work. The newspaper also covered our short-term accommodation expenses until we had found a flat of our own in Paris. David says:

'If I was in it for the money, I could quite easily have given information to hostile governments like Libya when I worked in MI5 or when I was released from prison. They would have paid millions for it. In fact, we were approached by an individual claiming to be a representative of the LIS when I was released from prison in France and most vulnerable to a recruitment approach. They offered me millions to betray my country in exchange for information, such as the Lockerbie evidence and the names of MI5 and MI6 agents in Libya. Despite my treatment at the hands of the Blair government, I turned them down. Looking

207

back, I have since come to the conclusion that the Libyan agent was in fact working for MI6 in a sting operation, designed to entrap me into committing treason.'

When David and I returned voluntarily to the UK in August 2000, we also turned down offers of large sums of money from Sunday newspapers for our story. Call us naïve, but we are not venal people.

Newsnight interview

On 25 August 1997, David gave an interview to Michael Crick for the BBC TV programme *Newsnight*. In it, he stated that:

- In preparation for the 1992 General Election, MI5 vetted candidates. The assessments but not the detail were sent to the Prime Minister with recommendations regarding any security threat the individual might pose, if he were made a minister.
- Tam Dalyell, the veteran Labour MP, had an MI5 file.
- PF1 was Eamonn de Valera, the first president of the Irish Republic; PF2 was Vladimir Ilyich Lenin; and PF3, Leon Trotsky.
- Former Prime Minister Ted Heath had a file for his rapprochement with the Eastern bloc.
- MI5 files were reclassified at the end of the 1980s under the 'Traffic Light' system. A green, amber or red card was placed inside the cover of each file to indicate whether it was open for enquiries, filing and observation (green), open for filing and observation (amber) or open for observation only (red).
- MI5 missed out on a chance to finish off the PIRA on the British mainland, after a series of successes in 1993 and 1994.
- David wanted to give evidence to the PM's ISC, even

suggesting that they could come to Europe and interview him if he could not return to the UK for fear of arrest and prosecution.

Chapter 13

The Fallout From the Story

In the week after the story broke, the government spin machine started attacking David's character in the newspapers. In an attempt to undermine his credibility, the papers variously stated that he was a 'Walter Mitty' character; too junior to know what he was talking about; motivated by a grudge; and a traitor. (In subsequent years we have seen the government use this approach against other whistleblowers, including Dr Kelly, Katherine Gun, and Clare Short.)

I was incensed by these attacks. They bore no relation to the man I knew. I gave an interview to the *MoS* in which I backed up David's disclosures and was highly critical of MI5 management. In the article I mentioned one minor 'operational' matter: 'how MI5 spent tens of thousands of pounds staking out an annual social weekend jamboree by the Socialist Workers' Party at Skegness'.[134]

At the same time, the government told Jonathan Holborow, the *MoS* editor, that it was threatening to 'send in the heavies' unless he disclosed what the *MoS* planned to run the following weekend. Holborow refused, citing free speech arguments, so the government obtained a temporary injunction against both David and the *MoS* at an impromptu hearing in a judge's home. It prevented the media from revealing any information about David's time in MI5 not in the public domain. Seven years

---

[134] *MoS*, 31 July 1997.

later, the 'temporary' injunction is still in place against David, although it has been dropped against the *MoS*.

While the government was making this threat, MPSB had conducted a counter-terrorist-style search of our Pimlico flat (although we were not to realise this until a month later, when under the headline 'MI5 sends in the "heavies" ', the *MoS* reported that MPSB had smashed up our home)[135]. In their quest for evidence, MPSB had smashed up furniture and lamps, pulled the bath apart, and ripped up the carpets. They found no evidence, but took sack-loads of personal possessions, including bed sheets, underwear, love letters and other personal memorabilia, even though the warrant only permitted them to take material 'which is evidence of an offence under the OSA or relating to money paid by the *MoS*'. Ironically, they had found my report of my meeting in June with Steve Canute, clearly entitled 'Meeting with Head of Personnel, Security Service (MI5)'. This they left carefully fanned out on the dining room table for me.

Around the same time, MI5's DG sent a letter to serving and former MI5 officers instructing them not to speak to the media in support of David. They were reminded of their obligations under the 1989 OSA and their crown servant contract and would face prosecution if they did so.

On 31 August 1997, early editions of the *MoS* carried the story of the injunction. At the time, editors rightly saw this as a gross infringement of the freedom of the press. The next edition led on my interview. That evening, Princess Diana died and the world's media was given over to the reporting of her death.

Some comments on the Paris crash

Before we look at the authorities' reaction to the disclosures, I would like to say a few words about the tragic car crash which

---

[135] *MoS*, 21 September 1997.

killed Princess Diana and Dodi Al Fayed under the Pont de L'Alma in August 1997.

Like many British people, when David and I first learnt of the deaths of Princess Diana and Dodi Al Fayed, we thought the crash in Paris was a terrible accident caused by paparazzi photographers pursuing the two at high speeds through the streets of Paris. Although Princess Diana – and her former lover James Hewitt – had both claimed to be under MI5 surveillance in the years before the crash, I knew that this was not true. I knew that MI5's surveillance teams had been deployed against legitimate targets during the periods in question. This begged the question: who exactly was following Diana at this time.

When the Squidgygate tapes had emerged in the mid-1990s, David made his own enquiries to see if it was possible that GCHQ had recorded their conversations. He learnt that prior to 1994, when GCHQ was put on a legal footing, it routinely tapped mobile phones without a warrant. (It was not clear how long after the practice continued.) His enquiries also established that it is very easy to tap mobile phones. Any surveillance team with a commercially available scanner can pick up the microwaves as they make their way from the handset to the telephone masts. This is not illegal. The 1985 IOCA and the 2000 Regulation of Investigatory Powers Act only apply to tapping on the public telephone network. As no warrant is needed in either of the above cases, private conversations can be intercepted without the involvement of the mobile phone company (who will not tap a phone without a warrant for fear of losing their government licence) and crucially without the knowledge of ministers who are supposed to hold the services to account.

'Having looked at the available evidence, I am personally inclined to think that MI6 paid to have Diana and Dodi involved in an accident in the same way they paid to have Gaddafi assassinated, using a "surrogate",' says David. 'Because Diana was either getting married to Dodi or she was pregnant, the authorities planned the crash to ensure

213

she was taken away from the Al Fayed family or that she lost her unborn child. The only reason I don't believe that the authorities didn't actually aim to assassinate her was that they did not want to make her a martyr at the expense of the royal family – as actually happened. While this was probably an operation which had been planned for a while, the timing of the car crash conveniently ensured that my disclosures were forgotten in the media coverage of the tragic events in Paris.

'If the authorities hadn't taken my evidence, I had planned to bombard them with further disclosures through the media until they did. Once Princess Diana was dead, we had no protection from the press. I managed to factor most problems into my plans but I could never have envisaged anything on this scale. It was always going to be an uphill struggle after that.'

The vast majority of the British people of course now believe that the crash was no accident. Although the British media continues to call the matter a 'conspiracy theory', there is compelling information to indicate that events were anything but accidental. For example, eyewitnesses to the crash reported seeing a white Fiat Uno in the tunnel at the precise moment when there was a bright flash of light which led to the crash. Mohammed Al Fayed's team have traced the white Fiat Uno to James Andanson, a paparazzo. In August 1998 former MI6 officer Richard Tomlinson gave a sworn statement about Andanson's connections to MI6,[136] which has a long record of using journalists and photographers as agents. Other paparazzi have backed up the story.

When interviewed by French police, Andanson claimed not to have been in Paris that night. Yet forensics carried out by Mohammed Al Fayed's security teams on the vehicle and the

---

[136] Tomlinson's statement to Herve Stephan, the French judge investigating the Paris crash, 28 August 1998.

214

crash tunnel indicated that the white Fiat Uno had been in the tunnel and had been sold just hours after the crash. This clashes with French police enquiries. When they went to interview Andanson, as a suspected owner of the white Fiat Uno in question, they found a white Fiat Uno but it was on blocks and had not been roadworthy for some time. These two pieces of forensics are not mutually exclusive. If Andanson had owned the white Fiat Uno seen in the tunnel, he could have sold it before French police came to interview him and replaced it with another, which the French police then tested. Anyone who thinks this is fanciful should bear in mind that intelligence operatives are trained to cover their tracks.

More worryingly, six months later Andanson was found dead in a burnt out car in the South of France, 400 miles from where he was supposed to be. The authorities have claimed that he committed suicide, although his death has all the hallmarks of an intelligence service assassination. Arson is used by less reputable intelligence operatives across the world to destroy forensics and cover their tracks in the same way they use car crashes to remove obstinate dissidents and other so-called subversives.

In fact, vehicle 'accidents' are used as a way of assassination precisely because they are such a common cause of death. It is very easy for the authorities to claim that anyone crying foul play is simply a 'conspiracy theorist'. Tomlinson has also provided some backing for this. He told the French judge that he had seen MI6 plans to assassinate Slobodan Milosevic, the former Serbian President, in a car crash by blinding his driver with a bright flash in a tunnel, exactly the same *modus operandi* used for the Paris crash. 'It was the ideal scenario,' said Tomlinson, 'the investigation would have concluded that it was an ordinary road accident.'[137]

French enquiries have also established that Henri Paul, the driver of Diana and Dodi's car and a security manager at the

---

[137] *Info Dimanche*, 17 September 1998.

Ritz Hotel, had bank accounts which received frequent cash deposits, indicating that he was working for a number of intelligence services. Tomlinson also told the investigating judge that, in 1992, he saw a file which confirmed that the security manager at the Ritz in Paris was an MI6 agent. However, he could not be certain that it referred to Henri Paul.

But if one matter convinces David and me that MI6 is implicated in the crash, it is the involvement of Oswald or Oscar Le Winter, a conman and intelligence nuisance with connections to MI6. In April 1998, Oscar or Oswald Le Winter tried to sell an alleged telegram indicating CIA and MI6 collusion in the assassination to the Al Fayed family for $20 million. Intelligence experts concluded the documents were crude forgeries. The CIA has denied that Le Winter ever worked for them in any capacity. MI6 has never made a similar denial. The sting using fabricated documents is a classic technique used by MI6's IOPs. It encourages the victim to use what appear to be intelligence documents to confirm what he is saying. When the documents are revealed as fakes, his entire case falls apart in front of the British public. Such exposure makes it more difficult for the public to accept genuine documents, should they later appear.

Nearly a year after the crash in June 1998, David was banned from a programme about it, following a letter from lawyers representing MI5 and the government. Never one to miss out on an opportunity to undermine David, the government lawyer commented: 'I am instructed that, in fact, the Security Service of which Mr Shayler was a member is not responsible for the protection of dignitaries.' But David had not told the programme any such thing. He had made it absolutely clear that although MI5 did not protect dignitaries itself, it did provide intelligence and assessments on the threat to any member of the royal family to help police. David had also worked closely with officers from SB and MI6 who do have a role in protection. It was yet another vindictive act on behalf of the authorities.

Life in exile

On 20 September 1997, a month after we went on the record, a month spent 'on the run' travelling around Europe, I flew back voluntarily from Barcelona to face arrest. I did not know when I would see David again, as the police could take my passport as a condition of bail if they decided to charge me. I was travelling with my lawyer, John Wadham of Liberty, who had informed MPSB that I was turning myself in and even which flight I was on. At first, they were happy for me to make my way to Charing Cross police station and be interviewed. At the last minute this changed, I believe on the instructions of MI5. When I arrived at Gatwick, five burly SB officers, some of whom I knew and liked, stepped forward as I reached the immigration desk. I do not know who was more embarrassed. I was arrested on suspicion not only of breaking the OSA but also of money laundering. The latter charge was based on the fact that David and I had a joint bank account.

I was held at Charing Cross and subjected to questioning for six hours but was not charged. However, I was required to return a month later on police bail. Two days later, SB arrested two of David's friends, Matt Guarente and Graham Dunbar, in dawn raids on trumped-up money laundering charges. They were also questioned and required to answer police bail. SB also attempted to arrest David's brother, Phil, but he was on holiday at the time. In an attempt to trace him, MPSB visited the offices of IBM, where Phil worked, and told his bosses that he was wanted for 'security irregularities'. The repercussions reached all the way to head office in America. He later attended Charing Cross police station voluntarily. He was arrested there and required to answer police bail the following month. Their 'crimes' were to have held money for us which could be sent on wherever we were in Europe. Matt and Phil were kept on police bail until December. Graham and I had to answer bail until March the following year, although none of us was ever charged.

Following my release I spent a week packing up our flat in

Pimlico, which had been comprehensively smashed up during the police search, and reassuring our families. In late September, I had mysterious instructions to travel to a small backwater in central France called La Souterraine, where David said he would meet me. On a dark, rainy night he came to meet me and took me to a remote farmhouse in an area called La Creuse. This was to be our refuge for the next ten months. During this time, we tried to resolve our situation, but found that neither the government nor bodies responsible for the intelligence services were interested in receiving our evidence.

The ISC and Cabinet Office review

When the story broke in the *MoS*, David offered to give his evidence to the authorities. As well as refusing to take his evidence, the government took out the temporary injunction to prevent the UK press from reporting any further disclosures. (This injunction is still in place over seven years later.) On 10 October 1997, John Wadham, the director of Liberty, wrote to Tom King, the Chairman of the PM's ISC, on his behalf. The committee is notionally responsible for holding the intelligence services to account, but cannot order witnesses to appear or documents to be disclosed. It ignored him, repeatedly refusing to take his evidence of conspiracy to murder on the part of the services. Even though the committee had declined to hear his information, this did not stop some of its members choosing to attack his character during the debate about the intelligence services in November 1998 (see below for more details). At that time, David was in prison in Paris awaiting the result of the UK extradition request and was therefore unable to defend himself.

In October 1997, the government tasked a Cabinet Office committee to look at many aspects of the intelligence agencies. John Alpass, a recent DDG of MI5, chaired the committee. In January 1998, Liberty wrote to the committee, asking that it look at our evidence as it might inform the committee's decisions with regard to the agencies. At first, the committee refused to take David's evidence because of the injunction, but backed down when the media pointed out the absurdity of this position. In refusing to take David's evidence, he provided yet further proof that there was no legal route to disclosure.

David takes up the story:

'In February 1998, I submitted a 6,000-word dossier detailing management problems in MI5 to the committee. In the covering letter, I mentioned that I had evidence of operational malpractice, which had led to the unnecessary loss of lives, but felt there would be real dangers in submitting such a sensitive document via the postal service, fax or e-mail. I therefore asked the committee to suggest a way in which I could submit the document to them. Although I did not refer to it specifically, I saw this as a way of making other parts of government aware of the MI6-funded plot to assassinate Colonel Gaddafi. As the committee did not reply either to Liberty or me, I was unable once again to submit my evidence.'

The negotiations

In late December 1997 David, represented by Liberty, entered into negotiations with the government to secure his return to the UK without arrest and imprisonment. As a pre-condition of entering the negotiations, he offered not to make any new disclosures or to write a book about MI5, and to pay back the expenses he had received form the *MoS* in order to survive abroad. He also voluntarily handed back the documents he had taken to prove his *bona fides*. MI5 had not even noticed that he had taken them. The authorities took two months to reply to the first draft of the negotiating terms sent to them. After that, Liberty sent the authorities a negotiating timetable. The authorities failed to meet any of the deadlines set and never once expressed an interest in getting round a table with David to try to resolve the issue.

In all the negotiations David made it absolutely clear that he wanted to give his evidence to ministers or the PM's ISC or even, as a last resort, to the head of MI5. In fact, he kept asking to meet the head of MI5 as he had vital information to impart about MI6's funding of Al Qaeda.

Before David had entered into the negotiations, the *MoS* and he decided to test the provisions of the injunction, which allowed them to make a legal disclosure about intelligence by submitting information to the authorities for clearance before publication. Once again, it only served to demonstrate that the instinct of ministers was to protect the services from proper scrutiny.

Parliament's response

Over a year later, after David had been thrown in prison in France at the request of the British government, Parliament was allowed for the first time to debate the annual report on the agencies – albeit a censored version – prepared by the PM's ISC. In the debate, the then Foreign Secretary, Robin Cook, chose to attack David – without overtly naming him – rather than explain the enquiries he had made to get to the bottom of David's legal disclosures about the MI6/Al Qaeda conspiracy:

'Today, the extravagant rewards that can be gained from an exclusive deal with a newspaper or book publisher can provide a bigger payout for disloyalty than the KGB ever offered. Moreover, it does not necessarily come with the same insistence on accuracy that the KGB might have required.'[138]

---

[138] Hansard, 2 November 1998, p. 584.

220

I wish Robin Cook luck with his own recently published memoirs.

In the same debate, Allan Rogers, a member of the ISC and MP for Rhondda, said:

'One person wrote to a newspaper to say that we had sought not to protect whistleblowers like himself, who spoke out in the public interest. I am wary of those who claim to be whistleblowers in the public interest, but who accept £80,000 or £100,000 or a contract to write a book... If the individual to whom I have referred had wanted to speak purely for love of country, there are mechanisms by which he could have done so. I accept that the mechanisms are not perfect.'[139]

David has never sought protection from the ISC. He has though asked its members to look at his evidence – which they have ignored – rather than condemning him on the word of the intelligence services. Mr Rogers is, of course, inaccurate regarding the sums he mentions. In addition, there are no mechanisms for bringing matters of public interest to the attention of those who matter.[140] If David had made his disclosures to the PM's ISC, he would still have been guilty of an offence under the OSA.

On top of all this, soon after the extradition attempt failed and David was released from prison in Paris, a member of the ISC, Michael Mates MP, erroneously stated on French television that David was motivated by spite, as he had been sacked from MI5.

If members of the ISC peddle this level of inaccuracy to Parliament, how can Parliament have any confidence in the ISC's claim to be an effective form of oversight of the agencies?

In addition, nearly all the subjects discussed in the debate

---

[139] Hansard, 2 November 1998, p. 598.
[140] The documents that MI5 was obliged to disclose at David's trial confirmed that there were no routes to making a legal disclosure at the time of David going on the record.

were issues David had raised in his original disclosures to the *MoS*:

- Accountability and effectiveness of oversight.
- The lack of personnel management leading to demoralisation of staff.
- File destruction.
- Adapting to post-Cold War threats.
- Whether the services represent value for money.

As such, they almost justify his decision to go on the record and make a wider audience aware of the shortcomings of the intelligence services. It is only the secrecy which protects the services that prevents us knowing how far they have reacted to David's criticisms. Once again, secrecy is being used to hide the potential embarrassment of officials, not to protect secrets.

Of course, if the ISC was properly exercising its functions, one of its members might have used this opportunity to tell us what it had done to investigate David's disclosures over the MI6-funded Al Qaeda attack on Colonel Gaddafi. It might for example be helpful to know whether the agencies co-operated with the ISC enquiries, if indeed there were any. Disclosure of this can hardly be said to damage national security. But it was never even mentioned. As Chris Mullin, MP for Sunderland, pointed out during the debate,

> 'People who serve on such committees [the PM's ISC] sometimes have the distressing tendency to go native after a while.'[141]

Letter to publishers

A month after this debate, on 1 December 1998, the government's

---

[141] Hansard, 2 November 1998, p. 604.

legal representatives wrote to all the major publishers in London asking them to abide by the terms of the injunction, which were attached to the letter. The letter sought to 're-emphasise the basis on which [the injunctions] were issued' but added the government's assertion that David's disclosures damaged national security. The judge who granted the injunction and the police investigating the case stated specifically in their reports that this was not the case. In addition, if the disclosures had damaged national security, the government would have been duty bound to prosecute the *MoS* under section 5 of the OSA. As *MoS* journalists were not even arrested, we can only conclude that there was absolutely no evidence whatsoever of damage to national security.

The letter was clearly designed to make publishers think that there would be damage to national security in anything they published by David, whether fact or fiction. This clearly goes beyond the terms of the injunction and is an infringement of the right to freedom of expression. Publishers wishing to act responsibly were therefore deterred from even speaking to him. In fact, one publisher had approached David shortly after his release from prison with a view to publishing the novel he had written, called *The Organisation*, but quickly dropped it after the letter was sent.

Chapter 14

The Israeli Embassy Bombing and the Gagging Orders

In October 1997, David and the *MoS* made their first submission under the injunction. The then Home Secretary, Jack Straw, was rather oblique in his response. However, it still opened up a whole can of worms, which may yet rebound on ministers, judges and MI5.

Background

When you step into any issue relating to the Middle East conflict, you will inevitably be accused of taking sides, of becoming a pawn in a political game. Some Jewish people have, for example, accused David of making his disclosures with regard to the Israeli Embassy bombing out of sympathy for Palestinian terrorists. So, first, let me state that David and I support the state of Israel (within 1967 borders) as the only true democracy in the Middle East. We have enormous respect for the Jewish people and their values, while condemning the Israeli government's continued flouting of UN resolutions mandating them to withdraw from the Occupied Territories.

Where innocent Israelis are victims of terrorism or their security is threatened, we have spoken out. This is why we felt that David should speak out about MI5's failure to prevent the

Embassy bombing in July 1994. We believed that MI5 was incapable of protecting the Israeli Embassy – a high-profile target at the best of times – from terrorist operations in the same way that the service was incapable of protecting the British people. This is another reason why David spoke out about the MI6 funding of Al Qaeda in Libya. If that country had become the first vehemently anti-Western Islamic extremist state, then only Egypt would have stood between Al Qaeda and Israel.

Directly because of David's allegations about MI5's bungling in the run-up to the Israeli Embassy bombing, the case of the two Palestinians convicted of conspiracy to carry out the attack, Samar Alami and Jawed Botmeh, was referred to the Court of Appeal and later the House of Lords. MI5 – and a number of other organisations – failed to disclose to the trial judge two documents vital to their defence, so vital that any jury member who had seen them would have been obliged to acquit the two. The trial judge never reached the stage of considering whether these documents would qualify for a Public Interest Immunity certificate or 'gagging order'.[142] Alami and Botmeh were therefore convicted in a wholly unfair trial.

At the time, David believed this was a cock-up on the part of MI5:

'I don't believe MI5 deliberately hid the document away to pervert the course of justice or cover up, for example, Mossad's unofficial activities in Britain, as some have suggested,' he wrote in *Punch* magazine, '...I do believe, however, that it was an honest mistake on the part of MI5 and others. Mistakes happen in the services just as they do anywhere else. The difference is the reaction to them. Where other organisations deal with problems, MI5 routinely uses secrecy to cover up its cock-ups... I cannot be so

---

[142] PIIs are ministerial certificates which prevent the defence from seeing material that might prejudice the national interest at trial. To be lawful, the trial judge must see the material and rule whether the state's decision to withhold it would lead to an unfair trial.

sure that Mossad did not frame the two, as there is evidence to indicate that they did.'

Samar Alami and Jawed Botmeh have remained behind bars for ten years because they were denied access to not one but *two* pieces of evidence which could have proved their innocence. At the same time, senior British judges in the Court of Appeal and the House of Lords failed to quash the conviction in the light of the new and compelling evidence.

Summary

Just after midday on 26 July 1994, a bomb went off in an Audi car outside the Israeli Embassy in London. That night, another bomb went off outside Balfour House, Finchley, the home to a number of Jewish groups and a deeply symbolic target since the Balfour Declaration in 1927 had led to the creation of the state of Israel 20 years later. In all, 19 people were injured but there were no fatalities. Shortly after, a previously unknown group calling itself the Palestinian Resistance Jaffa Group claimed responsibility for the attack.

In January 1995, police arrested Botmeh and Alami along with two other Palestinians, Nadia Zekra and Mahmoud Abu-Wardeh. Forensic work linked Botmeh to one of the cars involved in the incident, but only because he had helped an individual calling himself Reda Moghrabi to buy it. Despite this, Botmeh and Zekra were then charged with conspiracy to cause explosions and remanded in custody until the trial. Alami and Abu-Wardeh were released without charge.

Two months later, Alami was again arrested but this time she was charged with conspiracy to cause explosions, although she and Zekra were later released on bail. A month after she was released, police found low-density explosives (not linked to the Embassy bomb) in a locker Alami was renting from a branch of the Nationwide in west London. In June 1995, the

227

Anti-Terrorist Squad arrested Alami again and remanded her in custody. Later that summer, Abu-Wardeh was charged with conspiracy to cause explosions and was remanded in custody until the trial. When the trial began in October 1996, the judge immediately acquitted Zekra due to lack of evidence.

In December 1996, the jury acquitted Abu-Wardeh but Alami and Botmeh were found guilty of conspiracy to cause explosions and sentenced to 20 years each in prison.

How David heard of the failure to prevent the bombing

When David joined G Branch in October 1994, the fourth floor of Thames House was buzzing with a strange tale of how vital intelligence had been lost in the run-up to the attack on the Israeli Embassy in July 1994. He did not see the contents of the actual report but became aware that there was a Branch enquiry into the matter and heard accounts of what had happened from many different people in the section. They were all saying the same thing: in the weeks[143] before the incident, G9B/4 Jane Richards,[144] an officer in the counter-Iranian section, had received a warning of an attack on the Israeli Embassy in London. It was not an anonymous tip-off, the kind of tittle-tattle that routinely drifts across spooks' and hacks' desks and is worthless in investigative terms. It was a report from a reliable and well-placed secret source (presumably reporting on some aspect of the Iranian target, as G9B counters threats from the Iranian state and Iranian opposition groups).

Richards did not react to the report even though it came from a reliable source and the Israeli Embassy was assessed to be a prominent potential target for Palestinian terrorist groups

---

[143] In the *MoS* coverage of 2 November 1997, Nick Fielding claimed David had said it was 'days' before. He did not check this with David before it appeared. David has always made it clear it was some weeks before.

[144] The fictional name we used in the draft submitted to MI5 has been changed on the orders of the service.

and their fellow travellers. There are reasons for this. Most obviously, she may have been complacent. After all, at the time, there hadn't been an Arab terrorist attack in the UK for many years. She may have thought she had longer to react. But the point is, she didn't.

The issue of the missing warning was raised when G6, the agent-running section, failed to receive its feedback form. For each source report, there are three copies. One remains with the originating section, G6. Two further copies – one white, one blue – go to the desk officer, who checks the names of those who appear against service records. The officer then assesses, grades and comments on the new intelligence. The desk officer's white copy is filed on an investigative and/or personal file. The blue form is then returned to the agent-running section to provide feedback to the agent's handler. Once there, it is filed with other reports produced by the same agent. If the blue copy is not returned to the agent-running section within the month, it is chased it up.

In this case, G6 did not receive its blue copy, so in line with routine G6 approached Jane Richards to establish its whereabouts. She claimed to have passed it on but enquiries established that the service's document audit system, STAR, had no record of the report being handed on to another officer. G9B officers searched their section room only to find the missing report in a security cupboard belonging to G9B/12 Elizabeth Botolph. In the enquiry into the matter, Botolph denied putting it there. David explains:

'I do not claim to know exactly what happened but we can speculate. Panicked by the prospect of a career-threatening black mark for failing to warn others of the imminent attack, Richards hid the report in G9B/12's security cupboard. This was not difficult. Security cupboards generally remained open during the day and few officers followed the rules on locking them in short absences. Rather than draw attention to the report and her own failure to react,

Richards – I believe – hoped the report would be forgotten in the attendant chaos which accompanies any new post-incident investigative work.'

If the report had come in any other form, there would have been no reason for it to be traced. It could have been easily forgotten. Only the service's procedures for handling source reports caught Richards out.

Ministers abuse first use of submission under injunction

In accordance with the temporary injunction, in October 1997 the *MoS* submitted to the Home Office the draft of an article written by Nick Fielding[145] based on David's account. Later that month, the government wrote to the editor of the *MoS* to allow him to publish the article. In that letter, the Home Secretary did not deny the details of David's disclosure, but did state:

'Having discussed with the Security Service the allegations in the draft article I can say that it is not the case that such information as the Security Service had in their [*sic*] possession would have enabled it to prevent the Israeli Embassy bombing from happening. I can see, however, how Mr Shayler as a junior officer not involved in that area of work at the time, could have gained this mistaken impression. You should be aware that if I am asked about the article, that is how I shall respond.'[146]

A number of issues arise from this. It is clear that David's disclosures have not been independently investigated. Instead,

---

[145] Although Fielding had been given some details of the failure at his initial debrief in August 1997, he did not check the article with David before submission and publication in October/November 1997.

[146] Straw's letter to the *MoS*, 30 October 1997.

the Home Secretary 'discussed' the matter with MI5, an interested party in David's dispute with the authorities. Also, it is obvious that if the intelligence had not been mislaid, it could have been acted upon in some way:

- Security around the Embassy could have been increased.
- The Israelis could have been tipped off to be more vigilant.
- MI5 could have made further enquiries of the source and investigated the group named in the report and its members.

When put in a corner like this where there is no *independent* scrutiny, MI5 is incapable of admitting its mistakes. In this case, it has no other option than to present the information in the best light possible in discussions with government. If that means being 'economical with the truth' at the expense of the public interest, justice, the rule of law, and a whistleblower's reputation, then inevitably MI5 will react in this way.

I maintain that David did not take his original disclosures to the government for fear that exactly this would happen. In fact Straw – himself the subject of an MI5 file – should have been acting as an impartial referee between David and MI5. Instead, he wrote:

'such information as the Security Service had in their [*sic*] possession'

instead of

'The Security Service did have information in its possession warning of an attack on the Israeli Embassy.'

In fact, Straw did not deny the fact that intelligence existed – or indeed that it had been mislaid – merely the *interpretation* or assessment of that intelligence. As we have seen in the now-infamous September dossier in the run-up to the Iraq war, the authorities can cherry-pick intelligence to support any assessment

231

they want. In that instance, they sexed it up by omission. In David's submission, they sexed it down, again by omission.

Straw also denied an allegation that David had not even made. At no point did he say that the warning could definitely have prevented the bombing. In fact, until the actual perpetrator of the attack is detected – Alami and Botmeh were convicted only of conspiracy and have alibis for the day of the attack – the government is in no position to come to any definitive conclusion regarding the relationship between the document in question and the attack.

Interestingly, the press briefings seem to have gone further than what Straw was prepared to write in his letter. It would seem inconceivable that both the *Times* and *Telegraph* journalists misheard the Home Office briefing. Straw's letter to the *MoS* certainly did not say that David's claim was untrue, yet *The Times* and *The Telegraph* had clearly been briefed that it did:

'Further accusations of MI5 "bungling" from the former intelligence desk officer David Shayler were published yesterday after the Home Secretary decided that they were untrue and therefore could not damage national security.'[147]

'Jack Straw, the Home Secretary, allowed a newspaper to report that MI5 was warned about a bomb attack on the Israeli embassy in London because intelligence chiefs assured him that the claim was not true.'[148]

Cock-up and cover-up

Faced with public knowledge that a warning of an attack on the Israeli Embassy had not been acted upon – the cock-up – MI5 and the authorities tried to discredit David by briefing heavily against him off-the-record – the cover-up. But the

[147] Michael Evans, *The Times*, 3 November 1997.
[148] Michael Smith, *The Daily Telegraph*, 3 November 1997. See also Chapter 15, *The MI6/Al Qaeda conspiracy, part 2*, Foreign Secretary's comments.

authorities cocked it up again. In their desire to discredit David rather than listen to him, they had unwittingly admitted they had evidence relevant to any jury at trial: 'I can see, however, how Mr Shayler as a junior officer not involved in that area of work at the time, could have gained this *mistaken* impression.' The Home Secretary is in no position to judge whether this is a mistaken impression, as the actual perpetrators of the attack were not caught. In trying to undermine David's character, Straw unwittingly admitted that anyone could have gained this impression, including any jury member.

Further enquiries with Gareth Peirce, the lawyer for Alami and Botmeh, established that the document in question had not been disclosed at the original trial or been excused from disclosure by the trial judge and a PII certificate. Legal procedure had certainly been breached. Ministers should, of course, have ordered that the case be referred to the Court of Appeal immediately. It tarnishes the British legal system if victims of obvious miscarriages of justice are left to rot behind bars as if nothing has happened. But that is what occurred. David takes up the story:

'I have spent in total almost six months in prison for making my disclosures. That short period was bad enough. God knows how Alami and Botmeh felt, waiting to see if the government would acknowledge to a court information it had already given to the media, information that might still secure their release from prison.'

On reading the article in the *MoS*, Gareth Peirce wrote to the CPS to try to sort out their case. She was not to receive a satisfactory reply for a year.

Another undisclosed document

In July 1998, in David's last full week of freedom before he was arrested in Paris with a view to extradition, he met Paul

233

Foot, the investigative journalist who had taken an increasing interest in the Israeli Embassy case.

Foot had already had a piece published calling for the material to be disclosed to the defence immediately. David told Foot:

'There is another document which may not have been disclosed or was not covered by the gagging orders issued at the original trial. I recall reading it on my first day in G9A in October 1994. In it, a senior manager, Andrew Knight[149] recorded his findings based on his research into the investigation. This may sound hard to believe, but he assessed that the *Israelis themselves* were responsible for the bomb, in order to persuade the British authorities to increase the security around the Embassy.

'This is not as strange as it sounds. Shortly before the attack on the Israeli Embassy in Britain, nearly a hundred people had died in an attack on the Jewish Mutual Association building in Buenos Aires. As a result, the Israelis – worried at the best of times over what they still see as the large presence of former Arab terrorists who have sought asylum in London – were more paranoid about security than ever.'

Foot told David that this tied in with information he had heard. Alami and Botmeh had told police that they knew an individual called Reda Moghrabi, who had gone with Botmeh to buy the car which had subsequently been used to carry out the Israeli Embassy attack. Moghrabi had disappeared but the families of Alami and Botmeh now suspected he was an Israeli agent who had framed the two. Experts have commented that the actual attacks were likely to have been done by professionals, as no traces of the explosives were left. So were officers of Mossad, the Israeli equivalent of MI6, the professionals involved in the attack?

Mossad has no intelligence presence in Britain for the same reasons that Libya, North Korea and Iran are not allowed to have

---

[149] G9/1, G9/0, Paul Mitchell's deputy.

intelligence representatives in the UK. Their presence is likely to undermine rather than bolster the security of the British state. From time to time, Mossad asks to have an official presence in the UK but it is turned down each time on the recommendation of the British intelligence services, as it simply cannot be trusted. However, this does not stop Mossad from sending over undeclared, undercover IOs to gather information on Arab targets and their activities in Britain. From time to time, undeclared Mossad officers are detected by MI5 and quietly asked to leave the country. During our time in G Branch, an undeclared Mossad operative had moved to the north-east of England, where he had come to attention for threatening Arab dissidents. He was expelled on the recommendation of G9.

Alami and Botmeh have never disputed the fact that they had access to weapons and low-density bomb-making equipment. But they argue the material connected to them was left by Moghrabi to be used in experiments, a few days before the Israeli Embassy was bombed. As electrical and chemical engineers, the two explained they had tested the suitability of components and delivery methods of bombs to be used against the Israelis only in the Occupied Territories.

If the jury had accepted that the material was destined for the West Bank and the Gaza Strip, the two could not have been convicted of conspiracy to cause explosions under the PTA. At the time, PTA only applied to conspiracies to cause explosions in the UK (although the government has since changed this). More importantly, Alami and Botmeh's interest in explosives could have brought them to the attention of Mossad, the most likely arm of the Israeli state to have carried out any deniable attack in the UK. Mossad could therefore easily have framed the two.

There is further information to support this version of events. According to *The Sunday Times*, Mossad was in London to warn of an attack on the Embassy by Hezbollah a couple of weeks before it happened.[150] Were they putting out disinformation

---

[150] *The Sunday Times*, 13 July 1994.

235

to cover up their own attack on the Embassy? Or is it collateral (or corroboration) for the evidence which was kept from the jury who convicted Alami and Botmeh? Either way, this article supports the innocence of Alami and Botmeh.

Failure to disclose material at trial

Of course, the real reason for ministers' tardiness in this case became apparent a week after David's meeting with Foot in July 1998. The government knew that any jury trying David would see the public interest in divulging information pointing to a miscarriage of justice. It therefore decided to head David off at the pass. It requested his extradition, I believe, with two clear aims: to shut him up and to have him convicted before he was independently vindicated. In the context of the Alami and Botmeh case, I believe the government planned to refer their grounds for appeal to the courts only after David had been convicted.

Unfortunately for the government, things didn't quite go to plan. In November 1998, the French Appeal Court (and later the Supreme Court) refused to extradite David because it recognised that his offence was political. With no prospect of getting him back, the government finally had to do the decent thing and apply for a PII certificate to cover material which remained relevant but had not put before a jury or been seen by the judge at the original trial in late 1995. Shortly after David walked free from a French prison, nearly a year after Peirce first wrote to the CPS, a date was finally set for a PII hearing in March 1999.

In March 1999, the Home Secretary presented the signed gagging orders to the court. It is of great concern that MI5 did not submit this information at the original trial and that ministers have sought to keep it secret because:

• The mislaid intelligence warned of an attack, identifying a group unconnected to the two people convicted of conspiracy to cause the attack. Given that there is no firm evidence linking Alami and Botmeh to the actual bombing, this information would inevitably have created 'reasonable doubt' in the minds of jury members, who would then have been obliged to acquit the two.

- The other undisclosed document recorded a senior MI5 officer's assessment that the Israelis themselves were responsible for the attack, supporting the theory that Mossad framed the two. Under the rules of disclosure, a belief based on evidence is disclosable to the defence. Again, evidence of Mossad or Israeli involvement in the attack would have led the jury to acquit Alami and Botmeh.

The reliability of the convictions

The suppression of documents and departure from procedure would of course matter less if the case against Alami and Botmeh was conclusive. But it is far from it. There are many troubling aspects to the case. The trial judge acknowledged that the evidence was 'all circumstantial' and there was none to link the two directly to the actual attacks. The evidential case – where not actually indicating a miscarriage of justice – raises major concerns about the reliability of the convictions:

- Alami and Botmeh both have cast-iron alibis for the attacks. (Although this obviously doesn't acquit them of the conspiracy charge, it confirms that others were involved. These others could have planned and prepared for the attacks as well as carrying them out.)
- Evidence at the trial indicated that there was another man involved with Alami and Botmeh.
- All the witnesses to the buying of the car used in the bombing of the embassy confirmed that two men were involved. Botmeh immediately admitted he was one of

them, explaining that the other, Reda Moghrabi, had asked him to help buy a car, and he had obliged.

- When asked to draw Moghrabi, Alami and Botmeh drew a similar figure even though at the time they were in separate prisons and *incommunicado*.
- Uncontested handwriting evidence proved that the man who signed the purchase papers for the car was not Botmeh.
- The prosecution admitted that a hand-drawn map, which it had originally claimed was of a part of London, was actually of Sidon in Lebanon. Therefore it could not be targeting material for the London attacks.
- Israeli officials were, unusually, involved in the search for forensics around the Embassy.
- Discussions between British and Israeli forensic scientists about the explosives used to blow up the Israeli Embassy were also covered by PII certificates. Despite this, prosecution experts assessed that it was highly unlikely the type of explosive used in the attacks was TATP, the type discovered in the investigation into Alami and Botmeh.
- In his summing up, Mr Justice Garland remarked that, so far as the two accused were concerned, Moghrabi 'could have been a Mossad agent or a police informer'.
- When Peirce asked for the footage from the CCTV cameras covering the outside of the Embassy, she was told that they were not working that day. This seems doubly strange in the light of the heightened security alert following the attack on a Jewish interests centre in Buenos Aires the week before, in which 87 were killed and over 200 injured.
- An Israeli journalist reportedly approached a juror during the trial, prompting the judge to warn the jury and the media that undue influence on the trial would not be tolerated.

In the light of the above, combined with the two MI5 documents which are now covered by PII certificates, it is difficult to imagine that a jury would have found Alami and Botmeh guilty.

Vindication for David at the Court of Appeal

Although ministers were first made aware of the undisclosed documents in November 1997 and summer 1998, it took until the end of October 2000 for the Court of Appeal formally to hear the grounds of appeal, a full three years after the original disclosure. Although the Crown – supported by the Appeal Court – refused to disclose the first document in question to the defence, it did give the defence counsel, Ben Emerson QC, a summary of the report.

> 'Some months prior to the bombing of the Israeli Embassy in London on 26 July 1994, the Security Service and MPSB had received information from an agent source that a terrorist organisation, unconnected to these appellants, was seeking information about the location and defences of the Israeli Embassy in London for a possible bombing attack.'[151]

When pressed, prosecution lawyers admitted that the agent source was reliable and that the agent had named the terrorist group, although its identity was not revealed to defence lawyers.

Admittedly, the authorities have indicated, but presented no evidence, that the same source reported *after the attack* that this group did not carry out the bombing. But that only raises more questions than it answers. Unless MI5's witness is cross-examined, we cannot get at the truth.

In addition, the lack of further intelligence reports to be disclosed supports David's original allegation that an MI5 officer failed to react to the warning before the actual attack. If MI5 had properly investigated this intelligence at the time, the source would have been tasked to find more information. This information would have been the basis of further intelligence reports

---

[151] From the hand-written summary of the intelligence given to defence counsel at hearing, October 2000.

concerning the build-up to the Israeli Embassy attack. They would also have to be disclosed or presented to the judge under public interest immunity certificates.

In fact, further evidence of the security services' incompetence and inability to fulfil their legal duties has emerged as a result of the Court of Appeal hearing. No less than *seven* individuals – from a variety of police and intelligence organisations – failed to ensure that a document absolutely vital to a jury determining the guilt or innocence of Alami and Botmeh was disclosed to the trial judge. For one officer to mislay a document looks like 'misfortune'. For seven to mislay the same document looks like deliberate 'carelessness' or indeed a conscious attempt to corrupt the judicial process.

Anyone who disagrees with whistleblowing should ask whether MI5 would have ventured this information to ministers without David's intervention. The Home Secretary either did not know or did not see fit to include this rather pertinent information in his letter to the *MoS* in October 1997. That is a cover-up either on the part of MI5 to ministers or on the part of ministers to the public. Straw and Lander should be called before MPs to explain themselves.

The summary disclosed to the Court of Appeal also demonstrates that the authorities abused their powers under the injunction's submission process in order to protect the services from embarrassment and undermine David's reliability as a whistleblower, when vetting the article submitted through the *MoS* in October 1997.

In this context, free speech and the free flow of information can only be lawfully restrained under the Convention 'in the interests of national security',[152] yet ministers produced more details at the Appeal Court than during the original submission. This is proof that Straw either did not investigate David's original disclosure properly or that he withheld information vital to an understanding of David's disclosure.

---

[152] Article 10(2) ECHR, now incorporated into the HRA.

Either way, it is a clear example of being 'economical with the truth'. The relevant information about the detail of the document and the failure of officials to disclose it at trial cannot have been withheld 'in the interests of national security' because it was later disclosed in open court to three Appeal Court judges.

The future for fair trials and British justice

It is over seven years since David first disclosed the bungling in MI5 in the run-up to the Israeli Embassy bombing. Alami's and Botmeh's convictions should have been quashed then, a year into the sentence. They should have been freed, pending any retrial where all the evidence could be heard.

Although the Court of Appeal and the House of Lords have dismissed Alami and Botmeh's appeal, they simply ignored case law about the breach of due process at trial. They also ignored Straw's admission about David's original disclosure, which indicated that the undisclosed report would be likely to influence anyone's understanding of the facts of the case, including that of the jury. If British judges were interested in justice, they would have immediately quashed the convictions with a view to a retrial. However, as we have also seen in the Hutton Enquiry, they are rather more concerned with protecting the reputation of the intelligence services.

Alami and Botmeh's case is destined for the European Court of Human Rights. In the meantime, two people rot in prison. At the very least, they were convicted in a mistrial. More probably, they are the victims of a severe miscarriage of justice, because British spooks, ministers and judges cannot bring themselves to accept that the services made a monumental cock-up. Instead, they have done everything in their power to collude in an equally monumental cover-up.

Next time, there might not be a whistleblower to ensure the truth emerges. So what incentive will there be for MI5 to disclose vital material during trials, if they get away with it in this case?

It appears that we have given up on the notion of due process, fair trials and democratic rights in Britain.

Chapter 15

The MI6/Al Qaeda Conspiracy, Part 2

David had briefed the *MoS* with the bare bones of the plot in the summer of 1996 and again when preparing the disclosures of 24 August 1997. However, given the controversial and sensitive nature of the material, he had always wanted to submit it to the government for investigation. Since then, ministers and other responsible agencies like the PM's ISC and the Cabinet Office have consistently refused to take possession of David's evidence concerning the plot. Despite his repeatedly writing to them to inform them that elements of the services were operating outside the law.

As the authorities had shown no interest in taking his evidence, in late 1997 David met Mark Urban, at the time the BBC's Defence and Diplomatic Correspondent, and gave him a full, recorded interview about the MI6/Al Qaeda plot. Then, after he had entered into negotiations, David again tried to give his evidence to the British authorities, but they repeatedly refused to take it. By June 1998, Urban had stood up key aspects of the story. Although David urged Urban to submit the documentary to the authorities for immediate clearance under the injunction, BBC management appeared reluctant to face the government and the intelligence services head-on. They sat on the programme, while they debated it internally.

By July 1998 the government had shown no real will to come to a negotiated settlement with David. In frustration at the government's failure to discharge its democratic duties by taking his evidence, and at the same time faced with BBC inertia, in July 1997 David told the *MoS* that he was looking into setting up an Internet site to ensure that the crimes of the intelligence services could be properly exposed.

'Nothing will threaten the security of MI5 agents or staff,' he said, 'or compromise its working methods. But there are vital matters that need a public airing and the Internet is the way to do it.'[153]

David hoped the article would prompt ministers to take his evidence. As there was no response after a week, David again told the *MoS* that he intended to publish his disclosures – with due care for national security – on the Internet in the US, where it would be protected under the first amendment.

'I don't see how the Government can complain,' said David, 'when I've been trying to talk to them for months.'[154]

Three days later, his www.shayler.com site was hacked before it was even up and running. Verio aka Tabnet, the service provider in the US, said that the hacking was done by a professional after the password to gain access to the site was intercepted en route to David's computer. There is no actual evidence to indicate that the intelligence services were responsible but they are the likeliest culprits. Hackers do not normally attack anti-establishment websites, particularly when they are not yet up and running.

On 31 July 1998, David and I met the *MoS* in Paris, in an effort to get the MI6/Al Qaeda conspiracy out to a wider audience. On the strict understanding that the newspaper submitted the story to government, David gave the paper the details of the plot (without mentioning the names of intelligence officers).

---

[153] *MoS*, 19 July 1998.
[154] *MoS*, 26 July 1998.

Ministers refused the paper permission to publish the information in any meaningful form, while also denying the story. David also met Nick Rufford and David Leppard of *The Sunday Times* and gave them a briefing on the plot, with the same caveat. David comments:

'The denial and censorship do not add up.[155] Either the disclosure is untrue, in which case the government cannot cite national security reasons for suppressing the information. Or the disclosure is true, in which case the government has a duty to investigate exactly how British intelligence officers came to use taxpayers' money to fund terrorism and murder innocent civilians. The government has used the injunction and the 1989 OSA to restrain the freedom of the press, in order to protect itself from embarrassment rather than protect national security.'

David's arrest in connection with the Plot

Unbeknown to David and me, a couple of hours after he had legally[156] submitted his very serious evidence to ministers, those self-same ministers sent an urgent request to extradite David for his original disclosures, which had appeared almost a year earlier in the *MoS*. David says:

'In these circumstances, it is difficult to see how anyone could believe that our oversight arrangements work. Indeed, the act of imprisoning an individual who uses a legal route to report terrorism on the part of MI6, is hardly likely to encourage other individuals to use the system. It has all the hallmarks of despotism and tyranny.'

---

[155] The government's response was similar towards the BBC, when it approached ministers with Mark Urban's *Panorama* investigation, after the story was broken in *The New York Times* (see later in this chapter).

[156] Under the injunction, Order of Mr Justice Hooper, 5 September 1997.

The next day, 1 August 1998, the French DST, the equivalent of MI5 and SB, arrested David in the foyer of our hotel when he returned from watching his football team, Middlesbrough, lose 1–0 on Sky to Empoli in a pre-season friendly. He was held for over 24 hours in the Palais de Justice – most of the time in solitary – and denied access to a lawyer. The day after, he was transferred to La Santé prison in Paris's 14th arrondissement. At the instigation of the British authorities, he was held under draconian secrecy legislation and first saw a lawyer over two days after he had been arrested. He continued to be denied access to all other visitors for most of his time in prison.

But for David's quick thinking, I would not have known what had happened to him. He would have vanished. The DST asked him for his papers. Knowing I was waiting for his return in our hotel room, he told them his passport was in his bag upstairs (it was not). I therefore only knew he had been arrested when the DST came knocking on my door. I was not to see him again for over two months.

Two days after David was arrested, *The Daily Telegraph* splashed on disclosures he had given to its intelligence correspondent Michael Smith a few weeks before about security blunders concerning the IRA mainland bombing campaign. *The Telegraph* included some details of the failures but was blocked by the injunction from revealing how a number of attacks could have been prevented. Rather curiously, the paper – then edited by Charles Moore – called for David to be 'horsewhipped' in its leader column for providing information about security failures, which *The Telegraph* published in its news section.

David's solicitor John Wadham said:

'It's a strange coincidence that before this important story about this assassination attempt was going to break, the Government ensured that David was arrested and *incommunicado*.'[157]

---

[157] *The Daily Telegraph*, 3 August 1998.

The New York Times breaks the story

While David languished in a prison cell, and while the disclosure had been injuncted in the British press, a public-spirited individual passed the details of the MI6/Al Qaeda conspiracy to *The New York Times*. On 5 August 1998, it reported that the British media had been banned from reporting the plot.

> 'Did the British government try to assassinate Col Mummar Gaddafi, the Libyan leader, in February 1996 by planting a bomb under his motorcade? And did the plan go awry because agents from MI6, the foreign intelligence service, put the bomb under the wrong car, killing several Libyan bystanders?' it asked...
>
> 'A sweeping injunction has barred newspapers and television news programmes from publishing the embarrassing allegations about the inner workings of Britain's security services, brought up by a disgruntled former officer. The media have been forced to discuss the allegations without actually saying what the allegations are. "I've known these things for something like 16 months, and I am not allowed to publish any of it," said Jonathan Holborow, editor of *The Mail on Sunday*.'

The paper added that the government had told the press it could report the allegations *as long as it did not mention details, like the payment to Islamic extremists of around £100,000.*

The *Panorama* programme

The BBC began intense negotiations with the government for permission to show David's interview with Mark Urban. Only after threatening to challenge the temporary injunction through the courts, did the government back down. Two days after the publication of *The New York Times* article, the BBC was permitted to broadcast more details of the conspiracy in a *Panorama* special presented by Mark Urban. He confirmed that the Islamic group involved was the Militant (or Fighting) Islamic Group (FIG), led by Abdullah Al-Sadiq. Camille Tawil, an Arab journalist based in London, told the programme that shortly after the attack in February 1996, he received a fax from the group, claiming responsibility for the attack and naming the members of its team who had died in the attack:

> 'I felt it was credible information given to me but I wanted to verify the story. I contacted other Libyan groups and they gave me a similar account of what had happened. This is why I decided to publish the story.'

Panorama also reported:

> 'Libya has publicly accused Britain of giving refuge to the leader of the Militant Islamic Group. In response to our enquiry, the Foreign Office said it does not know whether Abdullah Al Sadiq is in this country'.

The programme also confirmed that MI6 did not get the vital permission from its ministers to carry out the attack – which is a legal requirement so the officers involved have immunity under English law.[158]

> 'Two well-placed people have told me that the Tory ministers running the department at the time gave no such authorisation. ...In short, that means Britain's intelligence service was operating completely out of control.'

Urban concluded:

> 'It is true of course that Shayler's knowledge of this affair

---

[158] Under the 1994 Intelligence Services Act.

248

depends entirely on what the SIS man, PT16/B, told him at their meetings. But certain pieces of this Libyan jigsaw cannot easily be argued away by SIS. There was an assassination attempt. Numerous Libyan sources confirm it. Britain did have a relationship with Tunworth. Any inquiry into David Shayler's allegation will be able to find the key CX report which detailed the plot against Gaddafi, so showing Tunworth's inside knowledge...

'Only a thorough-going inquiry would stand a chance of getting to the bottom of whether some intelligence officers played fast and loose with the rules. David Shayler has provided *Panorama* with other details about the Libyan operation and the people connected with it. Combined with our own information, it suggests that SIS have a very serious case to answer.'

The *Panorama* programme established that MI6 had operated outside the control of its political masters. In other words, unaccountable intelligence operatives were deciding British foreign policy, not a democratically elected government. When you think about it, this means that *middle-ranking intelligence officers have the power of life and death over an individual* without being accountable for their actions.[159] While that is all very well in a James Bond film, in the real world intelligence officers are now required to operate within the law.

Separate sources confirm the story

On 9 August 1998, the *MoS* added still further confirmation of the plot and the payments. It reported:

'David Shayler's revelations that MI6 tried to blow up

---

[159] As the MI6 officers involved aided and abetted murder and terrorism, they violated HRA, ECHR, Article 2, the right to life. None of the exceptions under Article 2(2) apply in this case.

Colonel Gaddafi were given strong credence by US intelligence sources yesterday. They insisted that, despite claims to the contrary, the British secret service was financing the group behind the attempt on the Libyan leader's life. [According to the US] the British service [MI6] turned to the Fighting Islamic Group [FIG] and its leader, Abu Abdullah Sadiq, who was living in London.'

A separate source, a former senior analyst with American intelligence, told the paper:

'I'm sure that British intelligence has all the plausible deniability that it needs. Certainly there were contacts between MI6 and FIG.'

Yet another source in Washington told the paper that MI6 had provided 'various kinds of support' to FIG, *including financial help.*

The same day, *The Sunday Times* reported that it had identified one of the perpetrators of the attack as Abd Al Muhaymeen. According to the paper, he was a Libyan 'fundamentalist' or Islamic extremist, to use MI5 phraseology, who had trained and fought in Afghanistan. On the day, he also chose the timing of the attack.

'He waited in ambush with a group of fedaydeen from a force known as the Islamic Fighting Group... The group appeared to be gaining in strength and daring, mostly due to the expertise of Afghan veterans such as Al Muhaymeen... As the convoy approached, Al Muhaymeen gave the word and the sounds of battle erupted. When it was over, Gaddafi had survived yet again. So had Al Muhaymeen. But several of their men lay dead on each side. So did *bystanders.*'

Foreign Secretary's comments

On 9 August 1998, Robin Cook, the then Foreign Secretary, told the BBC's *Breakfast with Frost* programme:

> '*The tale about the MI6 plot to assassinate Gaddafi is pure fantasy.* First of all, let's be clear about this claim that Shayler can bring down the government, [the claim appeared in *The Sunday Times*, but David never made it] the allegations are about something that is alleged to have happened not under this government but under our predecessor... I have pursued these allegations. I am absolutely satisfied that the previous Foreign Secretary did not authorise any such assassination attempt. I am perfectly satisfied that SIS never put forward any such proposal for an assassination attempt, nor have I seen anything in the 15 months I have been in the job which would suggest that SIS has any interest, any role or any experience over the recent decade of any such escapade. *It is pure fantasy.*
>
> 'I have already made my own enquiries. I have satisfied my mind. I see no basis for the reports in today's papers about any forthcoming enquiry. There was no SIS proposal to do it and I am *fairly clear* that there has never been any SIS involvement. I do wish people would recognise that what is being said here is that there is somebody who has left another service, not SIS, was never in SIS, is making allegations no doubt for his own reasons. We would like to see him back in Britain in order that we can pursue those charges that have been made against him.
>
> '*I am clear these allegations have no basis in fact* and secondly I am quite clear that the SIS operations that I have authorised have nothing remotely to do *with the kind of fantasy* that has been produced over the last two days.'

Without ever bothering to take David's evidence, Cook repeated from *The Sunday Times* an allegation that David had never made: that he could 'bring down the government', a tactic that Straw had used in the first use of the submission process in October 1997.

Cook also unequivocally denied the existence of any MI6 operation at all: 'The tale about the MI6 plot to assassinate Colonel Gaddafi is pure fantasy.' There is no mention here that Cook is claiming that *aspects* of the story may be fantasy – such as the payments, which the FCO later and wrongly claimed were the subject of the 'pure fantasy' jibe.[160]

Without bothering to hold a proper enquiry, he was uncritically putting out the MI6 line, adding: 'I am clear these allegations have *no basis in fact.*' However, governments do not usually issue urgent extradition requests on the basis of 'pure fantasy'. Nor can ministers legally ban information that is fantasy. After all, ministers had already indicated in off-the-record briefings at the time of the Israeli Embassy disclosure that disclosures on the part of former officers, which they accept to be untrue, could not harm national security.[161]

Indeed, when Cook said: 'I am absolutely satisfied that the previous Foreign Secretary did not authorise any such assassination attempt,' he merely confirmed a key aspect of the *Panorama* investigation; that MI6 did not have the permission of ministers to carry out the attack, making any actions by MI6 a criminal offence. Although Cook then claimed he was 'fairly clear' that there had never been any MI6 involvement and 'perfectly clear' there was no basis in fact, he did not relate how exactly he had established this or why he was 'perfectly clear' of one position but only 'fairly clear' about another.

Despite his claims, he obviously hadn't had time to organise and carry out a full inquiry, even though there were officers in MI5 who had been briefed about the plot, and who could have been interviewed. In fact, it appears that Cook – in the same way that Straw had done before him – went to the head of the

---

[160] Chapter 18, *The MI6/Al Qaeda conspiracy, part 3, The Observer* taken to court.
[161] Chapter 14, *The Israeli Embassy bombing and the gagging orders*. Ministers abuse first use of submission under injunction.

agency concerned (in this case, MI6) and asked if it had been involved in terrorist funding and murder. Not surprisingly, the latter appears to have denied it.

After the *Panorama* programme was shown, Mark Urban offered his evidence to Robin Cook, who refused to take possession of it, informing him that the matter was closed. As this was an allegation of murder and terrorist funding, Cook should have discharged his legal duty and immediately referred the matter to the police to investigate.

Libya confirms plot

On Wednesday 25 November 1998, Libyan TV broadcast footage of the assassination attempt. It showed Gaddafi leaning out of his open-topped car to greet the crowds, then mingling with the crowd. It then showed an object flying through the air, Gaddafi looking down, then suddenly being surrounded by bodyguards, who hustled him away. The TV zoomed in on the face of a man in the crowd, and his face was circled in red. Libyan TV named the assailant as Abdullah Radwan, a partner of Abu Abdullah Sadiq, the leader of the IFG. According to the report:

'Abdullah Radwan succeeded in reaching the front ranks and threw a grenade when the brother leader left the car.'

Libyan TV then showed an interview with Hasan Al Sadiq Al Shahh, an alleged accomplice of Radwan:

Questioner: Who entrusted you with the mission of entering the Jamahiriya [the People's Republic of Libya]?
Al Shahh: Abu Abdullah Al Sadiq.
Q: Did he give money?
A: Yes.
Q: How much money?

A: $20,000.

Q: $20,000?

A: Yes.

Q: What is the total amount of money you obtained from Abu Abdullah Al Sadiq?

A: Perhaps, $40,000 or $41,000.

Q: $41,000?

A: Approximately, yes.

Q: Where did the money you got come from?

A: I do not know. But there is a group in those countries.

Q: What countries are these?

A: Britain.

██
██
██
██ *

Our recent enquiries with Swallow Tail, a former intelligence officer who cannot be named for fear of reprisals,[162] have confirmed that the man caught by the Libyans in the attack was the agent Tunworth. This is further confirmation that an MI6 agent, whom we know was working to Watson in London, was involved in the plot. The officer also confirmed that ████████ was either killed during the attack that February or shortly after. This rather undermines the claims of ministers that they banned the story in order to protect national security, since the agent was clearly no longer at risk of reprisal and was not then providing intelligence to the British services.

Other than using the submission process to inform the PM about service abuses of power, David also wrote to ministers Tony Blair, Jack Straw, Robin Cook, John Prescott and the Attorney General on several occasions, asking them to investigate

---

*This paragraph, which is integral to the understanding of how the payments were made, has been removed on the orders of MI5, even though it is in the public domain.

[162] We can be sure Swallow Tail had the right access to know the identity of Tunworth as he was able to provide details of the operation which have never appeared in the public domain.

his disclosures of MI6's funding of Al Qaeda. At no point did any minister hear his evidence. In June 1999, David sent ministers *Secrets and Lies*, a document he had prepared on his case to counter the misinformation put out by the government. It provided details of the conspiracy but ministers still refused to call in the police or hold any kind of enquiry. And that would have been that, if it hadn't been for the public-spirited former intelligence officer who obtained the CX document issued by MI6 in December 1995 and put it on the Internet. That officer said:

'I've just about had it up to here with the lies of ministers. It is difficult to imagine a more serious abuse of power than MI6 funding our terrorist enemies with the result that innocent people are murdered in cold blood. If there had been a legal way of presenting that document to independent investigators, I would have used it. As there was not, I had to resort to the Internet. Thank God for modern technology.'

Chapter 16

Traitors, Agents and Dirty Tricks

In autumn 1999, when Melita Norwood and others were exposed as Russian KGB (Committee of Public Safety) spies by the publication of the Mitrokhin Archive, David and I were amazed by the public outcry.

After all, the British state has a lamentable record of prosecuting spies and traitors who gave information to the enemy, causing the deaths of dozens of brave British agents doing their best to defend the security of this country. Guy Burgess, Kim Philby, John Cairncross, Donald Maclean and Anthony Blunt – ex-public schoolboys to a man – all escaped prosecution. In the 1960s, George Blake was found guilty of three offences under the 1911 OSA and sentenced to 42 years in prison – three consecutive terms of 14 years, one year for every agent life lost as a result of his treachery – but he escaped from a high-security prison to Russia, where he lives to this day.

Melita Norwood was not prosecuted, even after MI6 had given MI5's K Branch details of her activities copied from the KGB archives by Vasily Mitrokhin in the early 1990s. She had not been prosecuted because a junior MI5 officer had ruled, without consulting ministers or other government departments, that there was not enough evidence to secure a conviction under the 1989 and 1911 OSAs. Of course, MI5 has never been an expert in evidence. That is the job of the police and the CPS. Even after Norwood confessed to her role on camera in 1999, she was never prosecuted for passing our nuclear secrets to the KGB.

257

At the time of the publicity about Norwood, David offered the government further evidence of a traitor who had never been brought to justice. In October 1999, David wrote to the then Home Secretary, Jack Straw, to alert him to the case of another individual who had betrayed the country.[163] David's letter exhorted him to name and shame under Parliamentary protection the individual against whom there was abundant evidence to indicate they had been involved in treachery.

Carole Maychell, KGB spy

Although ministers did everything to avoid taking this evidence, David had comedian and journalist Mark Thomas deliver it to the British Embassy in Paris by hand in November 1999. Straw even had the temerity to claim that suspected traitors had a lifelong right to privacy, when of course a public-spirited whistleblower like David did not. In brief, David's letter to Straw raised a specific case, concerning Carole Maychell, a former Territorial Army (TA) intelligence officer. Maychell's case has been widely reported in the media and at first sight would look like the kind of issue we should be supporting. In fact, the *MoS* drew parallels with David's case:

> 'Following the damning revelations of renegade MI5 agent David Shayler, her case is yet more evidence of the need for a review of the Official Secrets Act. Carole, a 38-year old secondary school teacher was the first, and now probably the last, British officer to be held in solitary confinement under the Act.'[164]

Her case became a minor *cause célèbre* with civil liberties groups because of what appeared to be the Army and MoD's heavy-handed approach to the case.

---

[163] David's letter to Straw, 12 October 1999.
[164] *MoS*, 3 January 1999.

Background

There is no dispute about certain facts in the case. On 21 November 1992, Captain Maychell – the third most senior woman officer in the TA intelligence corps – was asked to attend a personnel interview at the TA's Intelligence and Security Group HQ in Handel Street, London. Believing that she was to be offered promotion, she gladly attended. When she arrived, the Army's Special Investigation Branch and MI5 detained her in a locked interview room and interrogated her about two unauthorised trips to East Berlin in 1989 and 1990 where she met Peter Zuckermann, who had befriended her in England, and a man called Victor, who turned out to be a KGB officer.

She was then taken to Colchester prison, where she was held in solitary confinement for the next four months, after being charged under the Army Act. In January 1993, she was charged under the OSA after a classified document was found in her briefcase.

> ' "The MI5 interviews were terrible, with three men taking turns to interrogate me, belittling me and being very aggressive. Once I hadn't slept for four days when they took me in for questioning,"[165] she said of her illegal incarceration.'

In March 1993, she was freed on bail, after concerted protests from civil rights groups. Six months later, the CPS dropped all charges. Shortly afterwards, she was given a medical discharge from the Army. In 1999, the MoD settled out of court, giving her a reported £50,000 compensation for her illegal incarceration and the mental anguish it caused.

However, that is not the whole truth. It is clear there was a case against Maychell as her writ of habeas corpus was refused in February 1993 after the MoD said there was still 'a fairly

---

[165] *MoS*, 3 January 1999.

complex investigation to be done'. At the time, the presiding judge, Mr Justice Clarke held that the detention was not oppressive. British judges may not be the most liberal but even they would resist detaining an individual if there were absolutely no evidence against them.

The truth about Maychell

In fact, there was an abundance of evidence against Maychell. After the collapse of East Germany, information from the Stasi, the country's secret police, came into the possession of MI5 and the Army. It identified her as an agent of the East German intelligence service, who had passed secret NATO documents during the Cold War. When Maychell was first taken in for questioning, she admitted her contacts with Zuckermann and Victor. She was all too aware that she had broken the rules by making unauthorised trips and not declaring her meetings with hostile intelligence officers.

While David and I were still in the service, one of the officers who had been at the interrogation in London, Tom Potter, gave us further details. He told us that Maychell's commanding officer, who was part of the interviewing team, sat her down and ordered her to tell them everything. As she was a trained intelligence officer, Potter had expected her to be quite hard to break down, but she immediately began to confess. She provided details of all her meetings. She said she had copied many secret documents about NATO troop deployments, communications and other defensive measures and had passed them to the KGB. At the time, this was all up-to-date information and was therefore extremely useful to the KGB. Maychell provided so much information that she was detained for days.

However, Potter went on to say that her commanding officer had not informed her of her right to silence or her right to consult a lawyer before questioning. This meant that her long and detailed confession about her relationship with the KGB

260

was inadmissible in a court of law. Without that, there was no evidence to prosecute her. Potter tried to raise the question of her rights with his fellow officers before the interrogation, but his representations were dismissed.

Government sources have tried to claim that some of David's information is based on 'office gossip'. In this case, we don't just have the word of the officer involved in the interrogation. Maychell's example was used as a case study for MI5's Interviewing Skills internal training course, which both David and I attended. Officers were warned of the perils of not warning an interviewee of their rights.

I appreciate that Maychell cannot now be prosecuted for her crimes. However, her treatment stands starkly at odds with David's. She passed documents to the enemy, clearly damaging national security, yet she received £50,000 in compensation because MI5 and the Army made a mistake. The British people have a right to know how their taxes are squandered on traitors because officials are too incompetent to follow legal procedure. David comments:

'This really is the most basic mistake any interviewer can make. Anyone who has ever seen a British or American cop show on TV will know that a suspect has to be read their rights otherwise anything they say is inadmissible. Those with more suspicious minds might wonder whether this was done deliberately to spare the blushes of military intelligence in front of our defence partners. After all, it is highly embarrassing for all concerned that NATO documents finished up in the hands of the enemy.'

Peter Bleach, MI6 agent

In 2004, self-confessed arms dealer Peter Bleach aka James Gifran von Kalkstein was released from an Indian prison after pressure from the British government. It was the end to a saga

261

which, according to Bleach, began in July 1995 when he was
contacted by a Danish firm asking him for a quote to deliver
arms and ammunition to an unknown destination in South Asia.
In December 1995, he was convicted and sentenced to life in
prison for his part in smuggling 300 AK-47s, 15 Makarov
pistols, two sniper rifles, 24,000 rounds of ammunition, 10
rocket launchers and 100 anti-tank grenades into India. He has
since been released.

Bleach's life story resembles the plot of a bad spy novel.
He is tall and thin with grey hair. He has the distinguished,
patrician air that comes with a public school education (albeit
a minor one) and a career in the Army intelligence corps. He
has the charm and self-confidence to have smoothed his way
into the private security business before setting up his own
arms dealing firm, Aeroserve UK. At trial, he defended himself
with intelligence and flair. In court, he told how he thought he
was involved in a sting operation for MI5 and its executive
arm in the UK, SB. He said at the time of his trial:

'At every stage of this, I expected some big police action
to swing into operation. I expected all future meetings
would be under surveillance, we would all be arrested, and
I would be let out the back door of the police station.'

But, according to his account, when the crunch came MI5 and
SB deserted him. When he requested papers proving he was
given a 'brief' by MI5, the government altered the copy of the
SB officer's write-up of their meeting which was produced in
court. The press and MP Teddy Taylor in particular took up
his case:

'There is ... evidence that the British authorities tried to
cover up MI5's involvement by blanking out parts of
documents submitted to the court... It has emerged that
sections of notes of conversations between Bleach and the
officers were erased by Special Branch before they reached

the court. The sections referred to the involvement of MI5... Detective Sergeant Stephen Elcock was summonsed by Judge P K Biswas last week to explain why criminal proceedings should not be brought against him for allegedly tampering with the evidence and attempting to mislead the court.'[166]

And:

'The Government has been urged to intervene in the case of a British man found guilty yesterday of smuggling arms into India... Sir Teddy Taylor, Conservative MP for Rochford and Southend East, insisted yesterday that the British Government had evidence to prove Mr Bleach's claim.'[167]

Refutation of Bleach's MI5/SB role

It will come as a surprise to DS Stephen Elcock of North Yorkshire Special Branch to learn that he had asked Bleach to act as an intelligence agent (as Bleach also tried to claim at his trial). Or that DS Elcock had somehow obscured MI5's involvement in the arms drop, when all he had done was remove the name of an MI5 officer from the document for reasons of national security. In fact, Elcock had told Bleach in no uncertain terms that he risked arrest and a long prison sentence if he were so stupid as to become implicated in arms trafficking to a religious extremist organisation like Ananda Marg, a powerful, militant Hindu sect. Its orange-robed followers – who have an organised presence in Britain – advocate the eradication of state governments. Alleged persecution of the Ananda Marg has strengthened its members' conviction that the world needs to be cleansed by an Armageddon, and that they are the chosen

---

[166] *The Sunday Times*, 9 May 1999.
[167] *The Times*, 1 February 2000.

few destined to survive – one shared by such extremist cults as the Branch Davidians of Waco, Texas, and Aum Shinri Kyo of Japan, who famously released the poison gas sarin on the Tokyo underground.

In fact, it would be hard to imagine a more clearly stated warning of the dangers that Bleach faced. David took up the story in his *Punch* column:

'I met Steve Elcock in the course of my work in MI5; I've seen Bleach's MI5 file; and I've studied the uncensored version of the document that was presented to the court. Indeed, it was only slightly altered to protect the identities of British intelligence personnel mentioned in the report who had no information to add to DS Elcock's.'

At the time, David thought that Bleach was a fraudster who was out of his depth and tried to cover his tracks by claiming that he worked for the intelligence services. He wrote in *Punch* magazine:

'James Gifran von Kalkstein, as he is also known, is a fraud. In the Services I came across many of his type. They are the dark side of the Establishment. With the whiff of loveable roguishness about them, they live on the periphery of the world of intelligence and survive off the odd scraps of info and gossip that fall from the tables of their better off and better informed former school or army chums. With their assured accents and easy manner, they often succeed in conning those who have no real inkling of what goes in the intelligence establishment, including from time to time the odd newspaper editor or Channel 4 producer... If caught, they have to keep up the pretence in front of the jury in the hope that they will get off as a result.'

However, further research indicates that Bleach's protestations of working for MI5 or SB seem to be an elaborate ruse to deflect attention from the fact that he was smuggling weapons and ammunition on behalf of MI6.

Evidence of Bleach's MI6 role

There is, however, an abundance of evidence to indicate that Bleach was running guns to religious extremists on behalf of MI6.

When he was first arrested in 1995, the Indian Home Secretary described the incident as part of an 'international conspiracy',[168] clearly indicating that he believed that Bleach was not working alone. Although the Indian authorities believed Pakistan's intelligence service was involved,[169] a senior Bombay police officer involved in Bleach's arrest and interrogation claimed that Bleach had confessed to being a former MI6 operative who did small tenders for various governments.[170]

This has been supported by sources closer to home. A British military intelligence officer described Bleach as 'an international bits and bobs man',[171] the sort of euphemism that intelligence personnel use to describe their often less than savoury activities. The fact that he had an 'international' role again indicates that he worked for MI6.

His background is also typical of an MI6 agent: public school, Army intelligence corps, small businessman involved in the arms trade. However, the clearest indication that Bleach was working for MI6 comes from the efforts ministers made to secure his release.

In addition to the diplomatic manoeuvring behind the scenes, ministers seemed unembarrassed to make public statements in support of a convicted terrorist who had tried to supply arms to religious extremists hellbent on Armageddon. In July 2000,

---

[168] *The Straits Times* (Singapore), 25 December 1995.
[169] *MoS*, 31 December 1995.
[170] *The Straits Times*, 25 December 1995.
[171] *The Independent*, 9 July 1998.

Jack Straw, then Home Secretary, made a personal appeal on behalf of Bleach.[172] Three months later, he expressed concern at the long time taken for Bleach's appeal to be heard. 'In no sense has Bleach been abandoned by the British government,' he said.[173] A couple of months later, it was then Foreign Secretary Robin Cook's turn. He asked the Indian foreign minister to review the case.[174] In December 2000, Cook went a stage further and asked the Indian authorities in a formal letter to release Bleach.[175]

Given that the UK government is currently prosecuting a war on terrorism, why would ministers publicly support an individual who had knowingly entered into terrorism and then tried to embarrass Britain by claiming he was working for MI5 or SB, unless he was really an MI6 agent? And this begs the question: What exactly was MI6 doing sending arms to religious insurgents in a friendly country? and: Did that service have the permission of ministers to traffic arms to insurgents? If it did not, the officers involved should be prosecuted for illegal arms trafficking.

Bleach's release was presented as the right thing to do after the five Russian and Latvian crew members of the aircraft used to carry out the drop were freed in July 2000. Yet their case was very different to that of Bleach. All the evidence indicates that they were simply hired crew who had no idea that their cargo contained weapons and ammunition. By seeking the opinion of SB before the operation, Bleach had effectively admitted to knowingly taking part in an illegal arms drop, a wholly different situation.

Again, if Parliament has any respect for the rule of law, democratic accountability or world security it is imperative that MPs call Bleach and his MI6 handlers before the House and make them answer honestly and openly about his relationship with MI6 and that service's involvement in terrorism.

---

[172] *The Guardian*, 24 July 2000.
[173] *The Statesman*, India, 9 September 2000.
[174] *The Hindu*, 16 November 2000.
[175] *The Scotsman*, 9 December 2000.

It is also notable that Bleach used a tried and tested tactic to try to deflect attention from his MI6 role: blaming MI5. I believe that many of the instances in which MI5 is blamed in the media for undermining civil liberties are more likely to have been MI6, which seems to be a law unto itself.

Other MI6 dirty tricks

The Zinoviev letter

MI6 dirty tricks, particularly against the Labour movement, are nothing new. In June 2000, declassified papers released to the Public Record Office confirmed that in the 1950s the then head of MI6, Stewart Menzies, authorised the destruction of important files relating to the Zinoviev letter, blamed for bringing down the first Labour government in 1924. Menzies – in 1924 a junior MI6 officer and a Tory sympathiser – has long been suspected of leaking the letter to the *Daily Mail* on the eve of the general election, to stoke up Tory-inspired public fears of a 'red menace' about to overwhelm the country.

The letter – purportedly from Grigori Zinoviev, the head of the Comintern or Communist International, the Soviet Union's international propaganda arm, to the CPGB – urged the Party to incite the British proletariat to revolution. Its publication was a huge embarrassment to the Labour Prime Minister Ramsay MacDonald who had been the first Western leader to enter into treaty negotiations with the Soviet regime after the Bolshevik Revolution of 1917.

Without MacDonald's knowledge or permission, the Foreign Office sent an official note of protest in his name to the Soviet chargé d'affaires in the UK – which was handed to the press while MacDonald was out of London campaigning for re-election. When questioned about the note, the Labour leader was made to look a fool in front of the public in the run-up to a general election.

The declassified files reveal that the head of security at the

267

Foreign Office, George Carey-Foster, wrote to Menzies in April 1952, asking him how he wanted to deal with five files of material that had never been properly archived. Carey-Foster suggested that while some reports should be registered in the official Foreign Office archives, the most sensitive CX documents relating to MI6 should be destroyed. Menzies agreed and wrote back, saying that he had examined the proposals and saw 'no harm whatsoever in their being carried out, ie some papers to be registered and some destroyed'.

The letter was signed 'C' in the traditional green ink used by the head of MI6. Although official historians now believe that White Russians angry that the Labour government had legitimised the Soviet regime probably forged the letter, the missing MI6 documents mean that a cloud of suspicion will always hang over MI6's role in the forgery.

To us, this new information is a matter of history. To the voters of 80 years ago it would have been vital information, which could have informed the way they voted. Its disclosure demonstrates that we need a Freedom of Information Act to ensure that current and future evidence of the intelligence services' attempts to pervert our democracy can be released to the public before being destroyed. Otherwise, you're going to have to wait until 2072 for details of the MI6's payments to Al Qaeda, given how long it took to get to the truth of the Zinoviev letter. And that's only if unscrupulous officers haven't destroyed or tampered with the files.

MI6, The News of the World *and the compromise of a minister*

Although we believe MI6 has been far more active in destabilising the Labour movement, it is not averse to compromising Tory ministers when they don't do what MI6 wants. When evidence emerged for the first time in early 2004 that MI6 had played a role in destabilising democratic government, it was a Tory minister's resignation that the service brought about.

In 1973, Lord Lambton, the RAF Minister in Edward Heath's government, was forced to resign after being exposed in *The News of the World* for his affair with a night club hostess. Lee Tracey, a long-serving MI6 agent who had first come to the public's attention in the Profumo Affair, recounted how he had supplied a night-vision sight to *The News of the World* to photograph Lord Lambton smoking a joint *in flagrante* with the call girl on the orders of his MI6 bosses. It was only with specialist military equipment supplied by MI6 that the paper's photographer, hiding in a bedroom cupboard, was able to take good enough quality pictures of Lambton's activities. Tracey said in 2004:

'MI6 had its own agenda to expose Lambton and through a stringer [a source] on the paper offered them assistance. I got a phone call and was told to remove a classified night-vision device from a "certain department" and loan it to the newspaper. And that is what I did... I modified it with a special lens so it could be attached to a camera. Later, when I got the lens back, I was told the paper could not use the pictures because they were too gruesome but the people motivating it achieved their aims. I think the pictures taken with my sight were confiscated.'[176]

According to Tracey, MI6 was motivated by a desire to embarrass MI5, which had failed to act against the security risk posed by the peer's activities. Stephen Dorril, author of books on the intelligence services who has researched the Lambton case, said:

'MI6 was heavily involved in domestic operations during the Seventies, which is very strange for a foreign intelligence service. They appear to have believed that MI5 was not doing its job properly or at least was insufficiently influential to deal with security breaches involving public figures.'

---

[176] *MoS*, 18 January 2004.

Other MI6 corruption

MI5 and, particularly, MI6 carry out dozens of sting operations every year, largely without the knowledge or permission of ministers. In these, they pose as criminals and offer drugs and/or arms and ammunition to potential terrorists and crime lords. They then take the money and run without providing the goods in question. I have no problem with this. I am in favour of removing resources from terrorists and organised crime. However, it remains something of a mystery what happens to this money once it is in the hands of the services. The funds in question – which can come to tens of millions of pounds a year – either line the pockets of intelligence officers and their associates or are used to fund illegal or 'unavowed' operations on the part of MI6.

The money should of course be turned over to central government and used to finance the services' legitimate activities, saving the taxpayer up to tens of millions of pounds a year in the process.

MI6 and Army intelligence also use cut-outs or undeclared officers or agents to influence public opinion, inducing them to contact phone-in programmes, write in newspapers, and appear on radio and television. David and I personally experienced this when David appeared on BBC1's show *Look Who's Talking* to discuss whistleblowers in 2004. Members of the studio audience, who were supposedly concerned members of the public, afterwards admitted to David that they were part of the SAS. Ironically, David went some way to convincing them during and after the programme that he was a patriot, as he too had served his country to combat the IRA and had spoken out because of MI6 sponsorship of terrorism.

The undeclared use of intelligence and security service personnel is a perversion of democracy, using the 'false flag' of concerned public opinion to mask intelligence service propaganda. If the services wish to participate, then they should declare themselves in any debate, as happens in countries such as the US and France.

Chapter 17

The MI6/Al Qaeda Conspiracy, Part 3

In February 2000, *The Sunday Times* provided corroboration that MI6 had conspired with an agent in a plan to assassinate Colonel Gaddafi, when it reported that a leaked MI6 document, CX95/53452, had appeared on the website www.geocities.com/byanymeansnecessary2000.[177] When interviewed about the document, the then Foreign Secretary Robin Cook refused to confirm that it was genuine. David can though confirm that it is the document sent by MI6's R/ME/C to Whitehall departments and the intelligence services in December 1995. It refutes Cook's claims, which had caused many to believe that David had simply made the whole thing up:

> 'The tale about the MI6 plot to assassinate Gaddafi is pure fantasy.
> 'It is pure fantasy.'
> 'I am clear these allegations have no basis in fact.'

The MI6 report clearly demonstrated that an MI6 agent among the coup plotters was meeting his MI6 handler to discuss the assassination of Col Gaddafi 'in which he was involved':

> 'The coup plotters would launch a direct attack on Gaddafi and would either arrest him or kill him.'

---

[177] *The Sunday Times*, 13 February 2000.

'The military officer said that the plotters would have cars
similar to those in Gaddafi's security entourage with fake
security number plates. They would infiltrate themselves
into the entourage in order to kill or arrest Gaddafi.'[178]

Remember, Tunworth had already outlined his plans and his
request for finance to the resident MI6 officer in Tunis in
summer 1995. David's opposite number in MI6, PT16/B, had
then met Tunworth – in the full knowledge that the latter wanted
to assassinate Gaddafi – to obtain details of the operation, which
were published in the CX report. If this report had been a
record of a meeting between a Libyan terrorist and an IRA
member planning to assassinate Tony Blair which had fallen
into MI5 or police hands, it would have been accepted in a
court of law as clear evidence of a conspiracy between the two
to cause terrorism.

The MI6 intelligence report also confirmed that Sirte was
the site of the attack in February or March 1996, information
David had told Urban who had stood it up for the *Panorama*
investigation into the plot. It also established that the group of
coup plotters were at least looking for support from the British
state. (As a CX report going out to ministers, it could not detail
the illegal payments):

'The officer was disclosing this information in the hope
that if the coup was successful, the new government could
enlist HMG support.'

According to the report, Tunworth also admitted contacts between
the plotters and Islamic extremists, described as 'Libyan students'
and 'Libyan veterans who served in Afghanistan'. As already
discussed, veteran Libyan Islamic extremists who served in

---

[178] This also confirms David's account, which he learned from Moroccan and Egyptian sources
when in MI5 (and gave to Mark Urban of the BBC): 'Two of the reports indicated that the
attackers had tried to assassinate Gaddafi when he was part of a cavalcade but had failed as
they had targeted the wrong car.'

Afghanistan are considered by MI5 to be de facto members of Al Qaeda.

The CX report otherwise played down the agent's contacts with Islamic extremists, presumably because the report went to ministers who would have been appalled at the prospect of Islamic terrorists toppling Gaddafi, given that the former posed a greater threat to British lives. As we now know from the sexed-up dossier, it is not unusual for inconvenient pieces of information to be left out of official reports.

David is adamant that he was told in a briefing that Tunworth was leading a 'ragtag' group of Islamic extremists. David also briefed his boss at the time with this information and provided it in his sworn statement to the police. He has not been charged with perjury. Other media reports already quoted have established that the IFG were responsible. The Libyan TV broadcast also indicated that a leading member of the IFG might be Tunworth, as he led the attack in much the way that Tunworth outlined in the CX report.

The report also made it absolutely clear that the Permanent Under Secretary's Department – Sir Humphrey Appleby's equivalent in the Foreign Office – GCHQ, MI5; the MoD, and MI6 stations in Tunis, Cairo and Washington knew of the assassination attempt at least two months in advance. They would therefore have had copies on file. Did none of them bother to brief Cook with this rather pertinent information before he went on the *Breakfast with Frost* programme on 9 August 1998? Were our Sir Humphreys and our George Smileys deliberately keeping ministers in the dark? Or did Cook know about Tunworth but think he could get away with branding the plot 'pure fantasy' in the belief that documents detailing the relationship between Tunworth and MI6 would never see the light of day?

We also have to ask ourselves what role the PM played in all this, as the figure ultimately responsible for our services. What did he know and when did he know it?

Julie Ann and the bullies in government

The government had always claimed it was not in the business of preventing legitimate discussion of the intelligence services. But on 6 March 2000, that all changed when SB officers arrested Julie Ann Davies, a student at Kingston University, under the 1911 and 1989 OSAs, during a lecture at the college. She was held for several hours at Kingston police station but was not charged. She was later released on police bail. The university confirmed that it had complied with a search warrant, giving police the right to access Davies's computer at the university. Davies had recently visited David in France and had begun to rally support for him. She said at the time:

'During that meeting I became convinced that the man was genuine and so I felt the need to do something about his situation.'[179]

The day after the CX document appeared on the Internet, Davies circulated an e-mail to fellow campaigners and journalists. In it, she stated:

'You have probably heard about the document on the web that appears to back up David Shayler's allegations of an MI6 plot to assassinate Colonel Gaddafi.'

It is also clear from the context of the questions that police asked her that SB suspected her of putting the CX document on the Internet. Under questioning, Davies denied having anything to do with this. After keeping her on police bail for a number of months without charging her, SB eventually dropped the investigation. As a result of the police action, she was forced to drop out of her university course. She is currently suing police for wrongful arrest. As a result of disclosure in this case,

[179] *The Independent*, 7 March 2000.

police have provided her with the 'evidence' which led to her arrest. It consists only of three anonymous letters claiming that she put the document on the Internet. As they are anonymous, they would not be considered admissible evidence in a court of law.

Mr Peter Scott, Kingston University vice chancellor, said:

> 'The university, as an institution committed to freedom of expression, would be particularly concerned if it turned out that a discredited piece of legislation like the OSA was being used to suppress legitimate journalistic investigation and the public's right to know about alleged abuses by the security services.'

The arrest of Julie Ann Davies proved once again that ministers were rather more concerned with intimidating David's supporters and protecting the intelligence services from proper scrutiny, including criminal investigation, than free speech, one of the cornerstones of democracy. It was also a clear example of bullying. *The Sunday Times*, which had published the original article about the report and quoted from the document, had not been investigated, nor had any of its journalists been arrested in connection with the matter.

This is also clear evidence that material from CX reports can be published without causing damage to national security, as the government did not prosecute the paper or its journalists under section 5 of the 1989 OSA, where the Crown has to prove damage, for publishing and quoting from the report. But the bullying was set to continue.

The Observer taken to court

Having used the OSA to intimidate one of David's supporters for trying to expose terrorism funded by MI6, Blair's government then turned its sights on the elements of the press who were bravely trying to expose the conspiracy. Comedian and journalist Mark Thomas had agreed to deliver David's evidence about the conspiracy[180] to the British Embassy by hand in November 1999. As Straw did not even bother to reply, David briefed Martin Bright of *The Observer*. In February 2000, he reported that Straw had done nothing to ensure that there was a criminal investigation into PT16/B's activities.

The article also revealed for the first time in public that Tunworth was a senior member of Libyan intelligence, who had walked into the British Embassy in Tunis, and that reports quoting Moroccan and Egyptian intelligence sources had confirmed the assassination attempt shortly after it took place in February 1996.[181]

A Foreign Office spokesman changed the official position on the conspiracy, trying to play down Robin Cook's claim that the tale about the MI6 plot to assassinate Gaddafi was 'pure fantasy'. He told the paper:

'We have never denied knowledge of coup attempts against Col Gaddafi. We always described allegations of involvement as fantasy.[182] We have nothing to add or subtract.'

If the Foreign Office and Cook had been honest when the disclosure was first made, they would have said at the time:

'We are aware of a conspiracy to assassinate Colonel Gaddafi in early 1996. We are still making enquiries about any MI6 involvement.'

Tunworth was after all an MI6 agent who had by the time of the attack met David Watson, an MI6 officer, at least twice to

---

[180] The letter, dated 25 November 1999, was addressed to then Home Secretary Jack Straw.
[181] *The Observer*, 27 February 2000.
[182] From the CX report, we know that an MI6 agent was involved in the plot. Even on that basis – before we consider the payments to the IFG/Al Qaeda – MI6 was clearly involved. As this is still the position of the FCO, the current Foreign Secretary, Jack Straw, should rethink his department's denial of this plot.

discuss his plans. On that evidence alone, we can conclude that MI6 was involved. However, Tunworth could not have gone ahead with the plot without the backing of MI6, financial or otherwise. As we have seen, separate sources have confirmed payments were made to the IFG, the group Tunworth belonged to.[183]

On 14 March 2000, both *The Observer* and *The Guardian* were taken to court by the authorities. MPSB sought a court order to seize any notebooks and browse through *The Observer*'s computer for further evidence of breaches of the OSA on David's part. It sought from *The Guardian* the original of a letter David had written, which was published in the newspaper on 17 February 2000. As Nick Cohen, *The Observer*'s columnist put it:

'No one would dream of telling a newspaper about official corruption, incompetence or crime, if they thought the police – or in this case, the secret police – might read every jotting and e-mail.'

A couple of days later, DS John Flynn, from the financial investigations unit of MPSB, told *The Guardian* that there were 'reasonable grounds' for prosecuting Martin Bright and Roger Alton, the editor of *The Observer*, under section 5 of the OSA.

A month later, judge Martin Stephens ruled that the papers had to hand over any material, even though he admitted that the letter to *The Guardian* contained nothing that had not already been printed. David said at the time:

'The government is adopting the tactics of a totalitarian state by attacking the press in this way. If they really believe I have documents that could damage national security, why don't they come and talk to me about them, rather than intimidate journalists.'[184]

---

[183] See Chapter 15, *The MI6/Al Qaeda conspiracy, part 2*. Separate sources confirm the story.
[184] *The Observer*, 19 March 2000.

Even the then Foreign Secretary Robin Cook and the Foreign Office minister Peter Hain were reported to be horrified at such an attack on press freedom. But we have to wonder why they chose to speak out at this point. Did Cook know that if the documents were handed over then David might be prosecuted for disclosing details of the MI6/Al Qaeda conspiracy, allowing Cook's 'pure fantasy' lies to be examined before a court?

On 19 July 2000, Mr Justice Igor Judge heard the case for SB to access *The Observer*'s computer. He overturned the decision of the lower courts in his ringing defence of press freedom:[185]

'The Gaddafi Plot is either true or it is false, and unless there are reasons of compelling national security, the public is entitled to know the facts, and as the eyes and ears of the public, journalists are entitled to investigate and report the facts, dispassionately and fairly, without prejudgement or selectivity...

'If true, it is difficult to overestimate its enormity: a conspiracy to murder the head of another state, resulting not in his death, but in the deaths of innocent people who were not its intended targets... Again, if true, the circumstances in which such a plan was conceived and developed, and the identity of those who were informed about and approved it, or turned a blind eye to it, and equally those who were deliberately kept in ignorance, raise critical public issues about the activities of the security services and those responsible for them.'

The delayed police investigation

In March 2000, John Wadham and I had hand-delivered a statement – which David had prepared and indicated he was

---

[185] He also invoked a Frenchman, Voltaire, but not, strangely, an Englishman, Tom Paine, who had at the time of Voltaire written *Common Sense* and *The Rights of Man*.

prepared to swear to under oath – to the MPSB at New Scotland Yard. The police then refused to investigate the plot, claiming that conspiracy to murder did not amount to a crime in Britain. Again, this demonstrates what would have happened if David had violated the 1989 OSA section 1 and approached the Metropolitan Police directly with his disclosures in 1997.

Finally in December 2000, two and a half years after David had made the original disclosure, he was finally given permission by the authorities to give evidence to the police. DS Gerry Mackinnon and Detective Superintendent Lewis Benjamin working for SO1 of the Metropolitan Police, interviewed him and prepared a sworn statement, which he signed in early 2001. SO1 then undertook the first ever police investigation into the activities of MI6. You don't have to be a cynic to point out that by this time, MI6 had had plenty of time to destroy or tamper with the evidence. David and I have every confidence that the police in this case did their job thoroughly and professionally but by then, we believe, it was too late.

In February 2001, SO1 sent a report to the CPS. Prosecution sources said the authorities had decided there was a prima facie case, meriting further investigation.[186] In all, the enquiries took nine months. In November 2001, the Metropolitan Police confirmed that the MI6/Al Qaeda conspiracy was not 'pure fantasy':

'As you know, the Metropolitan Police Service undertook an assessment of the available material and submitted two reports to the Crown Prosecution Service, an interim report in February 2001 and a final report in September 2001. The police enquiry has been extremely thorough, examining all *relevant material*.'[187]

---

[186] *The Sunday Times*, 27 May 2001.
[187] Letter from the police to David, 9 November 2001. It was also slightly curious that the police wrote the letter, not the CPS, which now decides which cases go to court on the basis of evidence.

This clearly confirms that the police have gathered evidence – 'relevant material' – about the MI6 conspiracy, which confirms there is 'a basis in fact' for David's disclosures, refuting Robin Cook's assertion that: 'The tale about the MI6 plot to assassinate Gaddafi is pure fantasy [with] no basis in fact.' At the same time, neither the police nor the CPS sought to arrest David or bring charges for perjury or wasting police time, indicating that his detailed sworn statement was honest, reliable and true. On these available facts, any reasonable observer can only conclude that the FCO is lying and David telling the truth. In fact, we have challenged Cook to sign a sworn statement saying that the MI6/Al Qaeda plot was 'pure fantasy [with] no basis in fact'.

The CPS did conclude that there is not enough *evidence* to secure a conviction. But it took them two months to come to this decision after the nine-month investigation. Even then, the CPS sought to misrepresent the findings of the enquiry:

'Final advice from the Crown Prosecution Service has now been received, saying that *the material does not substantiate the allegation* made by David Shayler.'

The work of the police and the CPS is not to 'substantiate ... allegations' or otherwise. (Anyway, David made a number of allegations, not just one.) Its job is to judge whether there is enough evidence to secure a conviction in front of a jury *beyond any reasonable doubt*. That is a very high standard of proof. The usual test of proof for Parliamentary or judicial enquiries is 'the balance of probabilities'.

At the time, David commented:

'This is the first time that the police have investigated an allegation against MI6, partly because MI6 had a *de facto* immunity from investigation into allegations of crime on the part of the service under the Royal Prerogative. It demonstrates why MI6 was put on a legal footing in the 1994 Intelligence Services Act. The investigation was not

280

of course ideal. The police were only looking to gather admissible evidence, which could be used to secure a conviction of the two MI6 officers who planned and carried out the plot, rather than trying to assess all relevant material, including intelligence.'[188]

This whole process once again calls into question the oversight arrangements for the services and the ability of ministers and officials to discharge their legal duties. In the future, we will be seeking permission to have the recording – on which David's sworn testimony was based – published so that the British people and, it is hoped, Parliament can see for themselves the truth of his words.

Further confirmation of the plot

That, again, might have been that but for a book published by two French journalists shortly before David went to trial in October 2002. Guillaume Dasquié, publisher of *Intelligence On-line*, and Jean-Charles Brisard, a former adviser to French President Jacques Chirac, who worked for the French intelligence services, published *Forbidden Truth*. The book confirms that the IFG was the Libyan Al Qaeda cell responsible for the attempt on Gaddafi's life. The book added that the IFG also included Anas al-Liby, a leading Al Qaeda member who is wanted for his involvement in the African embassy bombings and remains on the US government's most wanted list with a reward of $25 million for his capture. Al-Liby was with Osama bin Laden in Sudan before the Al Qaeda leader returned to Afghanistan[189] in 1996. Dasquié said:

---

[188] David's press release, November 2001.

[189] Despite suspicions that he was a high-level Al Qaeda operative, Al-Liby was given political asylum in Britain and lived in Manchester until May 2000 when he eluded a police raid on his house and fled abroad. The raid discovered a 180-page Al Qaeda 'manual for jihad' containing instructions for terrorist attacks.

281

'Bin Laden wanted to settle in Libya in the early 1990s but was hindered by the government of Muammar Gaddafi. Enraged by Libya's refusal, bin Laden organised attacks inside Libya, including assassination attempts against Gaddafi.'[190]

This provides yet more evidence that Tunworth was involved with Al Qaeda. At the very least, MI6 and MI5's understanding of Al Qaeda was so limited that neither service realised the implications of Tunworth's proposed coup in Libya: by assassinating Gaddafi the West would have lost a valuable ally in the battle with Al Qaeda and instead would have had to face the threat of an Al Qaeda in control of Libyan oil.

Given the timing of the MI6 payments – along with the close relationship between the IFG and bin Laden – it appears that British taxpayers' money was used to fund Al Qaeda attacks in Libya. Ashur Shamis, a Libyan expert on Islamic extremism, also added support to David's allegation:

'There was a rise in the activities of the Islamic Fighting Group from 1995 [around the time of the first payment], but many in Libya would be shocked if MI6 was involved.'[191]

Issues raised by the MI6/Al Qaeda conspiracy

Nearly all experts who work in counter-terrorism – as opposed to people on the 'outside' – believe that assassinations, particularly in the case of heads of state, only serve to destabilise a region. This was a view held by the US National Security Council until George W. Bush became president. Although certain Third World leaders do not share our standards of democracy, they do provide a certain amount of stability to their country and

---

[190] *Asia Times*, 19 November 2001.
[191] *The Observer*, 10 November 2002.

region. Remove such a leader from power by assassination and you will only create a power vacuum, which will lead to unrest and violence as factions compete for power.

Under international law, assassination operations are illegal. The only moral argument for assassinating any dictator or terrorist is that such action would lead to considerably fewer deaths than leaving him in power to continue to support violence against the West. By 1996, Gaddafi had ceased to support the IRA or indeed any terrorism. There were, though, a few unconfirmed reports that he had provided funds to Palestinian resistance movements in the Gaza Strip and the West Bank, territories illegally occupied by Israel and subject to UN resolutions. In this context, Gaddafi was funding organisations fighting for their own freedom, not terrorists.

In addition, MI6 had given its blessing to an individual who was leading a group of Islamic extremists with links to the Al Qaeda network. If Tunworth, the individual the Libyans caught in the act, had succeeded in assassinating Colonel Gaddafi, his supporters would in all probability have set up an Islamic extremist state in North Africa, further destabilising a region already subject to violence from Islamic fundamentalists.

Once Al Qaeda had Libya, it would have been all too easy for the group to take control of neighbouring states like Sudan, Tunisia, Algeria and Egypt, which already have their own internal problems with Al Qaeda. In control of a state like Libya or a region like North Africa, Al Qaeda would have had:

- Ready access to Libyan funds, running into billions.
- Control of the Libyan oil industry, destabilising world oil prices.
- The ability to launch many more attacks like 11 September, killing and maiming thousands of UK and US citizens.
- A land border with Israel and therefore a greatly increased capacity to attack the state of Israel.
- The means to destabilise world security on an enormous scale.

In fact, we only have to look at the current problems in Iraq to see what could have happened had the MI6/Al Qaeda conspiracy successfully led to Gaddafi's assassination. In the absence of Western military and security forces in a post-coup Libya, Al Qaeda would have had an even freer rein than it now has in post-war Iraq. At the very least, MI6 failed to realise the implications of Tunworth's admitted association with Islamic extremists or his intentions, a coup leading to an Al Qaeda state in Libya. That in itself would be of enormous concern, for which MI6 deserves to be roundly censured. But the truth is, the agent duped MI6 officers into funding that potential Al Qaeda takeover. David explains:

'This was an act of terrorism, in which Britain became a state sponsor of Islamic extremism. To put this in context, the Provisional IRA tries to avoid harming civilians on the basis that it produces bad publicity (although inevitably civilians are maimed and murdered when bombs go off on our streets). Islamic extremists and Al Qaeda have no such restraint. MI6 consciously supported terrorists who pose a greater threat to the national security of the UK than the Provisional IRA ever did.

'Although my boss did not seem to want to know, I made it clear to him that it was his responsibility to take it up the management chain. This whole operation was clearly a violation of the rule of law that my recruiter had told me the services must observe.

'I could also clearly see that the relationship between Tunworth and MI6 was flawed. MI5 had no security record of Tunworth and MI6 had only a couple of traces or brief mentions. Yet less than six months later, after a handful of meetings, MI6 had given him £100,000 of taxpayers' money to assassinate a foreign head of state. There was no way that MI6 could in that time have established a close enough relationship with him to make any realistic assessment of his character and reliability – he really could have been anybody.'

If this sort of MI6 activity only went on abroad and did not affect British citizens, it might be less frightening for us. However, MI6 routinely operates in the UK. In addition to IOPs,[192] UKG (now PT16B/OPS) ran agents in the UK and UKZ carries out surveillance.

If our elected representatives are not allowed to access MI6 documents about the conspiracy then perhaps they should try using the US Freedom of Information Act to obtain final confirmation of MI6 funding Tunworth and the IFG and Al Qaeda.

Conclusions

As David went on the record precisely because of the MI6 funding of Al Qaeda, it is worth looking at what he would have said in his defence in court, had he been allowed one:

- **Cover-up:** There is overwhelming evidence to indicate that the then Foreign Secretary Robin Cook's statement protected murderers in the intelligence services and ensured that David was thrown in prison with a view to extradition. The media has been slow to put this to Cook and the head of Britain's intelligence services, PM Tony Blair. Once the MI6 document appeared on the Internet and the police recovered relevant material, it must have been clear to the PM that his Foreign Secretary had not told the whole truth to the British people. In that situation, he had a simple choice under the ministerial code: either correct the statement of his minister or enter into the conspiracy. This is a cover-up of monumental proportions. Its implications for our democracy and the rule of law are enormous.

---

[192] The Intelligence Operations section responsible for placing usually untrue stories in British newspapers. See Chapter 7, *Lockerbie, Lawson and misinformation*, MI6's Information Operations and *The Sunday Telegraph*.

- **Justice:** Although the deaths of a few Libyans may not carry as much weight with newspaper editors as the deaths of British citizens, they are still somebody's sons and daughters. They are human beings and not 'collateral damage' as some commentators have suggested. British ministers have a duty to protect life.[193]
- **Law and order:** Any attempt to assassinate a foreign head of state is an act of terrorism, banned by international law under the Protection of Privileged Persons Act 1869. How can we condemn Libya for bombing flight PA103 over Lockerbie or assassinating WPC Yvonne Fletcher if we resort to the same terrible tactics?
- **Terrorism:** Removing Colonel Gaddafi would have led to a more extreme despot taking over in Libya, which would in all probability have led to attacks on British, US, European and Israeli citizens. Al Qaeda members, enemies of the West then and now, carried out the attempted coup. By this time, MI6 knew that Al Qaeda was responsible for the attack on the World Trade Centre in 1993. At the same time, MI5 had set up a section, G9C, in 1995, specifically to investigate Islamic extremist groups, particularly Al Qaeda. It was therefore the height of negligence (some might say stupidity) for MI6 to give up to £100,000 of taxpayers' money to the leader of such a group.
- **Failure of accountability and oversight:** Under the 1994 Intelligence Services Act, MI6 could have submitted the plot to the Foreign Secretary for permission. With that permission, they would have been immune from prosecution. By not submitting, MI6 officers were deciding British foreign policy towards Libya, not the democratically accountable Foreign Secretary. After David's return to the UK, we approached the police to investigate the plot. They initially refused to take possession of David's evidence, in the meantime allowing those involved to perhaps doctor the evidence.

---

[193] HRA, Article 2, ECHR, the right to life.

- **Lack of transparency:** If we can only maintain our reputation for democracy through lying, cheating and obsessive secrecy, then I suggest we are not really a liberal democracy at all. If you want to live in the sort of country in which the intelligence services are allowed to work in absolute secrecy and literally get away with murder, I suggest you go and live in Iran.
- **Corruption:** If you want to live in a functioning democracy, you have a moral and democratic duty to ensure that the laws of the land are upheld and that they apply equally to every citizen of that country. When the PM and the Foreign Secretary give MI6 officers a *de facto* immunity by refusing to take evidence of their conspiring to murder, the politicians send a very clear message to MI6. And that message is: 'You are above the law. You can get away with it now and can get away with it in the future. In fact, you enjoy the same rights as KGB officers in the former Soviet Union.'
- **Waste of money:** In the attack, MI6 wasted £100,000 of taxpayers' money. These funds could have been better spent on schoolbooks and medicines.

Chapter 18

The IRA: MI5's Failure to Prevent Bishopsgate

When David decided to go on the record with the catalogue of crimes and incompetence of our intelligence services, he wanted to ensure that the lives of the British public were properly protected. The British people have a right to know when the intelligence services fail to prevent terrorist attacks – even when in possession of reliable information – as a result of bureaucratic inertia. We have already seen how MI5 failed to prevent two PIRA attacks in the North East in June 1993 and the attack on the Israeli Embassy in July 1994. The Bishopsgate attack in April 1993 is just one further example.

It was the most financially devastating terrorist attack in UK history, given that it cost the taxpayer £350 million. The attack also hit the heart of the UK financial infrastructure, gave PIRA world-wide publicity for its cause, and drove HMG to the negotiating table for the first time in the then 25 years of the modern conflict.

In July 2000, shortly before we voluntarily came back to the UK after three years in France, David submitted an article he had written about Bishopsgate for *Punch* magazine to ministers under the injunction.

Background

In June 1998, frustrated by the refusal of ministers to hear his evidence, David broke ranks in the *Spectator*.[194] He said that he had drawn up a dossier on MI5's operational inefficiency which detailed the McNulty attacks. He also claimed that the bomb attack in Bishopsgate 'should not have happened'.

Two years later, when David came to write a more detailed account of Bishopsgate for *Punch*, the authorities had often locked horns with the magazine over David's column. In January 2000, government lawyers representing MI5 twice wrote to *Punch* asking that it: 'take advantage of the proviso to the injunction allowing for the Crown to confirm that it does not object to publication of certain material'.[195] David would of course have done so, if his submissions in the past had been properly investigated. But, as we have already seen, ministers like Straw and Cook used them to attack David's reliability and put him in prison.

Other letters claimed that some of the material in David's *Punch* articles was damaging to national security. This was clearly rubbish as there was never any attempt to prosecute Punch under section 5 of the 1989 OSA, which makes it an offence for editors, journalists and others to make a 'damaging' disclosure of official information.

When the editor wrote back asking where the articles actually harmed national security, the government solicitor and his ever-anonymous clients refused to add any more detail, claiming that this would further compromise state security. If a disclosure has *actually* harmed national security, it has already been harmed. Nothing can change that. If through a disclosure national security has *not* actually been harmed, then further discussion might lead to harm. But that only serves to prove that the original disclosure did not harm the security of the state in the first place.

---

[194] The article received wider circulation because it was covered in *The Times* of 19 June 1998.
[195] Treasury Solicitor to *Punch*, 17 and 21 January 2000.

Further discussion of a disclosure which has already harmed national security might lead to *embarrassment*. For example, an MI5 agent may have been named to a terrorist group and been killed. That damages national security. If MI5 admits that its agent has been killed, then that does not further harm national security as the agent is already dead. His usefulness to the protection of national security ended with his death, as he could no longer provide further intelligence. If MI5 was to admit publicly that the individual had been one of its agents, then that would be merely embarrassing to MI5.

The editor of *Punch*, happy that David's column did not harm national security, decided to publish David's column and be damned. When ministers tried to use the injunction, commentators turned on the government. In turn, it was forced into an embarrassing climb down. As a result, *Punch* continued to publish David's column without submitting to government censorship. It had taken on the bullies and won. It was all clearly too much for Tony and his cronies. However, the authorities were clearly still looking for a way to get back at *Punch* and its proprietor Mohammed Al Fayed, who had caused them embarrassment for demanding an inquest into the death of his son and Princess Diana.

Submission of the article to comply with injunction

By July 2000, David had offered his information to ministers and a variety of bodies on a number of occasions. None had taken possession of his information. David explains:

'The editor of *Punch* and I agreed that there was a clear public interest in revealing the failures of the intelligence services which put life and limb at risk. The weight of the public interest came down more firmly on the side of publication because the government was conspiring with the services to ensure that information vital to the security

291

of the public was suppressed. That is a cover-up, in anyone's book. Even then, we behaved responsibly by submitting the draft article to the government censors for approval at around midday on Friday 21 July 2000, well in advance of the *Punch* print deadline the following Monday evening.

'I was quite prepared for the government to remove some of the detail of the Bishopsgate piece I had written. In fact, I had even highlighted the information which might cause the government concern. I wanted to include as much detail as allowed because I did not want the authorities to use any vagueness as an excuse to deny or mis-represent the failure, as had for example occurred with the submission regarding the Gaddafi Plot and the Israeli Embassy bombing.'

David therefore had no complaint with the thrust of the Treasury Solicitor's (TS) comments, communicated to *Punch* three days after the article was submitted to the authorities:

'As we discussed on the telephone the concerns often arise from the detail in the text, rather than its subject matter... My clients have been scrutinising the text over the weekend and are continuing to do so... [They] appreciate that you face tight publishing deadlines, and will therefore respond as soon as practicable with their comments on the text. I regret however that that is unlikely to be before close of business today. In the interim, I must ask that you take no further step towards publication of the article.'[196]

David was astonished that the authorities had been unable to resolve these 'concerns' with their unnamed clients in time for Punch's deadline. The authorities had already vetted similar information before Mark Hollingsworth reported it in *Defending*

---

[196] TS's letter to *Punch*, 24 July 2000.

the Realm: MI5 and the Shayler Affair, which was published in 1999.

In the ensuing telephone calls, *Punch* asked the TS to provide more specific information about where the article allegedly breached the injunction and agreed to remove much of the detail of the piece. The next day the TS wrote to *Punch* again, although by this time the article had already been self-censored by the editor and David and sent for printing. The self-censorship amounted to removing one paragraph from David's proposed original article but allowing the rest to be published because it could not represent a threat to national security.

The offending Bishopsgate article

In order to understand the Bishopsgate attack, I quote in full the article David wrote for *Punch*:

'It is Friday 7th August 1992, my first week in T2A, the newly formed MI5 section designed to investigate the Provisional IRA (PIRA, the MI5 term) on the British mainland. I am sitting in an office on the third floor of the MI5 office in Curzon Street, drafting the Sit Rep or situation report for Operation Witless,[197] the investigation into an active service unit (ASU) which has been followed moving suspicious trucks around West London. Reporting indicates the ASU is planning a large-scale attack in London, like the ones that took place six months earlier, at the Baltic Exchange in the City and at Staples Corner near the M1/M25 intersection.

'The Sit Rep will go out to all services involved in the operation, updating them on the state of play. That Friday evening, all is calm. The joint Met S Squad/MI5 A4 surveillance team has tracked the lorry to a trailer park in

---

[197] Real codeword changed on the orders of MI5.

North West London. The ASU is under control and it looks like any potential attack will be thwarted and the culprits caught red-handed.

'This is the last operation with the MPSB, the Metropolitan Police Special Branch, leading the intelligence investigation. Home Secretary Kenneth Clarke has already decided to switch the roles of MI5 and the MPSB for IRA investigations in Britain. After 1st October 1992, MI5 will be in charge and MPSB will support them. That night, an A1 special operation team makes a covert entry of the lorry yard and drills a hole in the top of the trailer. The search reveals that it contains up to 300 lbs of home made explosive (HME) and possibly detonators.

'In the MI5 jargon, this makes the lorry a VBIED, a vehicle borne improvised explosive device. It appears to hold well over twice the amount of ammonium nitrate and sugar – which when combined, form the explosive compound – that was used at the Baltic Exchange or Staples Corner. The intelligence services do not know the actual targets of the potential attack. Officers are though speculating that these might include key centres of the UK infrastructure or economy like the Telecom Tower, Tottenham Court Road, Oxford Street, Canary Wharf or even the MI5 building itself to hinder the service's efficiency before it takes over primacy.

'Now that the A1 Spec Ops team has confirmed that the vehicle is ready to be primed, it seems likely that any planned attack is imminent. Over the weekend, the heads of the services involved meet and agree to arrest the ASU when they return to pick up the lorry. Sure enough, in the following days, the ASU returns. The Met's SO13, better known as the anti-terrorist squad, take control of the operation from intelligence teams because "executive action", in other words, arrests, are imminent. They wait until the members of the ASU, around four or five individuals, some of whom have not been identified, further incriminate themselves by touching or checking the trailer.

'As the targets gather around the truck, the head of the surveillance team at the site tries to contact George Churchill-Coleman, then the head of the anti-terrorist squad and one of Britain's most recognised and senior policemen. The man *in situ* wants to brief Churchill-Coleman with the updates and ask for permission to arrest the suspected terrorists. He tries the Ops rooms on the 18th floor of New Scotland Yard. He tries the Ops room working in support at MI5's Curzon Street building. He tries Churchill-Coleman's mobile contact number. It is switched off.

'The NSY Ops room tries to track down the elusive head of Britain's terrorist policing. He is nowhere to be found. The officer at the site knows that if he gives the order without first clearing it with his boss, he will be to blame should anything go wrong. This is not a matter of legal procedure or a hard and fast rule. The officer at the scene can give the arrest order, if he wishes. He decides against this however, in view of any possible, future blame. He has his future in the police to think about and, in any case, the Met should be able to track down Churchill-Coleman shortly. The latter does after all know there is a serious, fast-moving, live counter-terrorist operation proceeding apace.

'But Churchill-Coleman does not get in touch. Suddenly the ASU start to file out of the lorry yard. One by one they leave. None of the tens of policemen and intelligence officers present dare to give the arrest order. As the final member of the ASU leaves the yard, he seems to have spotted surveillance. He smiles and does a cocky thumbs-up before climbing into a car and roaring off into the grim industrial estates of North West London. He has already been identified as Cyril "Jimmy" McGuinness. The Met has known him for many years for his role in routine but major vehicle theft. This is some of the first evidence that his tricks of acquiring, "ringing" – fitting a stolen vehicle with registration and chassis numbers of a legally registered

295

vehicle belonging to someone else – and selling on knocked-off cars and lorries has a more sinister purpose, that he is carrying out these tasks in support of PIRA.

'Although three people were later arrested in connection with the operation, they were released without charge. McGuinness was not among those arrested.

'Fast forward to 24 April 1993. I am at home in Clapham preparing for a party that will be attended by MI5 officers. At around 10:30 that morning, the windows of our flat shake. I joke to my flatmates that it's probably PIRA and I'll have to spend the best part of Monday writing and rewriting the brief for the DG, as it will inevitably be changed and changed back by my boss, Wendy Probit.[198] "No investigating terrorists for me for a couple of days. I'll only be involved in paperwork," I joke. I don't tell the others that MI5 was, as of the day before, following a three-man ASU led by Rab Fryers and Gerry Mackin. (Much later, they were both sentenced to over 20 years in prison for their part in other separate terrorist operations.) I wonder if that ASU has managed to slip its MI5 surveillance team and unleash a devastating attack on the centre of London. As the midday news bulletins go out, it becomes clear that an enormous bomb has gone off in the City of London. The scenes of war-torn devastation reminiscent of downtown Beirut are to dominate the television news and the papers for weeks to come.

'For the record, the bomb consisted of a tonne of HME and ten pounds of Semtex to help detonate it. It killed one person, Ed Henty, a *News of the World* photographer, and injured 36. It also caused £350 million of damage to a million and a half square feet of office space at the heart of the City. The damage briefly shut down a few of the international banks and exchanges in the City, including the 600 ft NatWest tower, one of the most familiar landmarks on the City skyline.

[198] T2A/2, David's MI5 boss from 1992 to 1994.

'In a single attack, PIRA cost the UK economy several times as much as the entire Troubles had cost over the previous twenty-odd years. In addition, it all took place in front of 1,000 international politicians, businessmen and officials who had gathered in the HQ of the European Bank for Reconstruction and Development in nearby Exchange Square.

'As publicity for the Republican cause, it was far-reaching. With only one death and that a photographer trying to get a closer photograph of the suspected bomb lorry, it had far fewer drawbacks than the incident in Warrington two months before. That had attracted enormous condemnation, as two teenagers had been killed after the advanced codeword warning (which accompanies just about every PIRA attack) had failed to get through to the authorities. Even the IRA's supporters in the Republic of Ireland and the Six Counties had been obliged to condemn such a senseless waste of life, though these same supporters had always been less bothered by attacks on the British infrastructure or economic targets, which the IRA seemed to have been carrying out almost at will for the previous six or seven months.

'On the Friday of the following week, police released video photographs of two men, their faces largely covered by hoods, jumping from the bomb lorry before it had exploded. They were circulated among the officers of MI5's T2A section and quickly identified as Cyril "Jimmy" McGuinness and his erstwhile sidekick, Damien "Redboy" McPhillips, another criminal well known to the Met for car crime. By this time, the two were also very well-known to MI5. They had not been arrested in the wake of Operation Witless's failure and had gone on to lead MI5 a merry dance for the following six months. The service had spent literally £millions on following them all over the country. It had also tapped their wide range of mobile phones and tried to effect "covert entries" (or burglaries) of their premises to gather evidence against the two.

'At the same time, Jimmy and Redboy had imported and exported stolen vehicles, either for their own profit or in support of the IRA's mainland bombing campaign. Stolen or "ringed" vehicles were being used increasingly on the mainland to either smuggle PIRA Semtex and weapons into Britain or to transport primed bombs to their targets, as happened in the Bishopsgate attack.

'Although MI5 had an abundance of information linking the two to car crime, it never gathered enough evidence to have them arrested and convicted in connection with terrorist offences. At the same time, the two appeared not to give two hoots that MI5 was devoting almost around-the-clock surveillance to them. At one point, McGuinness led an MI5 surveillance team into a dead end street and then blocked its escape. The unarmed surveillance officers became alarmed as McGuinness edged his car towards theirs, fearing he would draw a revolver and shoot them. Instead, he observed their fear, laughed, then turned the car around and fled, losing his MI5 tail in the process. Two months after the Bishopsgate attack, police released a photofit. It was clearly McGuinness. By that time, he had gone OTR – on the run – to the Irish Republic. There was no chance of extraditing him.[199]

'At the time of the Bishopsgate attack, relations between Special Branch and MI5 were at an all-time low. The MPSB had been set up over a century before precisely to deal with threats from Irish Republican extremists. MI5 had taken primacy against the IRA from the Met six months before, undermining SO12's *raison d'être*. Those six months had been a disaster for MI5, as it had adopted inaccurate and out-of-date warrants from the Met and had struggled to adapt its working practices to the fast-moving target of PIRA. That period had seen more IRA attacks on the British

---

[199] The material in grey is information that the authorities demanded be removed from the draft article in their letter of 25 July 2000 but was published in *Punch* (see also later in this chapter). It is very difficult to see how any of it damages national security.

mainland than ever before (or since). The devastation of Bishopsgate was, it seemed, the icing on the cake of MI5's humiliation.

'The police lost no time in convincing the press of this. Stories began to appear in newspapers almost immediately, attributed as ever to anonymous "insiders" and "security sources". A week later, the theory was supplemented with harder information, leaked I suspect by the Branch. *Cops rap MI5 "bungle"*, proclaimed the *News of the World*, displaying an MI5 report sent to police forces the evening before the Bishopsgate bomb. It warned patrolling officers to be vigilant and gave descriptions of three men, who "will almost certainly be armed". A senior City Police officer was quoted as saying: "We're certain the anti-terrorist boys had these men in their sights and lost them. Alarm bells rang as soon as their warning arrived with us. The timing of it and the fact there were detailed descriptions of three suspects can mean only one thing – a cock-up."

'All very reasonable, you might think, except – as with so much of the hall of mirrors that is the murky world of intelligence – this is entirely wrong. The subjects whose descriptions appear in that warning are Mackin, Fryers and another unidentified individual (U/I – to use the MI5 shorthand), not Redboy and Jimmy. Ironically, MI5's A4 surveillance teams were in the City the morning of the Bishopsgate blast following Mackin and the U/I. In fact, the many surveillance cars and "mobiles" on foot must have passed the lorry containing the bomb, possibly more than once, without noticing anything suspicious. I don't think there is any shame in that. It is difficult enough to control a fast-moving target well versed in the techniques of anti- or counter-surveillance without having to look out for other suspect vehicles as well.

'The truth is, the ASU which carried out the Bishopsgate attack is not identical with the ASU described in the MI5 report. The clue to what really happened is though contained in the report when it talks of '*at least one* PIRA active service unit ... currently active in London'. ▇▇▇▇▇▇▇

▇▇▇▇▇▇▇

▇▇▇▇▇▇▇ GCHQ was aware that there was at least one PIRA ASU currently active in London, but failed to circulate sufficient detail to enable their members to be identified by Special Branch or MI5.[200]T2A/1 and group leader, Paul Slim, had then spent many hours in discussion with GCHQ's Z1 section. It is responsible for 'Action On', the process of obtaining permission to use and disseminate – as opposed to simply reading and filing – GCHQ intelligence.

'Of the three UK services, GCHQ is the most *infra dig*. It has none of the glamour of exotic locations, which comes with working for MI6. And none of the occasional excitement open to MI5 officers in live terrorist operations. In 1984, during the protest outside the Libyan People's Bureau [LPB] in London, GCHQ had had its one chance to make a lasting contribution to anti-terrorist work in Britain.

It received information from Colonel Gaddafi's office in Libya to the LPB. It asked loyal Libyans to open fire on the dissidents or "stray dogs" outside the Embassy in St James's Street. As a prior warning of a possible attack, it was very useful intelligence or would have been, if it had been handed on in a timely fashion. But it wasn't as the nine-to-five bureaucrats at GCHQ had gone home for the night. As a result, the report did not go to the police or MI5 that day. In the meantime, WPC Yvonne Fletcher was fatally shot from a window of the LPB.

'Years later when I was working for MI5, officers still continued to encounter similar bureaucratic problems with GCHQ. Its staff seemed not to understand that intelligence was useless unless it could be deployed in the field. MI5

[200] The authorities asked that the original wording be removed but *Punch* did not receive this until after its print deadline. The magazine changed the wording to the white text now highlighted and published it. It is therefore public domain.

officers were well-trained in disguising sources. They had grown used to it in their work with Special Branch officers who were hardly ever allowed to see actual transcripts of bugging material or raw agent reports. MI5 officers were therefore well capable of disguising any GCHQ material so that the police – or any prying unauthorised eyes – would not be able to guess where it came from. Despite this GCHQ always displayed far too much caution over the dissemination, often refusing to allow MI5 to pass on vital intelligence at all or allowing only a version so watered down that it ceased to have the required impact with the organisation receiving it. I believe the latter occurred with the Bishopsgate intelligence.

'I was not actually privy to the discussions that night, although other officers in T2A briefed me shortly after. As far as I can gather, the GCHQ intelligence was only passed on to police in the form of "*at least one* PIRA active service unit..." No description of McGuinness was issued nor were the bobbies on the beat given any further indication of McGuinness's intentions. There was certainly no mention of the impending "spectacular" that weekend. I would hope that the authorities considered having McGuinness arrested that weekend, just in case, but it wasn't clear from the discussion in the week afterwards whether that option had been floated at all.

'So what happened to McGuinness and McPhillips after they went OTR in June 1993? As with other PIRA members who suspect that the game might be up, they stayed in the Republic until they thought the coast was clear again. In April 1994, the police let it be known that they knew the identity of the bombers and were still intent on putting them away. Around this time – I can't remember exactly when – McGuinness was finally arrested in connection with routine car crime. He was charged with a variety of offences, none of them relating to terrorism. Material taken from his property included lists of registration numbers belonging to MI5 surveillance vehicles.

'I do not know whether he was at least subsequently convicted of car crime as I left T2A not long after. One thing is for sure though. If he had been arrested in Operation Witless, he would probably have been convicted and sentenced to 20-odd years in prison. As a result, MI5 would have been able to more effectively combat the IRA on the British mainland from October 1992, when the service took primacy from MPSB. That means PIRA would have been less able to embarrass MI5, which was at the time struggling with its new role due to inefficiency and management failure, and been less confident in its efforts to cause mayhem on the mainland. And maybe, just maybe, Bishopsgate would never have happened at all and the IRA would have been forced around the negotiating table much, much sooner.'

Government's proposed redactions

In its letter of 25 July 2000, the TS asked *Punch* to remove the passages that are highlighted above in grey. These proposed amendments reveal a great deal about the authorities' under-standing of their role as censor,[201] which allow them to suppress free speech only in the context of protecting national security.

The proposed redaction of GCHQ's role in all this serves as a good illustration of all of the above. Knowing the article was to be submitted, David had included as much detail about GCHQ's role in failing to prevent Bishopsgate as possible. It was, he reasoned, up to the censors to make the case for banning it. In the absence of clear guidelines from the censors, *Punch* removed all the detail from the version of the article which eventually appeared on 26 July 2000:

'GCHQ was aware that there was at least one PIRA ASU

---

[201] Under the HRA.

currently active in London but failed to circulate sufficient detail to enable their members to be identified by Special Branch and MI5.'

In this form, the information is so vague that it is difficult to see how its disclosure could harm national security, particularly as the matter was already in the public domain. In an article based on a conversation with David about Bishopsgate, *The Sunday Express* had reported:

> '[Shayler] added that police had a "pretty clear indication" that the terrorists were going to carry out a large-scale attack in London but the information was wasted. "GCHQ is always worried about their sources of information being compromised and GCHQ never appreciates that intelligence has to be used to be effective," said Shayler.'[202]

In fact, in the TS's letter of 25 July 2000, the censors suggested that the GCHQ information be replaced with the following sentence from *Defending the Realm*, which had already been approved by the authorities:

> '[David] discovered that the culprits could have been arrested six months beforehand: a breakdown in communications between MI5 and Government Communications Head-quarters (GCHQ) prevented the Service from reacting to prior intelligence about the attack.'[203]

But this version was clearly designed to mislead. It conflated two separate events, the failure to arrest during Operation WITLESS in August 1992, and GCHQ's failure to allow other agencies to pass on its information in April 1993. This gave the appearance that GCHQ's failure was six months before

---

[202] *The Sunday Express*, 9 April 2000.
[203] Hollingsworth, *Defending the Realm*, p.4.

Bishopsgate when it in fact occurred shortly before the attack. The authorities were therefore asking *Punch* to knowingly mislead the British public by replacing accurate information with inaccuracies. That is irresponsible on the part of the government censors and points to a conscious cover-up of facts embarrassing to the intelligence services, similar to MI5 lying to government about the McNulty case. Indeed, when the two already published passages from *The Sunday Express* and *Defending the Realm* are put side by side, it is clear that *Punch* is not adding any detail to what is already in the public domain.

But the government ordered *Punch* to remove *any* mention of GCHQ from the original article as if it could hide the existence of GCHQ. As hard as they might try, the authorities cannot disguise the two GCHQ buildings in Cheltenham, which can be seen from the public highway, or hide Acts of Parliament. The 1994 Intelligence Services Act confirms GCHQ's legal existence. Again, this represents an untenable suppression of freedom of expression.

After all, it is hard to see how the following could in any way harm national security:

'Of the three UK services, GCHQ is the most *infra dig*. It has none of the glamour of exotic locations, which comes with working for MI6. And none of the occasional excitement open to MI5 officers in live terrorist operations.'

It certainly doesn't damage the security of the state and is the sort of comment anyone could make. But it gets worse. As we have already discussed, the authorities cannot lawfully suppress information already in the public domain. They could not therefore argue that the following, which they asked to be removed, breached the injunction:

'In 1984, during the protest outside the Libyan People's Bureau in London, GCHQ had had its one chance to make

304

a lasting contribution to anti-terrorist work in Britain. It received information[204] from Colonel Gaddafi's office in Libya to the LPB. It asked loyal Libyans to open fire on the dissidents or "stray dogs" outside the Embassy in St James's Street. As a prior warning of a possible attack, it was very useful intelligence or would have been, if it had been handed on in a timely fashion. But it wasn't, as the nine-to-five bureaucrats at GCHQ had gone home for the night. As a result, the report did not go to the police or MI5 that day. In the meantime, WPC Yvonne Fletcher was fatally shot from a window of the LPB.'

Because it had already appeared in the public domain:

'MPSB stated that MI5 had been responsible for the death of WPC Yvonne Fletcher outside the Libyan embassy in 1984. It claimed that the agency had failed to pass on vital intelligence, which was a telegram sent from Libya to the embassy in London. In fact, the telegram had been intercepted by GCHQ and not passed on at all, because it arrived outside their then office hours of 9 a.m. to 5 p.m.'[205]

Worse still from the point of view of the authorities, *government censors already knew the information was in the public domain* because they were responsible for clearing it for inclusion in *Defending the Realm*. Less understandable is the decision of the censors to ask for removal of the other paragraphs, which concern procedural problems between the services.

---

[204] Changed on the orders of MI5, even though the next passage from *Defending the Realm* confirms that the information removed is already in the public domain: 'In fact, the telegram had been intercepted by GCHQ and not passed on at all.'
[205] Hollingsworth, *Defending the Realm*, p.126.

Censorship of legitimate comment

I cannot even begin to imagine why the censors wanted to remove the second part of the passage highlighted in grey, which begins: 'Years later when I was working for MI5...' (see p.300). It is difficult to see how this passage would compromise sources, sensitive operational techniques or ongoing operations or otherwise compromise national security. It describes the procedures for disseminating intelligence. Police and intelligence services use similar procedures across the world, although usually with more respect for the need to prevent terrorist attacks and catch terrorists.

The week the article came out, convicted terrorists from PIRA were walking free from the Maze prison as part of the Good Friday agreement. If this did not spell the end of the armed struggle and much of MI5's interest in members of PIRA, then it certainly demonstrated that the authorities could see no near resumption of the armed struggle. Otherwise, why release terrorists likely to pose a threat to public safety?

The same argument applies to *Punch*'s decision to name the two men responsible for Bishopsgate, Cyril 'Jimmy' McGuinness and Damien 'Redboy' McPhillips. McGuinness knew he had been subject to MI5 surveillance in the past as the service had been obliged to disclose its surveillance logs on him when he had been charged (but never prosecuted) for routine car crime. If McGuinness knew so would his partner in crime, Redboy. McGuinness would also have been alerted to the intelligence services' interest in him by the publication of the photofit of the alleged Bishopsgate bomber in *The News of the World*. It bears a clear resemblance to him.

The TS's letter of 25 July 2000 provides one further insight into the minds of the censors. In the disclosures in *The Mail on Sunday*, David stated that MI5 spent its time endlessly poring over drafts at the expense of actually investigating and preventing terrorism. That letter provided further proof of this tendency:

'Delete: "OTR – on the run – to the Irish Republic" …
and substitute "slipped over to Ireland". Remove: "There
was no chance of extraditing him".
'Delete: "in the Republic" … and substitute "over there".'

Again, it is difficult to see how these amendments would protect
national security, particularly as one of them, 'There was no chance
of extraditing him', was a comment on the Republic of Ireland's
reluctance to hand over PIRA suspects to the British authorities,
rather than a piece of secret intelligence needing protection.

The Attorney General acts – against *Punch*

On 26 July 2000, *Punch* published David's article about the
failure of the authorities to prevent Bishopsgate. Instead of
taking steps to call the services publicly to account, the Attorney
General decided the magazine was to be the first publication
to be prosecuted under the injunction taken out against the
media and David in September 1997. David takes up the story:

'As usual, the thrust of the authorities' argument was that
the clear "brightline" had to be preserved. By this point,
because the services had failed to take my evidence when it
was offered, many media organisations had published or
broadcast my words without using the legal route to disclosure.
'If anyone is any doubt about this, then they should read
the version of the writ the government served on me in
December 1999.[206] It listed eight alleged breaches of the
injunction. I say "alleged" because ministers had not taken
legal action against the media involved, even though they
had breached the injunction – a criminal offence – by the
government's own admission.[207]

---

[206] An update of the order of Mr Justice Keane, 5 September 1997.
[207] Although a writ is a civil action, its breach is a criminal offence.

'By choosing to single out *Punch* for prosecution and ignore the actions of bigger publications which could hit back, the government was once again using the rule of law arbitrarily to persecute smaller publications who could not fight back.

'It is clear the authorities' action against *Punch* represented further persecution of those who embarrassed the services rather than an attempt to uphold the rule of law or prevent damage to national security.'

Punch taken to court

The HRA became law on 1 October 2000. In an early test of the Act, a couple of days later the Attorney General took *Punch* and its editor to court for publishing David's article about the Bishopsgate attack. Although government lawyers had claimed that:

'the purpose of an injunction is not ... to prevent criticism of the Security Service but is to prevent damage to national security',[208]

the prosecution argued that the injunction was taken out not to protect national security but to preserve the administration of justice. The Crown did not adduce any evidence of damage to national security caused by the article at any point during the hearings, although prosecuting counsel did try to submit an affidavit from the Attorney General after the prosecution had rested. Judge Silber refused to allow the evidence to be heard.

Despite this, Silber ruled that *Punch* was in contempt of court on the grounds of interfering in the administration of justice. Although the Appeal Court later overturned the conviction of the editor of *Punch*, the House of Lords re-instated it. The

---

[208] TS to *Punch*, 21 January 2000.

editor now has a criminal record simply for publishing an article which embarrassed ministers and the services. He is not taking his case to the European Court of Human Rights.

Support from a former MI5 officer

The authorities have also tried to undermine David by claiming he was a lone voice in MI5. They conveniently forget that I too worked there, was similarly frustrated and disgusted by what I saw, and that is why I supported him in blowing the whistle. The authorities also gloss over the number of disillusioned officers flooding out of the service. However, in July 2000, a month before we returned to the UK, another officer spoke out against MI5.

Jestyn Thirkell-White had joined MI5 at the same time as David. He had also worked with me in T5E, so he knew us both well. As well as being our friend, he was liked and respected in the service. However, by April 1996 he had had enough of the incompetence of MI5 and left to take up a new job at a merchant bank.

Jestyn stayed in contact with us when we were in France. While he had his reservations about David's going public, he agreed that *something* had to be done to improve MI5. As David's case developed, Jestyn became more and more incensed about the way he was being portrayed in the media – it bore no resemblance to the man he knew and liked. He also could not believe that the government had merely brushed David's allegations aside rather than hold MI5 and MI6 to account. Finally, he followed his conscience and took the brave step of approaching the journalist who had broken David's story, Mark Hollingsworth. He in turn talked to *The Guardian*, who planned to splash Jestyn's allegations of MI5's incompetence across the front page.[209] These allegations included the following:

---

[209] *The Guardian*, 22 July 2000.

SPIES, LIES AND WHISTLEBLOWERS

- He did not accept Jack Straw's statements that David's revelations had in any way damaged national security.
- He expected an independent enquiry because the allegations were serious enough to warrant proper investigation.
- MI5 officers wasted vital hours in the search for PIRA bombers dickering [*sic*] about with the wording of warrants, because of bureaucratic 'turf wars'.

By remarkable coincidence, on the day *The Guardian* was due to publish these allegations, a civil servant at the Cabinet Office called Colin Davenport was questioned by MPSB on suspicion of having leaked a copy of the book written by MI5's former DG Stella Rimington to *The Sun* newspaper. So while Jestyn's allegations and support for David did appear at the bottom of the front page of *The Guardian*, most news coverage that day was devoted to Rimington's book. The civil servant was never charged for this apparent breach of section 1 of the OSA. Indeed, in January 2003 he received a CBE.

Chapter 19

More MI5 'Bullshit' at the Bloody Sunday Enquiry

When intelligence documents which indicated that leading Sinn Fein member Martin McGuinness had admitted firing the first shot at the Bloody Sunday march were leaked to and published in *The Guardian* in 2001, it looked to any innocent and impartial observer as if McGuinness had been caught bang to rights. The paper said:

> 'One thing that bothers McGuinness about the Bloody Sunday thing was that he fired the first shot and no one knows this. This seems to be on McGuinness's conscience. He has spoken to Infliction about it several times.'

Although the document was dated 1984 and was only presented to the Saville Enquiry into Bloody Sunday with extensive 'redactions' – information blacked out supposedly to protect national security – David and I were, like many other readers, taken in by what appeared to be persuasive intelligence. Unlike them, I immediately revised my opinion when David shouted through to me one day:

> 'What does the name Infliction mean to you?'
> 'Bullshitter,' I instantly replied.
> 'Well, you'll be pleased to know that, according to today's

311

Guardian, he was the source of the claim that McGuinness fired the first shot on Bloody Sunday.'

I had first come across concerns about the source codenamed Infliction when I joined T5 in August 1993. David Kane, my predecessor, told me that it was well known that Infliction's information was suspect. He went through files with me and pointed out source reports from Infliction, whom he called a 'bullshitter'. He told me that Infliction was not trusted because:

'he always seemed to know something about everything, which was not usual. Agents and informers usually are able to give information on discrete issues only.'[210]

In my post as T5E/2, I saw Infliction's source reports. Each report was marked with words to the effect that his reliability was being re-assessed. As I said in my sworn statement to the enquiry:

'I do not recall ever seeing comments relating to an established source suggesting that their reliability was under constant review.'[211]

Meanwhile, David had also come across Infliction's reporting during his time in T Branch. While researching an IRA supporter, he had discovered that Infliction had reported that the suspect had influence within higher echelons of PIRA. Curiously though, the service had no other significant intelligence traces of the target, which would have been usual for an individual high up in PIRA's northern command. To resolve this, David asked an officer in T8, the agent handling section, for details of Infliction's reliability. He also branded the agent a 'bullshitter'. As a matter of course, David then discussed him with other MI5 officers in

---

[210] My evidential statement to the Saville Enquiry, KM12, 12 September 2002.
[211] My evidential statement to the Saville Enquiry, KM12, 12 September 2002.

T branch. They agreed with this view. To say that he was not trusted would be an understatement.

In fact T8 had recruited Infliction in the belief that he was providing accurate and reliable intelligence about leading members of the Republican movement, particularly in the PIRA northern command. On one occasion, MI5 went with his version of events, only for the service to be made to look stupid. As a result, it 'terminated' Infliction – ceased to employ him as an agent, rather putting a bullet in the back of his head. When David asked the T8 officer if anyone had gone through Infliction's reporting to assess which reports – if any – might be reliable, he smiled whimsically as he confirmed this, before confiding that Infliction had conned officers who had since risen within the service.

At the Saville Enquiry

On 8 May 2003, both David and I were cross-examined on the sworn statements we had given to the Saville Enquiry into Bloody Sunday. No solid evidence was put before us that might refute or undermine our testimony. However, under cross-examination, as a result of David's and my evidence, Infliction's handler, Officer A, was forced to admit on behalf of MI5 that he had been 'economical with the truth' when preparing his first statement, making no mention of MI5's formal assessment that Infliction was 'not fully reliable'. Rather embarrassingly for MI5, he was forced to issue a second statement, confirming that the service knew that Infliction had lied to them on occasions:[212]

> Counsel: by the time of this statement,[213] which is 16th January 2003, you are now providing information that, on occasions, Infliction had lied; is that correct?

---

[212] The verbatim cross examination took place on 8 May 2003.
[213] Saville Enquiry, witness statement, KA2.21.

Officer A: Yes, yes...
Counsel: You did not give the complete picture at all in your first statement to this Inquiry; is that correct?
Officer A: Well, that is why I was invited to make further statements, as I understand other witnesses have been.

Cross-examination also drew from a flustered and evasive Officer A an admission that he knew other MI5 officers – apart from David and me – had expressed the opinion that Infliction was a bullshitter, yet not thought this relevant to the enquiry:

Counsel: On occasions in fact he had been bullshitting; is that correct?
Officer A: What I say is that on a few – there were a few instances in which we assessed that he was bullshitting. And, as you say, that he had lied, and I described these issues yesterday.
Counsel: Indeed in that statement you introduce for the first time the information that some had initially suspected at least, that in fact Infliction was a fabricator; do you see that?
Officer A: Yes...
Counsel: Is there any particular reason why those views [of other MI5 officers] and those pieces of information, relevant I would suggest to Infliction's reliability, did not appear in your first statement to the Tribunal?
Officer A: It is – the first statement and this statement are not inconsistent. The second statement was, and this particular paragraph was an expansion of the remarks I made in the first statement.
Counsel: But you only confirmed that in fact there had been instances of [bullshitting] in your second statement once it had been made clear to you that another former member of the Security Services was giving information, that that was the status, according to some in the service, of Infliction?

314

Officer A: What I say in my first statement is that there was scepticism about – perhaps I could see again, it would be helpful, on the screen, what precisely I said there.

To say that there was 'scepticism about' Infliction is yet another example of MI5 being 'economical with truth' and sexing up intelligence by omission. Officer A's statement is a thoroughly dishonest piece of work. A statement to a public enquiry should be the truth, the whole truth and nothing but the truth. If his statement was signed under oath, Officer A should be charged with perjury and tried for his underhand attempts to pin the blame for Bloody Sunday on Martin McGuinness:

Counsel: Why did you not, presumably with your knowledge that the statement was going to be signed and sent to the Inquiry, why did you not tell the Inquiry the information that you knew they were looking for when you made your first statement, ie, comment or otherwise on your knowledge of the reliability of Infliction? It could only be because you did not want that information out unless you absolutely had to give it; is that not correct?

Officer A: I made the comment in my first statement, and indeed in my second statement, that Infliction was a reliable agent and overall he was a reliable agent.

Counsel: He is now, though, on your evidence, and has been a liar, a bullshitter, someone who was paid and someone for whom money, on your evidence, was extremely important. Someone who, in fact, withheld information from you; someone who in fact failed to give you complete information and someone who, on occasions, refused to answer your questions.

This all rather calls into question what MI5 considers to be a reliable agent. Most of us thought that this meant an agent was consistently reliable, not that he was reliable some of the time but then made things up and lied from time to time. The enquiry

315

also heard that the service had redacted – or blacked out – the phrase: 'Source description, reliability not fully assessed', when it submitted the report to the enquiry:

> Counsel: These are the two redacted pages of the report sent from London.[214] On the face of these two pages there is no assessment of reliability that could have been copied by the officer in Belfast. However, I believe you have in front of you a small bundle of unredacted documents. Is there a code there?
>
> Officer A: Yes, there is.
>
> Counsel: An entry in code. Can you tell the Tribunal what the entry, if decoded, would read?
>
> Officer A: Um, it would – which particular part of the code, all of it or the middle part?
>
> Counsel: The purpose of my question is to ask you whether there is, within that code, any assessment of reliability?
>
> Officer A: Yes, there is.
>
> Counsel: Can you tell me if decoded, what that assessment of reliability would read?
>
> Officer A: Reliability not fully established or not fully tested.

We really have to ask why MI5 felt the need to remove the assessment that Infliction's reliability was 'not fully established' from such a controversial document submitted to an official enquiry. It does not compromise the agent's identity and cannot have any implications for national security. The redaction was obviously designed to make the enquiry think that it was dealing with reliable intelligence, when it was not.

In a true democracy such an act would be seen as corruption or obstructing the course of justice. We have to wonder why no one from MI5 has been charged in this regard. After all, if the service is allowed to get away with it in this instance, what

---

[214] Saville Enquiry, document numbers G109.668 and G109.669.

incentive is there to prevent the service from doing it again, when there are no MI5 whistleblowers around?

The day after David and I gave evidence, further support for our information emerged from an unlikely source, Officer E, a woman described as David's former boss. We believe that Officer E is Wendy Probit, T2A/2, who managed David when he was in T2A. She told the enquiry that T Branch officers regarded Infliction's reporting as far from wholly reliable:

> 'Although I don't recall when I first heard this, I do have a general recollection that his reporting was considered by others to be of mixed reliability. As far as I recall, I gained this impression from hearing others comment on Infliction and/or his reporting.'

This also has implications for Officer A's statement regarding Infliction's reliability. He deliberately did not mention in his first statement that other MI5 officers had reservations about Infliction's reporting.

So did McGuinness fire the first shot?

New information

Declassified MI5 documents submitted to the Saville Enquiry have now provided further information about Infliction. In April 1984, Officer A sent MI5 HQ in London a note:

> 'Martin McGuinness had admitted to Infliction that he had personally fired the shot (from a Thompson machine gun on "single shot") from the Rossville Flats in Bogside that had precipitated the "Bloody Sunday" episode.'

According to the MI5 note, Infliction replied that 'it would be a big destabilising point' when asked about McGuinness's reaction,

317

should he discover that MI5 knew about the claim. Infliction then asked MI5 how and why it would 'make it known' and 'when would be the best time'. Under cross-examination on 7 May 2003, Officer A was asked why he did not question Infliction further about such a dramatic claim. He replied that it was not 'of immediate and critical importance at that time'.

Another document submitted to the enquiry, dated May 1984, recorded that Infliction no longer had access to the IRA when he provided the intelligence about McGuinness, though he was still working for MI5 on an *ad hoc* basis. Other documents point out that Infliction was paid between £15,000 and £25,000 a year, although it is not clear whether he still received this at the time he provided the McGuinness information.

Assessment

If I were sitting behind a desk in T5, assessing the report in question, I would be obliged to conclude that in intelligence terms it is worthless for the following reasons:

- Charitably, Infliction's reliability was 'not fully established' when he provided the intelligence, even though he had a long record of working for MI5. His reporting must therefore have been less than accurate. In fact, he was a 'bullshitter' known to invent information, presumably to boost his currency with the agent handling section, T8.
- The allegation was passed to MI5 some 12 years after the events of Bloody Sunday. It is not clear from the documents when McGuinness was alleged to have told Infliction, but the other MI5 reports released to the enquiry make it clear that Infliction no longer had access to PIRA in spring 1984, when he made the claim.
- Officer A did not take the allegation seriously when it was made, otherwise he would have asked for more details. There is no collateral or corroboration for the claim.

- From context, it almost appears that Infliction has made up his claim to create mischief. When asked about its effect, he is all too aware that it would be a big 'destabilising point' for the IRA. He also seems anxious to find out how this 'intelligence' is to be used by MI5, indicating that he lied to discredit McGuinness.
- Given that he no longer had a formal relationship with MI5, it may be that Infliction said it in the hope that he would be taken on again. It is clear from cross-examination of Officer A that he knew that money was 'extremely important' to the agent.

Lawyers for families of those killed and wounded on Bloody Sunday have asked the enquiry why Infliction has not been named or subpoenaed to answer questions about his rather dubious claim. McGuinness would after all have a good idea of his identity, if he really had confided to Infliction that he fired the first shot on Bloody Sunday. This and the blacking out of relevant information like the assessment of the agent's reliability has prompted the relatives of those murdered on Bloody Sunday to speculate why the material was released, if not to undermine their campaign for justice.

If Infliction made up the claim in the hope he could destabilise the IRA, he could hardly have envisaged it would be so closely scrutinised by an enquiry and former officers of the services, when it came out nearly 20 years later. He probably hoped it would be leaked to a newspaper without caveats, making its impact more devastating and persuasive than it actually was, which is, ironically, how the material first appeared in *The Guardian* in 2001. If David and I had not been in a position to give the public an authoritative inside account of Infliction, then it might just have worked.

Once again, Parliament must call the MI5 officers who tried to pervert the truth to answer for their actions under oath. We should also remember that Bloody Sunday – more than any other event in Ireland's violent and tragic history – was the catalyst which made many formerly law-abiding Catholics forswear British democracy and take up arms. Those responsible for the events of Bloody Sunday must be made to pay for their role in killing innocent civilians and contributing to nearly 30 years of civil war in the UK.

The real villain of Bloody Sunday

In October 2003, a former paratrooper known only as Soldier F was forced to admit under cross-examination that on Bloody Sunday he shot dead four Catholics.

By his own account, Soldier F killed an unarmed man, Barney McGuigan, as he went to the aid of a dying man, waving a white handkerchief, the recognised 'flag' of surrender. The former sergeant-major also conceded that he killed the man McGuigan was trying to help, Patrick Doherty, from behind. Although he claimed Doherty was armed with a pistol, other eyewitnesses have refuted this account. When asked by Michael Mansfield QC if he would admit shooting McGuigan to his wife and six children who were sitting in the public gallery, Soldier F just said: 'Yes'. At that point the inquiry was adjourned while McGuigan's sobbing widow was led from the public gallery.

Chapter 20

British Justice in Action

Countdown to imprisonment

David returned to the UK on 21 August 2000, hoping for justice and a trial within a reasonable time frame. After all, he had only been charged with the disclosures made to *The Mail on Sunday* on 24 August 1997 – not with any of his subsequent disclosures, not even the Gaddafi plot. The intervening three years had been more than enough time for the police and CPS to put their case together. However, the prosecution insisted on an interminable process of pre-trial hearings, in an attempt to ensure that David could say nothing in his defence when he eventually appeared before a jury.

David had to conduct his own case in the Old Bailey. As the pre-trial hearings had ruled out any defence under law, barristers were unable to represent him. At no point in the legal process was he allowed to adduce evidence, let alone freely cross-examine his accusers.

He was convicted on 4 November 2002, over two years after his return to the UK.

2001

18 February
Trial judge Mr Justice Moses dismisses an application by

321

government lawyers that the media should be banned from reporting a hearing in David's case, because part of the proceedings take place in secret. However, David and his defence team are barred from a two and a half hour hearing, in which prosecuting counsel Nigel Sweeney QC discusses the evidence against David relating to the documents he had taken and which he had voluntarily handed back to MI5. Sweeney said in open court:

> 'The material might not seem interesting or comprehensible but *if it got into wrong hands* it would mean all too much, and people's lives would be put at risk.'

Mr Justice Moses seems oblivious to the fact that the documents did not end up in the wrong hands. They were used by the journalists to verify David's statements, were not quoted, and had been kept in a safe.

26 April

Another pre-trial legal hearing takes place in front of Mr Justice Moses at the Royal Courts of Justice in the Strand.

Quoting from a House of Lords judgment in the case of George Blake, the former MI6 officer and traitor, Sweeney argues that:

> 'An absolute rule against disclosure, visible to all, makes good sense.'

In spite of this 'absolute rule against disclosure', Sweeney also argued that David had the right under section 7(3) of the OSA, governing rules for Crown Servants, to go to the Cabinet Secretary, to the Prime Minister or to the police. This was news to us. The document we signed on leaving MI5 stated that we could only go to MI5. Steve Canute, when discussing David's novel in 1997, had told him he must submit it only to MI5.

We heard about this alleged route to legal disclosure for the first time when Mr Sweeney raised it that day. But his position is illogical. On the one hand he stated that there was a 'clear bright line' against any disclosure; on the other hand he was saying that David could have approached a whole panoply of officials. But we had the proof over a number of years that no government officials would take the evidence when it was repeatedly offered. David had also had to gain permission from MI5 and MI6 to give his evidence about the Gaddafi plot to the police. But David was not allowed to say anything about all this.

At trial, MI5 was unable to disclose any service documents which laid down procedures for following this course of action or indeed any record of its existence. David comments:

'If there had been real avenues of complaint open to me under section 7(3), I would have used them. But I was always told in the service that any disclosure outside the service – even to ministers or the police – constituted a breach of section 1 the 1989 OSA. At no point during my service did anyone mention the alleged section 7(3) route of disclosure to government ministers. Indeed, it is not mentioned at all in the document which I signed on leaving and which I was never given a copy of. Nor does Stella Rimington mention it in *Open Secret* when she complains about her treatment at the hands of Whitehall.

'During the first induction course, TC101, new officers' attention was drawn to the 1989 OSA. If memory serves correctly, the course tutors had highlighted or put in quotations what we were told was the relevant section of the Act, section 1(1) and 1(2). I am absolutely certain there was no discussion of section 7(3) nor any attempt to draw my attention to it. In fact, there was not one mention of section 7(3) in the entire time I was in the service. I believe this is because not even the management of MI5 shares Mr Sweeney's construction of the 1989 OSA section 7(3). I was not allowed to mention any of these issues to the jury.'

Later in the legal process, we sought disclosure of the TC101 induction course to prove that MI5 does not interpret the OSA in the same way as the Court.

However, the trial Judge Mr Justice Moses turned down this request because it would clearly have undermined the interpretation of the OSA that he had already ruled on, without evidence. This goes to the heart of the unlawfulness of the 1989 OSA as section 7(3) gives former Crown servants – as defined by the OSA in section 12 but not former intelligence officers like David – the right to take disclosures to other Crown servants.

A year or two ago I was told by a trusted source that the Home Office lawyers had a crisis meeting the week after David returned to the UK in August 2000. They knew they were on the ropes, as the OSA's absolute rule against disclosure to anyone outside the intelligence services was incompatible with the ECHR. Then someone came up with the novel idea of using the section 7(3) argument against David. The Home Office held its breath, gave it a go, and was delighted to find that they had got away with it.

27 April
Under the headline: 'Why didn't you go to police? judge asks Shayler', *The Times* quotes Judge Moses as saying: 'Why not just go to the police?' even though Mr Justice Moses never uttered those words or that sentiment.

16 May
Mr Justice Moses rules that any unauthorised disclosure by a serving or former member of the security and intelligence services would put national security at risk, even though David wished to alert people to MI6's support for Al Qaeda. This means that David cannot use the defence that his disclosures served the public interest or that they did not damage national security.

Judge Moses also rules that the prosecution only has to prove that David:

- Worked for the service.
- Disclosed material 'relating to the work of – or in support of – the service'.
- Did so without permission.

There was no requirement even to prove that this was classified information. David tells the media:

'The implications of this decision are enormous. If this judgment is correct, the security services can take comfort from the fact that they are immune from whistleblowing [in all circumstances]. We hope that the Court of Appeal will restore to me the opportunity to run a defence concerning the illegality and malpractice of the intelligence services.'

18 July
The Guardian, *The Times*, *The Mirror*, the *Daily Mail* and other newspapers intervene in David's case, insisting a blanket ban preventing former MI5 officers from disclosing anything about their work was unlawful and in breach of the ECHR. Michael Tugendhat QC, acting for the press, told the Court of Appeal:

'In even the best run institutions, some responsible people think a cover up is preferable to a disclosure when in fact it is not. The avoidance of a breakdown in public confidence in official investigations (and in the accountability of the security forces) is a public interest of a very high order.'

8 September
The Guardian reports that the former head of MI5, Dame Stella Rimington, has called for radical reform of the OSA and an independent system to vet publications by former members of the security and intelligence agencies.
'I thought that they were being excessively and sometimes rather ridiculously careful,' says Dame Stella, referring to senior

MoD officials who vetted her book, after failing to stop her going into print. She says the absolute duty of confidentiality the OSA imposes on former members of the security and intelligence services is 'unrealistic'.

20 September
Three Appeal Court judges support Mr Justice Moses' ruling that there should be no defence of public interest or no damage to national security. David does manage to overturn the absolute rule against disclosure of section 1 of the OSA as judges grant that there is a defence of necessity.

However, Lord Woolf, the Lord Chief Justice – and a member of the legislature, the House of Lords – sitting with Mr Justice Wright and Mr Justice Leveson, rules that in David's case 'there was no necessity or duress as those words are ordinarily understood', despite not hearing any actual evidence. David says:

> 'If the defence of necessity had been available at the time of the offence – i.e. when MI6 had paid terrorists with connections to Al Qaeda to assassinate Colonel Gaddafi but before the attack took place – I would have used it. It seems highly undemocratic to criticise me for not using a defence which was not available at the time.'

As the defence was not part of the legislation at the time of the offence, the European Court may rule that David's conviction is in breach of Article 7: No punishment without lawful authority.

2002

21 March
Five Law Lords uphold the Appeal Court's ruling that the accused is not allowed to argue at trial that his disclosures did not damage national security or that his disclosures served the

public interest, even though his whistleblowing concerns the funding of terrorism and murder on the part of the services.

One of the panel of Law Lords is Lord Hutton, who later whitewashes the government's role in naming David Kelly and condemns the BBC for trying to get at the truth.

However, the problem was compounded by the fact that their Lordships allowed the Crown to introduce the following assertions into the pre-trial hearings, which were only supposed to be a discussion of the legal issues:

- The potential 'deaths of 50 agents', which has no basis in fact or evidence;
- A conversation the defendant had with the Head of Personnel, Steve Canute, on 17 July 1997, the contents of which are not only disputed, but also go to the very heart of the legality of the 1989 OSA.

The potential 'deaths of 50 agents' was not based on any witness statement. David's counsel, Geoffrey Robertson QC, disputed it but Lord Hutton and his fellow Lordships rejected his submission. Yet when the defence tried to introduce undisputed written evidence, which refuted the prosecution's assertions, their Lordships simply ruled it inadmissible.

We have to wonder why the House of Lords allowed the prosecution to make highly prejudicial claims with no basis in evidence at a pre-trial legal hearing, but then refuse to even consider written evidence from the defendant refuting the prosecution's arguments.

If the Law Lords and the trial judge were following the rules of natural justice, the HRA and the common law, they would have ruled that the prosecution was in breach of due process.

29 July
The Guardian reports that prosecution have indicated they will ask for the jury at David's trial to be vetted, as it was in the

notorious ABC trial in the late 1970s, where three defendants
– two journalists and an Army signals expert – received sus-
pended sentences for exposing the activities of GCHQ. The
jury was also vetted in the trial of the former MoD official,
Clive Ponting, in the 1980s.

It is not clear to this day whether the jury was vetted in
David's case.

11 August
Under the headline: 'MI6 faces court bombshell over £100,000
payment to Al Qaeda', the *MoS* reports that in a landmark
hearing, David will ask a judge to order MI6 to disclose classified
documents relating to the affair in order to plead a defence of
necessity. During the court case, this article is used against
David. The judge pores over it for evidence that David is
somehow going to damage national security in court while
ensuring that the disclosure, which was already in the public
domain before the article in question was published, is kept
away from the jury.

6 October
On the eve of his trial, David tells the *MoS*:

'I know all too well I'm taking on the Establishment, but
I am no traitor. All I am guilty of is exposing wrongdoing
at the highest level. As a result of that my life has been
changed irrevocably. This is not the prosecution of someone who has given away State secrets, but of someone
who has embarrassed the Government.'

7 October
Two years and two months after returning voluntarily to the
UK to face his accusers, David's trial is set to start. It is again
delayed by legal argument over whether the trial will be held
in camera.

The Evening Standard reports that David's lawyers have

accused ministers of trying to interfere in the trial by insisting that part of the proceedings are held in private:

> 'Ministers are demanding that trial judge Mr Justice Alan Moses agree in advance that the Old Bailey case go into private session without saying why and without hearing arguments to the contrary from the defence.
>
> 'On Friday Home Secretary David Blunkett and Foreign Secretary Jack Straw signed identical public interest immunity certificates under which the press and the public will have to leave court if sensitive security issues are raised. The certificates do not specify what information they are trying to keep secret on the grounds that to do so would cause the very damage the Government is seeking to avoid.'

Ministers who stand to be embarrassed by their failure to take David's evidence then claim:

> 'Publication of information of the kinds referred to would be likely to assist those whose purpose it is to injure the security of the United Kingdom and whose actions in the past show that they are willing to kill innocent civilians both inside and outside the UK in pursuance of their aims.'

In normal circumstances under English law such a disclosure in public prior to trial would be deemed to breach the principles of *sub judice* and lead to the trial being abandoned. As it is David's case, these rules – like so many others – have simply been ignored.

It is worth pointing out that – despite the long drawn out process and the wild claims from those who stand to be embarrassed – there has never been any evidence at all to indicate that David has damaged national security in any way.

9 October
After waiting for two stressful days, David is about to deliver his legal argument in front of the judge when Nigel Sweeney

QC again calls for an adjournment to argue that the legal arguments – yes that's right *legal arguments* – should be held *in camera*. How can legal arguments damage national security? The last time I looked the laws of the land and English case law were not security classified.

After a four-hour delay, David finally delivers his legal arguments.

At one point in his address to the court, David takes Judge Moses through all the relevant free speech case law.[215] It all confirms that a court can only come to a conclusion about a disclosure by examining evidence from both sides. A breach of secrecy or confidentiality is not in itself a reason to convict a defendant. It is also highly relevant to the proportionality of any punishment.

So David asks the judge what he thinks the European Court will rule in this case, in the light of the Article 10 case law and the absence of any evidence concerning the nature of the disclosure. Judge Moses refuses to answer, so David asks him again. He replies:

'Take your case to Europe, Mr Shayler.'

David later comments:

'At this point, I thought of saying: "Why? Have we given up on fair trials and human rights in the UK?" But I thought better of it.'

10 October
Mr Justice Moses rules that David still has no defence under the OSA. He refuses to rule on whether there is a difference between the ill-defined 'national interest' and 'the interests of national security', an issue vital to the lawfulness of the OSA.

---

[215] Under Article 10 of the ECHR and the HRA. The case law is now part of English law and trumps the common law, as it carries the sovereignty of an Act of Parliament.

He also ignores overwhelming evidence indicating that the OSA did not provide a route for serving or former intelligence officers to legally go to government or the police with details of MI5 malpractice and crimes. When disclosure belatedly took place just before the jury was sworn in MI5 was unable to produce any documents detailing the supposed legal routes to disclosure.

In fact, all the documentation supported David's argument that the OSA section 1 represented an absolute rule against disclosure and therefore fell foul of the European Convention because an absolute cannot be proportional. Proportionality is at the heart of the Convention and forms the essence of democratic fairness.

At no point during the legal process has David been allowed to put in evidence to support his arguments or to detail to the jury the efforts he made to raise issues of illegality with MI5 management while in the service or with the authorities after leaving the service. The trial is adjourned until the following week.

David sends a copy of his legal arguments to the Attorney General asking him to halt the prosecution on the grounds of public interest. The Attorney General refuses to do so on the grounds that David is allowed to adduce evidence, when this has already been ruled out.

Late October
The excessive and unnecessary secrecy of the British state is established to the British people. Disclosure of official documents proves that even the definitions of security classification – Restricted, Confidential, Secret and Top Secret – are classified Secret. They do not even refer to 'national security' in their definitions. The definitions which I saw on joining MI5 included specific reference to 'embarrassment' as a reason for classifying documents. These definitions are not disclosed to the Crown prosecutor, Nigel Sweeney.

Judge Moses rules that MI5 witnesses against David can give evidence behind screens concealing their identity. Intelligence

331

officers in police SBs give evidence in open court, so why can't intelligence officers from the Security Service? Police SBs do the same work and, in the case of MPSB, see the same intelligence as MI5 officers. As MI5 moves increasingly into evidential police work, such as organised crime and terrorism, they should be equally accountable.

Ironically, if an SB officer made exactly the same disclosure as David, he would have a defence of 'no damage', which was denied to David at trial. Clearly, the switch from police to MI5 responsibility has made the intelligence establishment immune from whistleblowing.

Last week in October
The Crown prosecutor, Nigel Sweeney QC, is allowed to make continuous assertions about the documents, claiming they were 'chock-a-block' with agent names, when they were in fact intelligence summaries just like the September dossier on Iraq's WMD, which was released to the public with no damage to national security. The truth is the documents he took did not reveal agent identities. Indeed, as David had never worked in an agent-running section, he never had access to such documents, which are rightly kept separate from the mainstream work of MI5. There was absolutely no evidence before the court to indicate that the documents contained agent names.

Like the Law Lords before him, why did Mr Justice Moses appear to allow the prosecution to make highly prejudicial claims with no basis in evidence or law, especially when a defendant representing himself is supposed to be given greater leeway by the trial judge?

31 October
David has to submit the questions he wishes to put to prosecution witnesses to the Crown prosecutor and the judge for vetting. Although they go to the heart of the lawfulness of any potential conviction, Mr Justice Moses crosses out the vast majority. The same happens with David's wish to speak in his own defence.

1 November
David is allowed to make a limited, vetted defence statement. Although he is not allowed to mention the MI6 funding of Al Qaeda, he tells the jury that he witnessed a 'heinous crime', which made him 'scared for his life'. The jury are interested but Mr Justice Moses does not allow them to ask questions.

4 November
In his summing up, the trial judge tells the jury that they are not allowed to make a perverse verdict – in other words, acquit a defendant even if they find him guilty on the facts, but find the law incompatible with justice.

David is found guilty on two charges of working for the service and talking about it without permission and another of disclosing telephone tap material in the Victoria Brittain investigation, even though it was clearly an unlawful operation. He faces up to six years in prison. He is bailed overnight.

5 November
Before passing sentence, Judge Moses allows me to take to the witness box to make a mitigation plea. This is the only time throughout the whole process when either David or myself is allowed to say anything about his motivation for blowing the whistle. Consequently, in his formal judgement Moses concludes that David thought he was acting in the public interest, and was not motivated by money. He then sentences David to six months in prison. Moses also accuses David of 'blinkered arrogance' for not seeking legal advice before going on the record, without ever bothering to check whether he had. In fact, David did seek legal advice from Bindman and Partners through Mark Hollingsworth in 1997. Bindman had advised that the OSA was an *absolute rule against disclosure* on the part of former MI5 officers.

6 November
Despite taking down Judge Moses' formal words in the courtroom,

most journalists report that David had 'sold agent lives down the river for money'.

2003

29 July
Three Appeal Court judges reject David's application for leave to appeal. He wished to appeal on the grounds that his Old Bailey trial was unfair in view of the 'unprecedented' restrictions imposed on him by the trial judge at the behest of the Crown prosecutor. Without hearing detailed argument, the Appeal Court holds that these restrictions relating to secrecy of documents and cross-examination of Crown witnesses 'only went as far as in the circumstances they had to go'.

19 September
At John Wadham's leaving party from Liberty, David approaches trial judge Alan Moses. They have the following conversation:

> Moses: (to friends standing nearby) This man turned to the camera and asked: 'How do you live with yourself?' during the documentary about his case. My wife then asked the same thing. (Laughs.)

> David: I said it the day that I did my legal arguments in front of you before trial. (Pause.) I said it because Annie was so upset. Anyway, it's gone to the European Court.

> Moses: Ah yes, well you'll win in Europe.

Moses then virtually apologises for putting David in prison, hinting that he had to. Diplomatically, David replies: 'It could have been worse.'

Nothing has changed between David's trial and the party. It is a clear vindication of David's arguments in court. It may also be grounds for appeal.

The inescapable truth is that David's prosecution had nothing to do with the protection of national security. It was about ensuring his conviction and the vilification in the newspapers that followed. It was all about protecting the reputation of the incompetents and criminals within the services; punishing David because he had dared to subject the services to unprecedented scrutiny; sparing the embarrassment of ministers who had been made to look like liars; and discouraging other whistleblowers.

In fact, let's be blunt. David's trial had all the hallmarks of a show trial in the former Soviet Union *pour encourager les autres*.

Chapter 21

Hutton and the OSA

When David was released from prison on the day before his 37th birthday – 23 December 2002 – we thought we had seen it all. But then, the intelligence case for war began to unravel. The whistleblower, Dr David Kelly, apparently committed suicide after questioning the claim that the Iraqis could launch WMD within 45 minutes of an order being given. Worse still, one of David's panel of Law Lords – Lord Hutton – was appointed to the enquiry into the circumstances leading to Dr Kelly's death. Before the enquiry began, newspapers praised Brian Hutton for his supposed independence. But they should have smelled a rat when Hutton also announced that he would be retiring once he had concluded his enquiry.

Hutton decided to blame BBC management practice for the events leading up to Dr Kelly's apparent suicide. Many saw Hutton's report for the whitewash it was. In exactly the same manner as in David's Law Lords hearing, Hutton didn't even look like he was trying to get at the truth. He appeared to cherry-pick the information which suited him and ignore the rest. The findings of his enquiry have already had a chilling effect on free speech in Britain.

In his chairmanship of the enquiry, Brian Hutton also failed to establish in any way how the OSA may have contributed to 'the circumstances surrounding the death of Dr Kelly', precisely because he had denied David – and therefore Dr Kelly – a public interest defence or a right to take information to Parliament

337

under the OSA. If Kelly had enjoyed these rights when he learnt of ministerial attempts to sex up the dossier, he would not have found himself in a position where he felt he had to alert the media in a clandestine manner and, by extension, he would not have had allegedly to take his own life.

The Hutton Enquiry failed on two major points:

- Evidence concerning the OSA was not heard.
- Witnesses were never cross-examined over whether Kelly was threatened with prosecution.

Given his harsh and selective criticism of BBC management practice and its alleged failure to get at the truth, the ultimate irony – some might say hypocrisy – of the enquiry must be that Hutton's standards of enquiry were far more lax.

The failure to hear evidence

Before the Hutton enquiry began, a number of independent sources told journalists that Dr Kelly was threatened with prosecution under the 1989 OSA and that Kelly feared losing his civil service pension. I challenge ministers to name a single case of an official being stripped of their pension for a breach of civil service rules. However, that sanction is invariably enforced to punish those convicted of OSA offences. If convicted, he could have lost his pension as well as facing up a two years in jail.

We can be sure that Hutton did not take possession of all relevant material, as David wrote to him on 28 August 2003 asking to give evidence about the implications of the OSA:

'I am also probably the only person in the country who has been in the same situation as Dr Kelly... At any trial, he would not have been able to argue that ... his disclosures were in the public interest. I mention all this as it may provide some insight into Dr Kelly's state of mind. He would have been aware of the seriousness of his situation regarding the OSA.'

At trial, the prosecution would only have had to prove that Dr Kelly was a government contractor; that he had said something 'damaging' relating to 'the work of, or in support, of the intelligence services';[216] and that he had done so without permission, to secure a conviction under the Act. Since it is part of the work of the intelligence services to provide intelligence and assessment for JIC papers, Kelly had clearly broken the law when he discussed the 45-minute claim, and any assessment of it, with journalist Andrew Gilligan.[217] In practice, under the OSA the prosecution would only have had to prove that the material Kelly discussed with Gilligan was classified, which it was, to obtain a conviction for 'damaging national security'.

Lord Hutton was well aware of this because – as we have already seen – he was one of the Law Lords who ruled that there was no public interest defence to the OSA and indeed no right to take disclosures to Parliament.

Any objective judge would have been duty-bound to explore this in some detail, particularly with witnesses such as Tony Blair, who has an appalling record for threatening journalists with prosecutions and writs in relation to the OSA. The enquiry was an excellent opportunity to ask Blair under oath whether he, or his officials or ministers, ever threatened Kelly with the OSA. Yet the Prime Minister was never asked the question at all, let alone under oath.

In fact, none of the witnesses at the enquiry gave their statements under the usual judicial rules of evidence. Liars were not open to charges of perjury. Witnesses could 'be economical with the truth' without the fear of committing a crime. At the same time, Brian Hutton did not compel government departments to provide relevant documents under penalty of obstructing the

---

[216] Section 1(9) 1989 OSA.
[217] Although the authorities had given Kelly permission to discuss certain matters with the media, the 45-minute claim did not fall within his remit.

course of justice for failing to do so. The whole set-up was a recipe for any officials, ministers or intelligence officers to lie with impunity and 'forget' to submit vital documentary material. Anyone who thinks this fanciful only has to remember what happened at the Saville Enquiry or the Stephens Enquiry. In both cases, the security forces withheld vital evidence.

The meaning of Hutton's failure regarding the OSA

Lord Hutton and his fellow Law Lords denied to whistleblowers the use of a public interest defence under the OSA. Therefore, Dr Kelly didn't have a leg to stand on, when he was reportedly threatened with prosecution. With a public interest defence, he could have told any jury that he was trying to prevent the UK entering an illegal war on the basis of sexed-up intelligence. Instead, he was facing a two-year prison sentence and, at the age of 59, the loss of his pension, as well as the prestige accrued through a long and successful career. This is bad enough for our democracy and our security but there are other knock-on effects of Lord Hutton's failure to bring the OSA into line with democratic standards.

Dr Kelly – and other dissenting voices, particularly in the intelligence services – had no legal route to alert Parliament to the misrepresentation of the intelligence used to justify war, again as a result of Lord Hutton and his fellow Law Lords' failure to observe the minimum democratic standards set out in the HRA. Instead, a majority of our MPs voted for an illegal war. They were then rather embarrassingly obliged to hold a Foreign Affairs Select Committee and an ISC inquiry after the invasion of Iraq. It was rather like holding an appeal for a condemned man after he had been executed, and then being amazed that justice was not served. Did not even one elected representative think this might be necessary *before the war*?

In the absence of any legal route to independent scrutiny of their concerns, MI6 officers were obliged to raise their concerns anonymously in the press. For this, Health Minister John Reid claimed that 'rogue elements in the intelligence services' were trying to undermine the government. But where were they supposed to go? Perhaps, as was suggested at David's trial, they should take their evidence directly to the PM or the head of the service they belong to. But then we are back to the vexed question of the PM investigating allegations against himself, either directly or via an approach from the head of the service involved.

Kelly and the OSA

Although Hutton did not cross-examine or gather evidence about the OSA, its spectre inevitably hung over his enquiry. In fact, it would be fair to say that there was a conspiracy not to mention the OSA: the British authorities love for it dared not speak its name.

The enquiry was, for example, also presented with a document written by John Scarlett, the then Chairman of the JIC and current head of MI6, which referred to subjecting Dr Kelly to a 'security-style' interview. Security interviews are not carried out for breaches of civil service discipline, as a former deputy head of MI6 like Scarlett well knew. They are designed to deal with more serious matters – where an individual is suspected of a criminal offence, more often than not under the OSA. These interviews are conducted under caution – the interviewee must be warned of his qualified right to silence and that anything he does say may be used in evidence against him – by intelligence service interrogators.

A MoD minute submitted to the enquiry raised the possibility of prosecution for talking to the media. It concluded:

'Finally, a reminder of what CDS and I stated on 12 June about unauthorised leaks to the media... *In addition to*

341

being disciplinary offences, they could also lead to prosecution after criminal investigation [my italics].'[218]

The enquiry also established that an excerpt from Alistair Campbell's diary referred to a 'plea bargain'. If Dr Kelly was not threatened with prosecution for a criminal offence like the OSA, why would Campbell use this specific phrase to describe the government's plans for dealing with him?

Around the same time, Sir Richard Dearlove, then the head of MI6 (aka 'C'[219]) also told the enquiry that discussing a CX report with a journalist would be a 'serious breach of discipline'. Discussing an intelligence report with the media would, of course, constitute a breach of the OSA. Lord Hutton would have known this after hearing arguments in David's prosecution. Indeed, Lord Hutton was given an obvious and excellent opportunity to ask if Kelly had been threatened with prosecution under the OSA, when the director of personnel at the MoD was asked at the enquiry whether Dr Kelly had been notified for purposes of the OSA.[220]

Yet Lord Hutton did not seek to cross-examine any of these witnesses over whether Kelly's actions might be seen as a breach of the 1989 OSA or whether he was threatened with it.

Given the above evidence, are we still expected to accept that Dr Kelly took his own life because his reputation might have been compromised in the future, as Hutton concluded in his report? Or does it seem more likely that he took his life, if indeed he did (the Hutton Enquiry was used to avoid having a full inquest into Kelly's apparent suicide) because he was facing prosecution under the OSA, loss of his pension at the age of 59 and up to two years in prison?

Hutton's enquiry did of course establish that vital meetings were not minuted. Was the decision at least to threaten Kelly

---

[218] From the Permanent Under-Secretary of State at the MoD, Sir Kevin Tebbit, to senior officials, dated 10 October 2002. See Hutton Report, paragraph 27.
[219] 'M' in the Bond films.
[220] 11 August 2003, Richard Hatfield's evidence, Hutton Enquiry.

with an OSA prosecution raised, but not minuted? More importantly, why didn't Hutton at least ask his witnesses this? We shall never know.

In fact, the inadequacy of the House of Lords ruling in David's case has led to further arrests of individuals who have served the public interest. Although OSA section 1 charges against Katherine Gun, a transcriber from GCHQ, were eventually dropped – even though she admitted disclosing a classified document to a journalist[221] – she still had to spend a purgatorial eight months awaiting trial.

The available evidence shows that the OSA may finally have driven an honourable man to his death. Ironically, the man chosen by the PM to conduct an investigation into Dr Kelly's death was not objective, because he knew he had already failed to reform the Act. Hutton appears to have hoped that no one would notice he hadn't asked about the OSA, rather as he did when refusing to hear evidence about the OSA in David's case or when he refused to accept that the government had sexed up the September dossier by making its claims rather more certain than the intelligence services believed them to be.[222]

The truth is – be it *Spycatcher*, David's disclosures or Andrew Gilligan's report – British judges simply do not understand the importance of free speech, particularly with regard to disclosures about the crimes, misdemeanours and abuses of democratic rights on the part of the intelligence services. They have never bothered to take evidence and allow cross-examination of intelligence service witnesses, which could get to the truth about how national security is actually damaged.

That ignorance, and lack of appreciation of the responsibilities which come with living in a democratic society, pose a far

---

[221] In the document, the US government tasked the British signals intelligence station to spy on our allies in the run-up to the UN debates on Iraq over a second resolution.

[222] As well as brushing up on human rights law, Hutton clearly needs to brush up on his modal verbs. 'Can' does not mean the same as 'may' or 'might'; 'is capable of' is not the same as 'may be capable of'. The phrase 'intelligence indicates that Saddam might' means just that: the services have intelligence to indicate. It does not mean that the statement is a reflection of established fact, no matter what Lord Hutton may say.

greater threat to our democracy than the actions of a BBC reporter or a GCHQ or MI5 whistleblower, especially when they are proved to be right. We may not have to put up with this nonsense for too much longer, though. Help is at hand – in the form of the HRA.

The legality of the Law Lords' status

How do you confuse a Law Lord? Ask him if his position is compatible with the HRA and the European Convention, which it incorporates into English law with the full sovereignty of Parliament. This is not a joke. It is in fact a Morton's Fork, the debating equivalent of checkmate. In this case, if the Law Lord answers: 'No', he admits that his role is 'unconstitutional' or incompatible with the HRA. If he answers: 'Yes', then has he understood the full import of Article 6 of the ECHR, the right to a fair trial?

Article 6 of the ECHR states:

'In the determination of his civil rights and obligations or of any criminal charge against him, everyone is entitled to a fair and public hearing within a reasonable time *by an independent and impartial tribunal established by law.*'

Yet the Law Lords are clearly not independent of the legislature (or Parliament) because they sit in the House of Lords, which has a responsibility for scrutinising Bills of Parliament and voting on them. And they cannot be impartial because they hear arguments in court about legislation they have in effect already passed. (When Law Lords like the Lord Chief Justice Woolf sit on the Court of Appeal, as happened in David's case, that court also fails the independent and impartial test for a tribunal under the HRA.) Halsbury's Laws of England, the lawyers' bible in this country, confirms this. It clearly states:

'The final court of appeal in England is part of Parliament
... the Lord Chancellor is a member of all three branches
of government and the Law Lords are members of the
legislature.'[223]

It does, though, go on to claim that a variety of factors operate
to insulate the judiciary as a whole from political pressures,
such as not speaking in debates. Although the individual Lords
of Appeal may not have debated – for example, using David's
case, the 1989 OSA – they inherit the decisions of the chamber
when they become members of it rather in the way new owners
of a company must honour existing contracts, no matter how
loathsome, inconvenient or unjust they find them. In fact, by
not speaking in debates, Law Lords tacitly support all legislation
which is passed by their fellow Lords. Given this tacit support,
they are not impartial when they rule on the legislation.

Neither the House of Commons nor the government authorised
the hearing of appeals by an Appellate Committee of Law
Lords. The House of Lords simply took it upon itself to hear
appeals in 1948, but only as a temporary measure. This procedure
has since become normal practice. As the procedure was not
endorsed by the sovereignty of an Act of Parliament, the right
of the Law Lords to hear appeals is clearly not 'established by
law' in terms of the Court's composition, jurisdiction and
function as the final court of appeal. At just over 50 years old,
it can hardly be said to be one of our long-standing, constitutional
traditions.

The implications of this are enormous. It means that the Law
Lords' rulings have no basis in law. Under the current arrangements, any one who has gone before the Law Lords could
argue at the European Court that they were denied their Article
6 rights to a fair hearing, since interested and partial Law Lords
judged their case. It also raises questions about the legality of
the body of case law that their Lordships' created. If their

---

[223] Halsbury's Laws of England (Constitutional Law and Human Rights section).

345

position was not democratically constituted, then neither were their rulings.

Their Lordships' ignorance of their own failure

In November 2002, the Law Lords submitted their comments regarding the proposed Supreme Court to ministers.[224] Needless to say, Lord Hutton was on the side of the Law Lords who branded change leading to a Supreme Court as 'unnecessary' and 'harmful'.

The paper their Lordships submitted adds: 'The present arrangements work well.' The truth is they do not. As the Labour Party's Consultation Paper, which was authored by Jack Straw and Paul Boateng when in opposition and gave rise to the HRA, recognised:

'Other countries which have incorporated the Convention have had as many cases before the ECHR. What marks out the UK's record is the serious nature of the cases brought and the absence of speedy and effective domestic remedies.'

Of course, New Labour is a different animal in office. 'Nothing in this proposal intends or implies any criticism of the way in which the current Appellate Committee [the Law Lords] or its members have discharged their functions,' Lord Falconer told Parliament in 2004.[225] Yet the Law Lords *should* be criticised as our final court of appeal. It is after all their fault that the UK is found to be in breach of the European Convention – which was drafted by two Englishmen in the wake of the horrors of the Second World War; has nothing to do with the political structure of the EU; and is the collected democratic wisdom of

---

[224] *The Times*, 5 November 2003.
[225] Hansard, 10 February 2004.

over 40 countries – on far more occasions than any other signatory.

In fact, since the HRA was implemented in 2000, the European Court of Human Rights has ruled against the UK on more occasions, not fewer. From 2000 to 2003, we have been found to be unlawful in 87 cases, as opposed to 41 cases between 1998 and 2000. Even though it takes four or five years for a case to be judged by the European Court, the Law Lords were supposed to have taken the HRA and the Convention into account from 1998, when it was first passed. We should therefore expect a decrease in the number of rulings against the court. But the figure has gone up significantly. That is proof that the present arrangements, as well as being unconstitutional, do *not work at all* let alone 'well'.

Chapter 22

The War in Iraq: Blair's Waterloo

In September 2002, the British government allowed a JIC assessment to be made public for the very first time, when it published the now infamous *Iraq's Weapons of Mass Destruction* report, aka the September dossier. It may turn out to be the last, not because it harmed national security but because it amply demonstrated just how useless MI5 and MI6 are. More embarrassingly for Blair, he used the dossier as an opportunity to 'pay tribute to our Intelligence and Security Services for the often extraordinary work that they do'.

Talk about getting egg on your face. We all now know that the 'extraordinary work' of the intelligence services proved to be anything but. The intelligence indicating that Iraq was trying to obtain uranium from Niger, for example, was based on forgeries containing laughable and childlike errors (which made George Bush look an even bigger fool than usual, when he used it in his annual State of the Union address in 2003). We also know that the claim that chemical and biological weapons could be deployed in 45 minutes of an order being given was sexed up by omitting that this intelligence only referred to battlefield munitions rather than long-range warheads which could be used against UK interests. In fact, not one piece of current intelligence about the Iraqi threat turned out to be true. That is a lamentable record on the part of MI5 and MI6.

But it didn't just take in the PM, the Cabinet and MPs. Many newspaper commentators used the dossier to claim that opponents of the war were naïve fools blithely promoting peace in ignorance of the threat that Saddam posed to our lives. They have been made to look like, well, naïve fools – not least for taking Blair at his word.

When will they learn? Just because intelligence is secret does not make it reliable. Just because a new piece of intelligence comes from a source who has reported reliably in the past, it does not mean for certain that it is gospel truth. I just wish the government had taken David's evidence years ago. But as we all know, the Cabinet and Parliament, particularly the PM's ISC, would rather ignore unpalatable truths than actually give whistleblowers a fair hearing.

Blair gets it wrong again and again

As well as putting British lives at greater risk from Al Qaeda than they ever were from Saddam, the invasion and the continuing occupation of Iraq are an expensive business, running into billions. In addition to the thousands of innocent Iraqi civilians who have already died, many British soldiers have surrendered their lives not in defence of our country or our security but on the whim, prejudices and naked ambition of a PM who has repeatedly used misrepresentation and spin to try to justify an unjustifiable war. There is, for example, absolutely no truth whatsoever in Blair's private claims made to MPs before the vote on war that Saddam supported Al Qaeda. As any Middle Eastern expert or counter-terrorist officer will tell you, leaders like Saddam and Colonel Gaddafi of Libya have even more to fear from Al Qaeda than the UK or US.

Blair continues to claim that Saddam was a threat to world peace. This appears to be an act of faith on the part of the PM. It bears no relation to any objective assessment of the available intelligence. Swallow Tail has told us that the formal assessment – endorsed by the JIC – of the threat posed by Saddam barely changed in ten years. In fact, it is the same as when I was in G3 assessing Middle Eastern threats. To summarise – and I am not quoting here – the assessment said:

'Due to the UN sanctions operating against Iraq, we (MI5) believe it is highly unlikely that Saddam will carry out or sponsor terrorist attacks. In fact, we assess that he will act as a brake on any terrorist groups, which currently have links to the regime, as their actions will reflect badly on Saddam.

'Although we continue to receive intelligence from reliable sources, indicating that Saddam may have nuclear, chemical and biological WMD programmes, none of it has been corroborated. Intelligence also indicates that the Iraqi regime continues to seek to procure the raw materials necessary to produce WMD, although there is little reliable intelligence to indicate that this has been successful. We assess that he may therefore have some incipient WMD programmes but is still a long way from producing the actual weapons.'

It is clear that MI5 did not believe that there was any 'smoking gun' which could justify defensive military action. In fact, Blair missed out the most vital line from the September dossier, which would have been included in any normal JIC assessment and indeed was included in earlier papers on Iraq:

'We assess that the regime of Saddam Hussein poses no direct threat to British interests.'

But it gets worse. In February 2003, a month before the war, the JIC warned Blair that an invasion of Iraq would *increase* the danger of WMD finishing up in the hands of terrorists, namely Al Qaeda, which they assessed posed the greatest current threat to the lives of British citizens, a far greater threat than Iraq:

'Al Qaeda and associated groups continued to represent by

far the greatest threat to western interests, and that threat would be heightened by military action against Iraq... Any collapse of the Iraqi regime would increase the risk of chemical and biological warfare technology or agents finding their way into the hands of terrorists, including Al Qaeda.'[226]

When the PM's ISC quizzed Blair on this extraordinary omission, he told them:

'[There was] obviously a danger that in attacking Iraq you ended up provoking the very thing you were trying to avoid... You had to ask the question, "Could you really, as a result of that fear, leave the possibility that in time this developed into a nexus between terrorism and WMD in any event?" ... This is where you've just got to make your judgement about this. But this is my judgement and it remains my judgement and I suppose time will tell whether it's true or it's not true.'

If nothing else, this demonstrates that Blair has become so obsessed with spin that he thinks it is acceptable to spin the case for a war. If he was going to use intelligence to justify war, then he was duty bound to publish the intelligence services' counter-arguments. Would any MP, journalist or member of the public have supported war if they knew that the experts were saying that WMD might end up in the hands of Al Qaeda? At least, they have the defence of ignorance. Blair *knowingly* put British lives at risk of future nuclear, chemical and biological attack from Al Qaeda so he could pursue a target which posed no direct threat to British interests.

And it is no good the PM asking us to trust his judgement. To use the PM's phrase, 'time' has already told us his judgement was very wrong on two counts: he was wrong that the invasion

---

[226] *Iraq's Weapons of Mass Destruction, Intelligence and Assessment*, the ISC, September 2003.

would not lead to an upsurge in the Al Qaeda threat; and he was wrong when he concluded that:

> 'The assessed intelligence has established *beyond doubt* ...
> that Saddam *has continued to produce chemical and biological weapons*, that he continues *in his efforts to develop nuclear weapons*, and that he has been able to extend the range of his ballistic missile programme.'[227]

We knew this claim was sexed up before the war even started, as it did not accurately reflect the intelligence in the September dossier, which said:

> 'There is intelligence that Iraq has *sought the supply of* significant quantities of uranium from Africa.'

All I can say is: 'Thank God, Saddam did not have any kind of WMD.' Given the level of Al Qaeda activity in Iraq now, can you imagine what that group could have done with nuclear, chemical or biological weapons, not just in Iraq but closer to home? I don't want to be led by a man whose judgement is so arbitrary that he can be certain, but wrong, that Saddam had continued to produce WMD yet ignore the very real threat of the chemical and nuclear weapons – which he was certain existed – falling into the hands of Al Qaeda.

In the Foreword, Blair said:

> 'I also believe that, as stated in the document, Saddam will now do his utmost to try to conceal his weapons from UN inspectors.'

This only served to raise another issue of enormous embarrassment to Blair. Saddam could not comply with the UN resolutions asking him to co-operate over his chemical and biological

---

[227] *Iraq's Weapons of Mass Destruction, Intelligence and Assessment*, September 2002, Foreword.

weapons, as he didn't have any. International observers assess that up to a million Iraqi lives were lost because UN sanctions – pushed by the UK and US – against Iraq were also predicated on false intelligence. The truth is Saddam did comply with the UN's mandates. He allowed their inspectors into Iraq. They couldn't find nuclear, chemical and biological weapons because there weren't any to find. It now appears that Saddam encouraged whispers about his putative WMD stocks merely to intimidate Iraq's old enemy, Iran. In addition to the deaths of civilians and British troops, Blair's hands are also stained with the blood of the innocent Iraqis who died as a result of the sanctions, after he took office in 1997.

The ISC and the heads of service

Even the PM's ISC was obliged to conclude:

> 'The 45 minutes claim, included four times, was always likely to attract attention because it was arresting detail that the public had not seen before... The fact that [the 45-minute claim] was assessed to refer to battlefield chemical and biological munitions and their movement on the battlefield, not to any other form of chemical or biological attack, should have been highlighted in the dossier. The omission of the context and assessment allowed speculation as to its exact meaning. This was *unhelpful to an understanding of this issue.*'[228]

They should, though, tell it like it is. It was not merely 'unhelpful'. It was a deliberate perversion of the truth designed to scare any reader into supporting the invasion in the belief that they and their children were in direct and imminent danger

---

[228] Paragraph 86, *Iraq's Weapons of Mass Destruction, Intelligence and Assessment,* the ISC, September 2003.

of dying a horrible death from nuclear, chemical or biological attack. Some individuals have tried to claim that the 45-minute intelligence did little or nothing to convince the public of the case for war. Yet the government spin machine ensured national newspaper headlines screaming such words as '45 Minutes from Doom'. Did this really have so little impact? The claim was given extraordinary prominence in the September dossier. It was mentioned in the foreword, the executive summary and twice in the main text as well as being used to justify the invasion before Parliament.[229]

Not surprisingly, the PM's appointees cleared him of 'sexing up' the dossier and indeed any wrongdoing. Yet no one appears to have quizzed the PM over how he could square his ignorance of the true nature of the 45-minute claim, a boast he has made to Parliament, when he wrote in the Foreword to the September dossier:

'We cannot, of course, publish the detailed raw intelligence. I and other Ministers *have been briefed in detail on the intelligence and are satisfied as to its authority.*'

Both statements cannot be true. We also know from the Hutton Enquiry that 'ownership' of the document passed to No. 10. At that point, it was the responsibility of Blair to ensure that it accurately reflected the intelligence on which it was based, particularly as he intended to use it to justify a war in which innocent civilians were inevitably going to be maimed and massacred. Individuals with genuine leadership qualities gather the facts then check them before committing. A true leader would recognise his mistake and resign.

I wonder, though, how Blair could come to a conclusion about the reliability of MI5 and MI6 information when he had failed to take possession of David's evidence indicating that MI5 often formed assessments on the basis of very little

---

[229] George Bush also used it to justify the invasion in a speech in late September 2002.

intelligence. Or that MI5 often got it wrong with regard to the implications of its intelligence, as it did in the case of Victoria Brittain? Or that MI5 sometimes gave ministers false information to cover up its mistakes, as it did in the McNulty case.

Not surprisingly, the PM's ISC concluded after a secret enquiry that the heads of MI5 and MI6 had distorted the threat posed by Saddam Hussein – mainly by the sin of omission. This stands at odds with the well-placed sources we have talked to. They have told us that senior intelligence officers were universally opposed to the inclusion of the 45-minute claim.

When similar claims were made in the press, Blair pointed out that the heads of service, MI5's Sir Stephen Lander and MI6's Sir Richard Dearlove signed off the September dossier, so they must have been happy with it. Yet the intelligence about the 45-minute claim came from MI6, so Dearlove can hardly claim that he did not know the detail of intelligence provided by his service. Nor can Lander claim that MI5 had not seen the document, as it assesses all security intelligence. When attending the JIC, the heads of service have briefs from desk officers to deal with this kind of detail. Having been told by Lander during his visit to my section, G3A, in 1996 that he did not bother to read these detailed briefings, perhaps we can assume that he had not done so in this case. Still, we have to ask why the heads of service put their names to the September dossier when they *knew* it sexed up the case for war, if no pressure was put on them. That is the $64,000 question.

Cynics may point out that Lander resigned at the time the September dossier was published and Dearlove has opted for early retirement, but I'm sure that these events are entirely unconnected to the dossier.

Scarlett and the dossier

Dearlove's resignation paved the way for John Scarlett to be appointed head of MI6 in 2004, even though he took full responsibility for the inclusion of the sexed-up 45-minute claim before the Hutton Enquiry. He also insisted that ministers had *not* put pressure on him to sex up the dossier, although he did it in such a way that, had there been a jury, they would have been left in no doubt he was being 'economical with the truth'.

If a junior MI5 desk officer had so appallingly bowdlerised a report, especially one of such prominence, they could never seriously be considered for promotion again. If we accept Scarlett's own admission that ministers like Blair put no pressure on him to sex up the dossier, we have to conclude that he consciously and deliberately exaggerated the case for war in a public document as he had seen the 'battlefield munitions' assessment of the 45-minute claim. How can we now trust the new head of MI6 to report intelligence reliably to Whitehall, in secret, where there is no scrutiny or oversight?

Yet in the world of Blairism, a monumental mistake is not punished but rewarded. David has always said that the intelligence services are anything but meritocratic, with those not rocking the boat more likely to be promoted than those who stand up for what is right. Scarlett's appointment has provided more than ample proof of that. As a result, the people of Britain are seeing all too clearly that there is nothing they can do to stop Blair's arbitrary use of power. In this case, it just looks like he is thumbing his nose at public opinion, in the full knowledge that the people are impotent.

However, a well-connected intelligence source who is close to the former head of the JIC, and former MI5 head Sir Stephen Lander among others, has indicated that Scarlett only signed off the September dossier under protest:

'He was so angry at the misrepresentation of intelligence in the September dossier – and we are specifically talking about the 45 minute warning – that he thought long and hard about going on the record with his concerns. He did not do so as a result of legal advice regarding his civil

357

service contract and pension rights as well as facing up to two years in prison for breaching the OSA'.[230]

The truth is senior intelligence officers not only feared prosecution under the OSA. They also feared that Tony Blair would seek retribution against any service blowing the whistle on him, either by cutting its budget or transferring its responsibilities. As PM, Blair can allocate the intelligence budget not on the basis of where resources are needed but on the basis of who has best supported the Blair project, including all its spin and misrepresentation.

Gilligan, Dissidents and the 45-minute claim

Various leaks to the media indicated that the 45-minute claim came from Iraqi dissidents or exiles. Many journalists speculated that Iyad Allawi, the head of the Iraqi National Accord (INA), was the source of this claim. Allawi is now the interim Prime Minister of Iraq. In October 2004 he finally admitted that he contributed to this claim. Allawi has clearly gained power and influence as a result of this wholly unfounded intelligence being used to overthrow Saddam. For such reasons, when David and I were in MI5 we were taught to be particularly sceptical about intelligence provided by dissident sources, as it seldom turned out to be true. In fact, you could argue that anyone including dissident intelligence in a JIC-style dossier without collateral did so *in the full knowledge that it may not be true*, especially:

- If that individual had claimed to have examined the sourcing in detail, as Blair had in the Foreword to the September dossier.

---

[230] As a 'notified person' for the purposes of the Act, the chairman of the JIC would be treated like a member of the intelligence services. He would not therefore be allowed to argue that his disclosures were in the public interest or that they did not damage national security.

- Given that the 45-minute claim was received when the dossier was in preparation yet still lacking in convincing up-to-date intelligence. The timing of its arrival in MI6 seems rather too good to be true.

If the PM did check the sourcing of the intelligence as he claims[231] and he knew it came from a dissident source, this means that Gilligan's infamous 6.07 am broadcast on the BBC's *Today* programme was near as damn it 100 per cent true:

John Humphreys: The government is facing more questions this morning over its claims about weapons of mass destruction in Iraq. Our defence correspondent is Andrew Gilligan. This in particular Andy is Tony Blair saying they'd be ready to go within forty-five minutes.

Andrew Gilligan: That's right, that was the central claim in his dossier which he published in September, the main erm, case if you like against, er, against Iraq and the main statement of the British government's belief of what it thought Iraq was up to and what we've been told by one of the senior officials in charge of drawing up that dossier was that, actually the government probably, erm, knew that that forty-five minute figure was wrong, even before it decided to put it in...

JH: When you say 'more facts to be discovered', does that suggest that they may not have been facts?[232]

AG: Well, erm, our source says that the dossier, as it was finally published, made the Intelligence Services unhappy, erm, because, to quote, erm the source he said, there was basically, that there was, there was, *there was unhappiness because it didn't reflect, the considered view they were putting forward, that's a quote from our source and essentially, erm, the forty-five minute point, er, was,*

---

[231] Blair also gave a conflicting statement to Parliament that he did not know about the sourcing of the 45-minute claim. The two statements cannot both be true.
[232] No one could ever claim that intelligence is the same as established fact.

*was probably the most important thing that was added.
Erm, and the reason it hadn't been in the original draft
was that it was, it was only, erm, it only came from one
source and most of the other claims were from two, and
the intelligence agencies say they don't really believe it
was necessarily true because they thought the person
making the claim had actually made a mistake, it got,
had got mixed up.*[233]

Even Gilligan's claim in the same broadcast that:

'Downing Street, our source says ordered a week before
publication, ordered it to be sexed up, to be made more
exciting and ordered more facts to be, er, to be discovered'

is true to the extent that:

- The PM's Foreword[234] does sex up the case against Iraq,
  when compared with intelligence in the dossier.
- Hutton and Butler have established that the government
  asked the services to find more intelligence after the first
  draft of the dossier was circulated because it was 'intelligence
  light'.
- Scarlett's reply when cross-examined at the enquiry appeared
  to be rather less than honest about government pressure.

Yet Hutton concludes:

'The allegation reported by Mr Gilligan on 29 May 2003
that the Government probably knew that the 45 minutes
claim was wrong before the Government decided to put it
in the dossier was an allegation which was unfounded
[because] the 45 minutes claim was based on a report

---

[233] *The Today Programme*, BBC Radio 4, 29 May 2003.
[234] *Iraq's Weapons of Mass Destruction, Intelligence and Assessment*, September 2003, par 76.

which was received by the SIS[235] from a source which that Service regarded as reliable...[236]

'In the context of the broadcasts in which the "sexing-up" allegation was reported, and having regard to the other allegations reported in those broadcasts, I consider that the allegation was unfounded as it would have been understood by those who heard the broadcasts to mean that the dossier had been embellished with intelligence known or believed to be false or unreliable, which was not the case.'[237]

What intelligence outsiders do not realise is that the services often use the description 'reliable' for agents they have had a long-standing relationship with or for agents who say what the services believe is true, which is not the same as having proven reliability. As we have seen, an MI5 officer tried to argue at the Bloody Sunday Enquiry that an intelligence source, Infliction, was 'reliable', even though the officer knew his agent had a proven track record of lying and withholding information. Again, if Blair's statement in the Foreword about examining the sources in the September dossier is true, it was the case that 'the dossier had been embellished with intelligence known or believed to be false or unreliable'. And even if we are generous to Blair and accept his statement to Parliament that he knew nothing of the sourcing, Defence Secretary Geoff Hoon and others have admitted to knowing the provenance of the 45-minute claim. Why didn't they insist that caveats were included with the claim or indeed just tell the PM?

In fact, the claim that battlefield WMD could be deployed within 45 minutes of an order being given was not actually new information in September 2002. Iraqi military manuals dating from before the First Gulf War included similar details about the deployment of battlefield chemical and biological

---

[235] Secret Intelligence Service or MI6.
[236] Statement by Lord Hutton, 28 January 2004, par 48(2).
[237] Statement by Lord Hutton, 28 January 2004, par 48(8).

weapons. Any expert would have assessed that the claim may have been recycled rather than new information.

The dossier and the OSA

We now know that so-called intelligence included in the 'dodgy' dossier, was based on a 12-year-old PhD thesis. We also know that Blair gave it to journalists[238] and passed it off as 'further intelligence' and 'it is the intelligence that [the security services] are receiving' to Parliament on 3 February 2003.[239]

By using material which *purports* to be intelligence[240] such as the PhD thesis, Blair may well have breached the OSA. He could also be prosecuted under section 1 of the Act for using intelligence without permission. In its Annual Report 2002–3, the ISC confirmed:

'[The submission] process was not followed when a second document was produced in February 2003. Although the document did contain some intelligence-derived material it was not clearly attributed or highlighted amongst the other material, nor was it checked with the Agency providing the intelligence or cleared by the JIC prior to publication.'

As a 'notified person' Blair will also have signed a 'non-disclosure document for the purposes of the OSA' similar to the one David and I signed. This would make him liable under section 1 of the OSA. He will be all too aware that he is 'liable to be prosecuted under the Act' if he communicates security and intelligence material to unauthorised persons unless he has 'previously obtained *the official sanction in writing* of the

---

[238] *Iraqi Weapons of Mass Destruction, Intelligence and Assessments*, September 2003, par 131.
[239] Hansard, column 2,5, 3 February 2000.
[240] The 1989 OSA section 1(2) is absolutely clear about this: 'The reference to subsection (1) above to disclosing information relating to security and intelligence includes a reference to *making any statement which purports to be a disclosure of such information or is intended to be taken by those to whom it is addressed as being such a disclosure.*'

Service' whose intelligence he is using. If he cannot produce written permission, then the Attorney General has to insist that he is prosecuted under official secrecy legislation. Like David, he has no defence.

Since Blair has relied heavily on the OSA – to a far greater extent than his two Conservative predecessors – to suppress dissent and persecute whistleblowers and journalists, he can hardly claim that he did not understand the 'lifelong duty of confidentiality' it imparts to certain officials with regard to unauthorised disclosures. If you live by the sword, you cannot complain when you die by the sword.

But there is one far more important issue that comes out of all of this, which has so far only been tentatively expressed. Intelligence services and governments do not have a bottomless pit of money and staff at their disposal. Like any other organisation, they have finite resources. Their job is to ensure that they make optimum use of investment and personnel. Any CEO who committed his organisation to enormous investment in one area on sparse information of questionable reliability, at the expense of other recognised and more lucrative markets, only to be *proved* to have made the wrong decision would inevitably have to resign.

In this case, the PM has invested heavily in a war in Iraq at the expense of investigating Al Qaeda, which continues to be responsible for indiscriminate terrorist attacks across the world. I wonder how many man hours went into the argument, planning, preparation, justification and execution of the unjustifiable war in Iraq. Would those billions not have been better spent on tackling an organisation which poses a *direct and known* threat to the lives and security of the people of this country rather than an indirect threat based on misinformation and propaganda? Ironically, if Tony Blair allows himself to remain CEO of the UK after getting it so wrong, isn't he just another fat cat rewarding his own failure?

Whichever way you cut it, the PM has done far more than any whistleblower to undermine our national security. Without the existence of WMD of any kind, he cannot deploy the self-defence argument in justification of the war. Without it or a second UN resolution authorising an invasion, Blair is a war criminal, no matter what selective legal advice the Attorney General gave him. As he has signed the International Criminal Court treaty, he cannot plead ignorance. He should be indicted at The Hague forthwith.

No matter what half-cocked conclusion any enquiry comes to, world peace is too precious to be left to a man who at best is of questionable judgement and at worst has lied to justify a war in breach of international law. We simply cannot get away from the fact that we went to war on the basis of:

- Exaggerated assessments, in some cases, of forged intelligence documents.
- JIC assessments of the real and objective threat, which the PM kept from the public.
- Supposedly reliable agents, some of whom were reportedly dissidents, who stood to gain from overthrowing Saddam.
- Intelligence which has now proved to be untrue.
- The word of Tony Blair who once again asked us to trust him.

Yet the man responsible remains in power.

Chapter 23

Where We are Now: Conclusions and Recommendations

Autocracy and the media

At the moment, intelligence reporting works like show business reporting. Instead of a 'PR' giving the story to the press and ascribing it to 'a friend' of the star, the services brief journalists non-attributably, with the information sourced to 'an intelligence insider' or 'intelligence sources'. It's a bit like the lobby briefing system, where No. 10 briefs the press but the information is sourced to 'No. 10 insiders' or 'well-placed ministerial sources'. In neither case are the authorities held accountable for what they say to journalists. Blair's henchmen have smeared in this way many whistleblowers, including David; Dr David Kelly (apparently to the point of suicide); Elizabeth Filkin, the former Parliamentary commissioner; Martin Sixsmith, the erstwhile director of communications at the Department of Trade and Industry; and even Black Rod.

The truth is, the vast majority of intelligence and lobby journalists cannot or do not check their information. They have to publish what they are told. If they have qualms about or wish to verify the unattributable claims, then refuse to publish because the information supplied is incorrect, they are excluded from the charmed circle. Over the last seven years, only rarely have journalists checked a story about David before publication, even though checking so-called 'facts' – a terrible phrase, the process involves verifying *allegations* – should be the bread and butter of news reporting. Of course, once a 'fact' is published, journalists researching follow-up stories using newspaper databases, usually against a tight deadline, accept it uncritically.

Coercing the press into using non-attributed stories to attack dissent is the action of an autocratic state led by a despot. A democratic leader – or indeed a democratically accountable intelligence service – would stand up and make their comments on the record, where they could be checked by journalists and openly and objectively examined by all. Non-attributable briefings are given precisely so that information can be distorted or invented.

Very few intelligence journalists have MI5 or MI6 sources who are independent of the official briefings. In fact, under section 1 of the 1989 OSA, any intelligence officer talking to the media without the permission of their boss would commit an offence. By asking questions of that source, any journalist would be inciting or conspiring with an MI5 or MI6 officer to break the law. The OSA means that journalists researching stories about the services simply cannot do their job properly. We have seen what happens when journalists and activists try to expose the murky workings of the services: they are hit with injunctions, like *The Mail on Sunday*; threatened with prosecution, like Julie Ann Davies and Martin Bright; or finish up with a criminal record, like James Steen, the former editor of *Punch*.

Academics and journalists who peddle the intelligence services' line cannot be objective. In the absence of a credible Freedom of Information Act, they are dependent on the services to provide them with the (selective) information they need to do their job. They cannot criticise the services for fear of losing this access.

The truth is, when ministers and MPs – and editors and journalists – slavishly follow the diktat of the secret state, they do so because they are scared of the intelligence agencies, not because the services' demands represent the right thing to do.

The situation requires cross-party action so that the lawless elements of the intelligence establishment do not single out and smear any brave party leader who stands up to them. Eventually and inevitably, they will get on the wrong side of the services, as Thatcher did when she pushed the 1989 Security Service Act through Parliament, (and only then as a result of Harriet Harman's and Patricia Hewitt's ECHR ruling which was binding on the UK government).

Once this happens, prime ministers realise just how dispensable they are. Thatcher barely lasted a year after the services she had so praised turned on her for making them observe the minimum standards required in a democracy.

The OSA

As Sir Humphrey Appleby said to Jim Hacker in *Yes, Minister*:

'The Official Secrets Act is not there to protect secrets, Minister. It is there to protect officials.'

And one might add, ministers – from embarrassment. The programme was written and broadcast a quarter of a century ago, yet its subject matter is still as relevant today. It is alarming that neither Tory nor Labour governments in that time have dealt with issues which are integral to the good government of this country.

When David tried to demonstrate at his trial that 'embarrassment' was used as a reason to classify documents, MI5 withheld the definitions of 'security' classification, which referred specifically to 'embarrassment to HMG', from the Crown prosecutor. This was an illegal interference in the right to receive information and the right to a fair trial. Under the HRA,[241] ministers and intelligence services may only withhold

---

[241] ECHR, Articles 10 and 6.

information 'in the interests of national security'. Sparing ministers and senior intelligence officers from embarrassment does not fall within this category.

The truth is that Blair read David wrong in the beginning because he listened to the advice of MI5, an interested party in ensuring its mistakes and crimes were covered up. Blair then used the OSA and a flurry of writs and threats to spare himself embarrassment rather than protect national security.

Never before have British intelligence documents appeared in public without authorisation – as happened with the MI6 CX report confirming the MI6/Al Qaeda conspiracy and the Bazelya letter from MI5 to the Foreign Office – to the enormous embarrassment of the authorities. Blair bears a heavy responsibility for this. Those documents only appeared on the Internet because principled journalists and intelligence personnel were trying to get at the truth, as a result of:

- Blair's failure to hear David's evidence.
- The misleading statements made by his ministers about David's disclosures.
- The lack of a legal route to independent scrutiny of evidence of the crimes of the services.

Britain has the most draconian secrecy legislation anywhere in the Western world. While I do not argue with the need for a law to prosecute traitors who betray the country to its enemies or to protect real secrets, such as the identity of agents, the law also needs to protect whistleblowers. After all, America faces an even greater threat from terrorism than the UK, but it does not have an OSA, and it allows intelligence whistleblowers to give evidence of wrongdoing and incompetence to Congressional Committees.

MI5 and MI6 have over the last 15 years focused increasingly on work which used to be done by the police: terrorism, arms, trafficking and organised crime. Why should the intelligence services now be any less accountable than the police? And why should intelligence whistleblowers have any less protection under the law? It cannot be 'necessary in a democratic society' to deny an intelligence officer from MI5 a defence against disclosure, when an intelligence officer from Special Branch, Army intelligence or the Northern Ireland Police Service Special Branch making the same disclosure would have a defence – that there was no damage to national security – even though the latter three have regular access to the same sensitivity of material.[242]

The issue of 'damage to national security' is itself a vexed question. It has never been defined for the purposes of the law. We saw time and again in David's case the lawyers and judges muddling it with 'harm to the national interest' – a very different concept. The restraint of free speech is only permissible in a democracy in order to protect the former, not the latter.[243] The 'national interest' is a vague concept like 'the good of the people', which is often employed by totalitarian regimes in order to excuse human rights abuses. All too often in this country, successive governments cite 'national security' to draw a veil over embarrassing facts they want to hide from us.

The OSA should be repealed and replaced with a National Security Act, in which the Crown must prove any disclosure – no matter who makes it – caused the following damage to the security of the state to secure a conviction:

- The compromise of an agent. This damages national security because the agent's future intelligence about threats to the state is lost.
- The compromise of a sensitive technique. This damages national security because suspects can evade techniques which would not otherwise have been known to them. They would therefore be in a stronger position to carry out or aid terrorism which damages the security of the state. This

---

[242] Sections 1(1)a and 1(3), 1989 OSA.
[243] Article 10, ECHR and the HRA.

does not include telephone taps and many other techniques regularly featured in spy and police dramas.

- The compromise of ongoing operations, allowing suspects to evade surveillance and/or arrest and therefore continue to undermine national security.

It is worth pointing out to British ministers, judges, MPs and journalists that national security can only be compromised when certain types of classified information end up in the hands of the enemy. How could documents left in the safe of *The Mail on Sunday* damage national security? Did the information get into terrorist hands by process of osmosis, telepathy or radiation? In that safe, those documents posed a lesser risk to national security than documents carried across London in a 'secure' briefcase by MI5 and MI6 officers, especially when those officers are blind drunk, as has happened in recent years.

I challenge ministers to identify a single instance of an agent, a sensitive technique or an on-going operation, which has actually been compromised as a result of David's disclosures. And it is not good enough for ministers and officials to claim that will only further compromise national security. If national security has been compromised by a disclosure, it has been compromised. If national security has not been compromised by a disclosure, then further discussion might compromise it but that only serves to prove that the original disclosure did not damage the security of the state in the first place.

It was obvious during David's trial process that Mr Justice Moses, the Lord Chief Justice, Harry Woolf, and five Law Lords, including Brian Hutton did not know – nor did they seek to find out – how national security is damaged. How could they come to a conclusion about balancing David's right to free speech against the interests of national security[244] in the absence of evidence, let alone the absence of cross-examination of that evidence?

---

[244] The democratic test of the HRA under Article 10(2) of the ECHR.

The failure of Parliament and Freedom of Information

The Iraq war has not just shown up the shortcomings of the PM and senior judges like Lord Hutton, but also the lack of rigour in the Cabinet and Parliament. The Butler Enquiry established that about 17 Cabinet members agreed to go to war without actually seeing the documents used to justify the invasion. At the same time, our elected representatives – in both the Conservative and Labour parties – voted for a war without making any enquiries of their own. They endorsed Blair's decision to go to war without knowing any of the detail or sourcing of the claims made in the September dossier.

All tyrannical regimes have assemblies which are supposed to hold the rulers to account. Formed from committees of state or party flunkeys, they work in secret to rubber stamp the decisions of their dictatorial leaders. Our Parliament, and the PM's ISC in particular, is no different. Any committee that seeks to condemn a whistleblower on the word of the intelligence services before it has heard his evidence is clearly run by, and for, Establishment apparatchiks rather than servants of democracy.

As we cannot trust ministers, MPs and judges to get at the truth, it is time to open up those files. MI5, MI6 and GCHQ continue to retain intelligence – including personal and private information – illegally gathered under the terms of the HRA.[245] Those affected, which includes Conservatives like Teddy Taylor and Ted Heath and, according to Swallow Tail, Jeffrey Archer and Jonathon Aitkin, as well as many left-wing ministers, MPs and activists, have a right to compensation for the unlawful invasion of their privacy. Telephone taps, bugs, surveillance reports and the vast majority of intelligence summaries can be released to the victims of unwarranted state surveillance without any damage to national security whatsoever. This would of course embarrass the services, but that is a different matter.

---

[245] Before MI5, MI6 and GCHQ were put on a legal footing in the 1989 Security Service Act and the 1994 Intelligence Services Act. The HRA is retrospective.

The PM's ISC has failed to respect democratic rights. We have found ourselves in the position of having a committee appointed by the PM being required to investigate him. That is bad enough. Worse still, Swallow Tail has told us that at least one MP on the committee is working to an MI6 brief. This MI6 agent of influence muddies the waters on behalf of the service and feeds in misinformation, where necessary. He was principally responsible for ensuring that the committee did not hear David's evidence.

If the ISC lets MI6 literally get away with murder – and funding our terrorist enemies like Al Qaeda – then it will let the services get away with anything. After all, it is hard to imagine a more heinous crime. The PM's ISC should be scrapped and replaced with a proper oversight committee, elected by MPs, with the power to call for documents, subpoena witnesses, interview under oath and directly investigate the services' abuse of their powers. This is not left-field thinking – look at the scrutiny brought to bear on the American intelligence services in the last few years.

The future for MI5 and MI6

The existing intelligence infrastructure should be abolished.

As well as failing to understand its duties with regard to a democracy, particularly free speech, freedom of information and the need to follow legal procedures, MI5 is incapable of protecting us effectively. In fact, as I have shown in this book, David and I during our years in the service saw it fail to stop four terrorist attacks when it was in possession of reliable intelligence:

- The Bishopsgate attack in April 1993 (although in this case, GCHQ and the head of the Anti-Terrorist Squad must shoulder some responsibility).
- The McNulty attacks on two fuel installations in the Newcastle area on 9 June 1993. Rather than admit to the

mistake, senior MI5 officers deliberately lied to government to cover it up.

- The Israeli Embassy attack in July 1994.

These are just cases we saw in our time and in our sections in MI5. How many other failures have there been?

In addition to allowing thousands of Al Qaeda members into the UK in the 1990s, MI5 clearly failed to gather enough security intelligence on Richard Reid, the trans-Atlantic shoe bomber, otherwise it would have stopped him from carrying out an operation that could have killed hundreds of innocent people.

US investigators have established that Reid was an Al Qaeda operative who travelled from Europe to Israel, Egypt, Turkey and Pakistan using an alias identity, Abdul Ra'uff. Their enquiries have also established that Reid was trained in using explosives and played a role in researching and reconnoitring potential targets for future attacks. We wonder just how much MI5 knew of his role.

An organisation like MI6, which is prepared to fund our terrorist enemies then cover it up cannot claim any legitimacy or public confidence. MI6 should be abolished and, as happened in South Africa, a Truth Commission should be set up to investigate its activities. Agents and officers who confess to their crimes and misdemeanours will be given immunity from prosecution. Those who do not should be tried, according to the evidence against them.

The future for counter-intelligence

Instead, we need a dedicated Counter-Terrorist Agency (CTA), which can work at home and abroad, to replace the myriad organisations which currently combat terrorism. They would gather intelligence *and* evidence against suspects, ensuring that no one escaped trial, as has happened so often with spies, traitors and terrorists as a result of the services' turf wars and ineffectiveness. As a priority, the CTA would recruit human sources, the only way consistently to gather effective, pre-emptive intelligence about terrorist attacks. The CTA's responsibilities would also include arms and drugs[246] trafficking and counter-proliferation.[247]

As the skills required to gather intelligence are very different from those needed to analyse intelligence – and to remove the conflict of interest in a service assessing the value of the information it has collected – the investigative and assessment functions should be split into separate agencies. The CTA's intelligence would be assessed by an independent Research and Assessments Agency (RAA), which would replace the JIC and sections in MI5 like T2C, T2D and G3A.

In any case, it is high time outside consultants objectively assessed the performance of our intelligence officers – be they SB, MI5, MI6 or Customs officers – including the most senior levels. The new CTA would provide an ideal opportunity to carry out this exercise. Officers who have the interpersonal skills, drive and strength of character to conduct or co-ordinate operations and recruit agents would be transferred to the CTA. Officers with genuinely analytical minds – as opposed to those who blithely follow the party line – and good writing and paper skills would form the RAA. The dead wood – and there is an abundance of it – would be offered outplacement advice.

At the moment, MI5 officers are paid significantly less than MPSB officers doing a similar job. MI5 staff receive 10 per cent more than a Home Office employee of the corresponding civil service grade. If you pay peanuts, you get monkeys. CTA officers would be paid a decent wage – with help, such as cheap loans to buy property in and around London – for protecting our lives and risking their own.

Where managers and investigators are capable, efficient and

---

[246] The proceeds from drug trafficking are now used to fund terrorism. Better still, just legalise and tax the drugs trade.
[247] The services' term for countering the threat from WMD.

effective, there will be a need for fewer of them. If we are to have a national security budget, it is imperative that good money is not thrown after bad. If the same useless bureaucrats are in charge, this situation will continue. Both the CTA and the RAA would be headed by a CEO-style figure, who could be held responsible for the successes and failures of their agencies. They would be directly accountable to the PM and be properly overseen by a committee of Parliament, elected by MPs. As in the US, officers would be allowed to raise concerns about illegality and incompetence with the revamped parliamentary committee, without comeback on their careers within the service. As constructive criticism is the lifeblood of democracy, the lives of the British public would be properly protected from threats like Al Qaeda.

Responsibility for the gathering of political, economic and counter-espionage intelligence could be transferred to a small, discrete agency answerable to the FCO, who would also assess its information. Vetting, naturalisation, alien registration, document security, and the human resources and IT function for the new agencies should be farmed out to dedicated sections, or even the private sector, rather than wasting the talents of mainstream intelligence officers. The companies chosen would make decisions without prejudice, for fear of losing their contract.

We must also accept that in an age of international terrorism, our fight against it cannot be limited by national boundaries. The European Union must therefore have its own counter-terrorist body to at least ensure that intelligence about terrorism is co-ordinated, consistently assessed, and acted upon in a coherent manner.

The future for democracy in the UK

Many have criticised Blair for his 'presidential' style of government. Yet the US president has far less power over ordinary Americans than the British PM has over the citizens of this country. There is, for example, no OSA in the US. Although he voted against the removal of a public interest defence from the 1989 OSA when in opposition, since he has come to power Blair has used this act repeatedly to persecute journalists, activists and whistleblowers trying to expose the British state's sponsorship of terrorism in Libya and Northern Ireland. He is a hypocrite. Even worse, he has given succour to the enemies of democracy working in MI5, MI6 and Army intelligence.

Democracy is without doubt the best way to run a society. But in Britain, we now have an enormous democratic deficit. Take the free vote and democratic representation, for example. Blair has just over 40 per cent share of those who voted. That is about 23 per cent of the eligible electorate. Yet he has over 60 per cent of the seats in the House of Commons, giving him power way beyond his electoral standing.

The beginning of democratic society is the written constitution, the contract between the citizen and the state. A Bill of Rights protects the liberties of the people over those rulers who try to assume excessive power. In other Western democracies, independent judges stop the advance or abuse of power. In Britain, our senior judges are part of Parliament so they are not independent or impartial, the test of a judiciary in a democracy. The chamber they belong to, the House of Lords, is appointed in effect by the PM. As its members are not elected, it does not reflect the will of the electorate.

As we have seen in the Hutton Enquiry and David's case, British judges have been rather too prepared to accept untruths and assertions on the part of the state, rather than gather all the evidence; objectively assess it; and then come to an informed conclusion. Conservative, establishment-minded judges in the Weimar Republic did not stand up for *habeas corpus* when Hitler jailed innocent Jews, political activists and homosexuals without trial.

We are not there – yet.

But we are rapidly moving in that direction. Blair has promoted laws to imprison people without trial in Britain for the first time outside war. No other signatory of the ECHR has followed suit. More worryingly, anti-terrorism laws are now being used to arrest and detain political activists demonstrating, for example, against international arms fairs held in London.

The Law Lords' right to hear appeals has no basis in law or justice. The HRA is no Bill of Rights. In both instances, we fail the democratic test. British citizens therefore have no real protection against a dictatorial PM. In theory, we are protected from tyranny by the sovereignty of 'Parliamentary democracy'. In practice, there is no such thing. Either Parliament is sovereign or the people are. The two cannot both be sovereign. We are a Parliamentocracy,[248] not a democracy.

Under the coercion of the whip system, Parliamentocracy means that MPs can vote to take away hard-won liberties, overturn judges' rulings in favour of democratic rights,[249] and legislate against the interests of the people as a whole.

If our elected representatives in Parliament were truly independent of government the whole situation might not be so bad. But the whip system means that the government controls 'Parliamentary democracy'. In turn, the PM is no longer 'first among equals' in the Cabinet. He can ruthlessly use secrecy legislation and non-attributable briefings to suppress dissent from within it. Or he awards sinecures, baubles and gongs to keep dissent under wraps rather than to reward exceptional achievement.

In the end

We also have to ask how many millions of pounds of taxpayers' money have been squandered in the pursuit of David to spare Blair, his fellow ministers and the intelligence services from

---

[248] Democracy means the rule of the people from the Greek 'demos' meaning people and 'kratos' meaning 'power'. Parliamentocracy is a variation on that.
[249] This happened with the removal of a public interest defence from the 1989 OSA.

embarrassment. This sounds like a great deal of money. But think of the cost of the investigation when we first went on the record, tracking us around Europe, searching our flat, and arresting me, David's brother and two of his friends. Think of the hours of legal work involved in the negotiations, the injunction, the failed extradition and the two-year-long trial. Finally, think of all the legal action taken against journalists who have covered his case and against supporters, like Julie Ann Davies. That is a wasteful odyssey for any PM to make.

If Blair was genuinely concerned about threats to our security, why did he not take David's evidence demonstrating that the actions of MI5 and MI6 had undermined the security of this country? The implications of the disclosure about MI6 funding of Al Qaeda are so enormous that ministers, MPs, editors and journalists must not be allowed to get away with off-the-record or unsubstantiated ministerial denials. There must be a proper, independent enquiry. If ministers really believe David is a fantasist, they should welcome it in the certain (if erroneous) belief they will be vindicated.

In one of the last e-mails he wrote before his apparent suicide, Dr Kelly talked of 'dark actors playing games'. In February 2004 government minister Dr John Reid stated that there were 'rogue elements' within the intelligence services. Bizarrely, even the Queen has talked about 'dark forces', according to former royal butler Paul Burrell. It is clear that there are officers within MI5 and MI6 who are working to their own agenda rather than the protection of this country, its people and its democracy.

What you have read in this book is only the tip of the iceberg.

Abbreviations

ASU	Active Service Units
AWOL	Absent Without Leave
CEO	Chief Executive Officer
CIG	Central Intelligence Group
CND	Campaign for Nuclear Disarmament
COBRA	Cabinet Office Briefing Room
Comms	Communication systems
CPB	Communist Party of Britain
CPGB	Communist Party of Great Britain
CPS	Crown Prosecution Service
CSSB	Civil Service Selection Board
CTA	Counter-Terrorist Agency
DCI	Detective Chief Inspector
DDG	Deputy Director General
DG	Director General
DS	Detective Sergeant
ECHR	European Convention on Human Rights
ECtHR	European Court of Human Rights
EPV	Enhanced Positive Vetting
ESO	External Security Organisation (Libyan)
FBI	Federal Bureau of Investigation
FCO	Foreign and Commonwealth Office
FIG	Fighting Islamic Group
FRU	Forces Research Unit
Garda	Republic of Ireland police force

GCHQ	Government Communications Headquarters
GD	General Duties
GI	General Intelligence
HMCE	HM Customs and Excise
HME	Home Made Explosive
HMG	Her Majesty's Government
HMP	Her Majesty's Prison
HOW	Home Office Warrant
HRA	Human Rights Act
HSB	Head of Special Branch
IED	Improvised Explosive Device
IFG	Islamic Fighting Group
IMG	International Marxist Group
IMO	International Miners' Organisation
INA	Iraqi National Accord
IO	Intelligence Officer
IOCA	Interception of Communications Act
IOPs	Intelligence Operations section (MI6)
IRA	Irish Republican Army
ISC	Intelligence and Security Committee
JIC	Joint Intelligence Committee
KGB	Russian Committee of Public Safety
Linen	Telephone intercept
LIS	Libyan Intelligence Services; Libyan Interests Section
LPB	Libyan People's Bureau
MFA	Ministry of Foreign Affairs (Libyan)
MI5	Security Service
MI6	Secret Intelligence Service
MoD	Ministry of Defence
MoS	*The Mail on Sunday*
MPSB	Metropolitan Police Special Branch
MT	Militant Tendency
NCCL	National Council for Civil Liberties (now Liberty)
NCIS	National Criminal Intelligence Service
NSA	National Security Agency

NSY	New Scotland Yard
NUM	National Union of Mineworkers
OC	Officer Commanding
OP	Observation Post
ORBAT	Order of Battle
OSA	Official Secrets Act
OTR	On The Run
PBIED	Person Borne Improvised Explosive Device
PF	Personal File
PFLP–GC	Popular Front for the Liberation of Palestine – General Command
PII	Public Interest Immunity (certificate)
PIRA	Provisional Irish Republican Army
PM	Prime Minister
PTA	Prevention of Terrorism Act
PPSF	Palestinian Popular Struggle Front
PSI	Public Services International
RA	Republican Army
RCG	Revolutionary Communist Group
RCP	Revolutionary Communist Party
RIPA	Regulation of Investigatory Powers Act
RUC	Royal Ulster Constabulary
SAS	Special Air Service
SB	Special Branch
SDS	Special Duties Section
Sigint	Signals intelligence
SIS	Secret Intelligence Service
Sit Rep	Situation Report
SM	Senior Management
SO13	Metropolitan Police Anti-terrorist Squad
SS	Security Service
SSR	Security Service Report
STAR	Document audit system
SVR	MI5's equivalent in Russia
SWP	Socialist Workers' Party
TA	Territorial Army

T&GWU	Transport and General Workers' Union
TC	Training Course
TS	Treasury Solicitor
U/I	Unidentified Individual
VBIED	Vehicle Borne Improvised Explosive Device
WMD	Weapons of Mass Destruction
WPC	Woman Police Constable
WRP	Workers' Revolutionary Party

Index